Law and Economics and the Labour Market

NEW HORIZONS IN LAW AND ECONOMICS

General editors: Gerrit De Geest, *University of Ghent and University of Antwerp, Belgium and University of Utrecht, The Netherlands*; Roger Van den Bergh, *University of Rotterdam and University of Utrecht, The Netherlands*; and Paul Fenn, *University of Nottingham, UK.*

The application of economic ideas and theories to the law and the explanation of markets and public economics from a legal point of view is recognized as one of the most exciting developments in both economics and the law. This important series is designed to make a significant contribution to the development of law and economics.

The main emphasis is on the development and application of new ideas. The series provides a forum for original research in areas such as criminal law, civil law, labour law, corporate law, family law, regulation and privatization, tax, risk and insurance and competition law. International in its approach it includes some of the best theoretical and empirical work from both well-established researchers and the new generation of scholars.

Titles in the series include:

Inflation and the Enforcement of Contracts
Shirley Renner

Law and Economics and the Labour Market
Edited by Gerrit De Geest, Jacques Siegers and Roger Van den Bergh

Law and Economics and the Labour Market

Edited by

Gerrit De Geest

Professor of Law and Economics, University of Ghent and University of Antwerp, Belgium and Researcher at the University of Utrecht, The Netherlands

Jacques Siegers

Professor of Economics, University of Utrecht, The Netherlands

Roger Van den Bergh

Professor of Law and Economics, University of Utrecht and Professor at the University of Rotterdam, The Netherlands

NEW HORIZONS IN LAW AND ECONOMICS

Edward Elgar

Published by
Edward Elgar Publishing Limited
Glensanda House
Montpellier Parade
Cheltenham
Glos GL50 1UA
UK

Edward Elgar Publishing, Inc.
136 West Street
Suite 202
Northampton
Massachusetts 01060
USA

A catalogue record for this book
is available from the British Library

Library of Congress Cataloguing in Publication Data

Law and economics and the labour market / edited by Gerrit de Geest, Jacques Siegers, Roger van den Bergh.
(New horizons in law and economics series)
Includes index.
1. Labour laws and legislation—Economic aspects. 2. Law and economics.
I. Geest, Gerrit de. II. Siegers, Jacques J., 1948–.
III. Bergh, Roger van den. IV. Series.
K1705.6.L39 1999
344.01—dc21 99–26391
CIP

ISBN 1 85898 697 4

Printed and bound in Great Britain by
Creative Print and Design (Wales), Ebbw Vale

Contents

Figures

Tables

Contributors

Jürgen G. Backhaus, Professor of Economics, Faculty of Economics and Business Administration, Department of Economics, Rijksuniversiteit Limburg, Maastricht, The Netherlands.

Matthias Beck, Department of Economics, St. Salvator's College, St. Andrews, Scotland.

Peter Chrubasik, Otto-von-Guericke-Universität Magdeburg, Fakultät für Wirtschaftswissenschaft, Magdeburg, Germany.

Simon Deakin, Reader in Economic Law, Faculty of Law and ESRC Centre for Business Research, University of Cambridge, England.

Gerrit De Geest, Professor of Law and Economics, Faculty of Law, University of Ghent and University of Antwerp, Belgium and Researcher, Economic Institute/CIAV, Faculty of Law, University of Utrecht, The Netherlands.

Oliver Fabel, Professor, Full Professor of Management at the Faculty of Economics and Statistics, University of Constance, Germany.

Lonnie Golden, Assistant Professor of Economics, Penn State University, Delaware County, Media, PA 19063, USA.

Roman Jaich, Universität Gesamthochschule Kassel – FB 6- Angewandte Sozialwissenschaften, Rechtswissenschaft, Nora-Platiel-Strasse 5, D-34109 Kassel, Germany.

Teun Jaspers, Professor of Law, Faculty of Law, University of Utrecht, The Netherlands.

Guy Mundlak, Haifa University Law School, Mount Carmel, Haifa 31 905, Israel.

Bernhard Nagel, Professor, Universität Gesamthochschule Kassel – FB 6- Angewandte Sozialwissenschaften, Rechtswissenschaft, Nora-Platiel-Strasse 5, D-34109 Kassel, Germany.

Jacques Siegers, Professor of Economics, Economic Institute/CIAV, Faculty of Law, University of Utrecht, The Netherlands.

Roger Van den Bergh, Professor of Law and Economics, Economic Institute/CIAV, Faculty of Law, University of Utrecht, The Netherlands.

Ann-Sophie Vandenberghe, Researcher, AWSB, University of Utrecht, The Netherlands.

Frank Wilkinson, Senior Research Officer Department of Applied Economics and ESRC Centre for Business Research, University of Cambridge, England.

Steffen Welzmiller, Otto-von-Guericke-Universität Magdeburg, Fakultät für Wirtschaftswissenschaft, Magdeburg, Germany.

Foreword

This volume consists of a selection of anonymously refereed papers presented at the Utrecht Workshop on 'Law and Economics and the Labour Market', held at Utrecht, 30–31 May 1997, organized by the Economic Institute/Centre for Interdisciplinary Research on Labour Market and Distribution Issues (CIAV), Utrecht University, in cooperation with the Netherlands School for Social and Economic Policy Research (AWSB) and under the auspices of the the European Association of Law and Economics (EALE).

The general purpose of this workshop was to bring together researchers from the three different research programmes that are studying labour law: labour economists, legal economists and legal doctrinists.

Labour economics literature, is traditionally – and by definition – the part of economics that studies labour market phenomena. The focus is more on labour contracts than on labour law, but this nuance is less important than one may think. Before regulating labour contracts, policymakers should understand the economic logic behind the variety of contractual arrangements.

Another branch of economics, law and economics, is of course relevant too in that labour relationships are to a great deal governed by legal rules. Until now scholars who were working in the core of law and economics did not pay too much direct attention to labour law. Yet indirectly, two branches of the law and economics literature are of special relevance: economic analysis of contract law and the economic theory of regulation. The policy recommendations of the first one should in principle hold for labour law too, since labour law is after all a special subdivision of contract law. The policy recommendations of the modern economic theory of regulation should be valid too, since many rules in labour law are of an imperative nature ('regulation' in the terminology of economists).

Thirdly, labour contracts are studied by traditional legal scientists. Of course legal doctrine is a research programme of a different kind from the first two. Some legal doctrinists still pretend not to say anything on optimal law but just to describe the existing law. Yet, it is now generally accepted in legal theory that legal doctrine has a normative component too. Legal writers fill up gaps and influence legislators and courts, and are influenced by what they think the law ideally should be. It is a sort of human knowledge that influences and shapes labour law.

Until now, labour economists and legal economists have been working relatively isolated from each other. In contrast there have been intensive cross-overs between for instance law and economics and insurance economics (see for example Geneva Papers on Risk and Insurance and the conferences organised by the Geneva Association), law and economics and public choice (in Europe many scholars attend conferences of both the European Association of Law and Economics and the Public Choice Society) and law and economics and modern industrial economics.

The gap between law and economics and legal doctrine seems to be even more vast. Labour law scholarship is too often still based on old-fashioned economic theories (over-emphasizing the problem of monopolization, stronger and weaker parties etc).

The editors of this volume hope to help bridge this gap a little bit.

Gerrit De Geest
Jacques Siegers
Roger Van den Bergh

1. Labour law and economic theory: a reappraisal

Simon Deakin and Frank Wilkinson

1.1 INTRODUCTION

This paper reassesses economic arguments for and against labour law regulation in the light of recent developments in contract theory, institutional economics, and the theory of the firm. Early analyses of labour law in the law and economics tradition took a position which was largely hostile to labour market regulation. It was argued that trade unions used labour law to cartelize the labour market (Posner, 1984) and that employment protection legislation interfered with efficient incentive structures operating at the level of the individual contract of employment (Epstein, 1984). These arguments were linked to the wider public-choice critique of state action (Rowley, 1985) and to libertarian attacks upon attempts to legislate for social justice (Hayek, 1979), as well as to macroeconomic models which saw labour market regulation as a cause of unemployment. The critique of labour law therefore spanned a range of theoretical positions. A consensus developed according to which the solution to 'rigidities' caused by labour law lay in 'deregulation', the removal of all or part of the legislation of the welfare state, and the encouragement of labour flexibility. These policies have been practised, to varying degrees, in most advanced economies in the 1980s and 1990s.

However, economic theory has been rediscovering some of the benefits of market regulation. A sophisticated view of contract suggests that there are significant barriers to both static and dynamic efficiency in situations of repeated or long-term exchange. Where workers invest in firm-specific skills, an appropriate incentive structure should incorporate a degree of protection of the employee against arbitrary treatment by management, and some guarantee of continuing employment. This has highlighted certain efficiency-enhancing effects of legislation governing termination of employment (Levine, 1991; Levine and Parkin, 1995) and workforce representation (Rogers and Streeck, 1994). Similarly, formal analyses of strategic behaviour have shown that in the presence of asymmetric information, private bargaining will not necessarily produce optimal outcomes (Aghion and Hermalin, 1990). From the broader perspective of evolutionary and institutional theories of the firm (see Hodgson, 1998), there is a need for a deeper understanding of the institutional preconditions of economic exchange and learning, which include a role for the important but ill-defined notion of 'trust' (Deakin and Wilkinson, 1996).

As in the 1970s and 1980s, a number of different theoretical perspectives may again be converging around a new consensus concerning regulatory policy in the labour market. This is to the effect that a good case for public-regulatory intervention in the labour market can be made, given the limited capacity of private contracting to generate certain static and dynamic efficiencies. This would be consistent with Coase's view 'that there is no reason why, on occasion ... governmental administrative action should not lead to an improvement in economic efficiency' (Coase, 1960, p. 119). Such a view implies that the issue of regulation versus deregulation cannot be decided *a priori*, but requires instead a more detailed empirical analysis of the sources of transaction costs and of impediments to effective contracting in particular contexts. There should also be a clearer acknowledgement of the importance of non-market institutions as solutions to coordination problems, and of the need of such institutions for legal underpinning. This new labour market theory has the potential to influence public policy at an important juncture in the debate over labour flexibility and the future of the welfare state.

1.2 LABOUR LAW AS A FORM OF MARKET REGULATION

For present purposes we define 'labour law' as a type of regulation of the employment relationship which derives principally from the state, in the form of social legislation and of private law, and from conventional sources, such as collective agreements or arbitral awards. Much of labour law has a protective purpose, although there is disagreement as to how far this protective element forms an essential part of labour law (see Mitchell, 1995). Labour law is distinct from the private law of property, contract and tort. Although these private law concepts continue to play an important role both in guiding the courts and in providing a definitional structure for legislation, public regulation has ensured that labour law has achieved a qualified autonomy from the private law of obligations (Wedderburn, 1987).

Three related features of labour law regulation illustrate its separation from private law. The first is the recognition of the employment relationship, or contract of employment, as a distinct *object of regulation*. The contract of employment is subjected to norms which are specific to that contract, as opposed to contracts of a different type (such as sale, lease, and so on). This does not necessarily mean that the general principles of contract law cease to have any role at all in constituting the contract of employment; however, their influence is reduced in favour of norms of a more specific kind. As a result of the separation of the contract of employment from general contract law, it is necessary for labour law to develop criteria of identification (such as 'control', 'integration' or 'economic reality' (see Deakin and Morris, 1995, ch. 3)) which serve to define the relationships to which these specific norms apply.

The second feature is the emergence of distinctive *forms of regulation*, known as *labour standards*. Labour standards can be thought of as being either substantive, procedural or promotional in nature (Mückenberger and Deakin, 1989; Sengenberger, 1994; Deakin and Wilkinson, 1994). Substantive standards are those which directly regulate the individual employment relationship (Kahn-Freund, 1983), for example by setting minimum wages, maximum working hours, basic health and safety standards, and so forth. It is normal for these standards to take the form of a 'floor of rights' or set of minimum provisions on which other conventional sources of terms and conditions can improve, but from which they may not derogate, except under prescribed conditions (Wedderburn, 1992).

Procedural standards – referred to by Kahn-Freund as 'indirect regulation' – do not govern directly the terms and conditions under which labour is contracted, but instead provide legal support for mechanisms of collective negotiation and/or representation of workers and employers. These would include laws enabling trade unions to operate free of the doctrine of restraint of trade and of the economic torts; laws providing for arbitration or conciliation of labour disputes; laws placing employers under a duty to bargain with certain representatives of the workforce, or to consult with them over certain decisions; and laws providing for co-determination.

Promotional standards are concerned with enhancing labour market opportunities through training, job creation and other forms of 'active labour market policy'. These may take the form of subsidies to employers, targeted expenditure, and adjustments to the social security and tax systems (Sengenberger, 1994). They span the divide between the core, juridical forms of labour law intervention, on the one hand, and instruments of public economic governance, on the other.

The third element in the emergence of labour law is the existence of institutions which are specific to that field of regulation, which operate to produce, monitor and enforce labour standards. Such institutions include specialized labour courts, trade unions, employers' associations, machinery for the determination of pay, conciliation and arbitration mechanisms, and a variety of other forms.

1.3 LABOUR STANDARDS AND REGULATED COMPETITION

Labour standards undoubtedly aim to regulate competition in the labour market, and for some this would be a sufficient basis to condemn them on grounds related both to efficiency and to fairness (Heldman, Bennett and Johnson, 1981; Epstein, 1983, 1984; Posner, 1984). However, it is important to clarify at the outset an important feature of labour standards, which is that they rarely displace contractual autonomy completely. The scope for statutory standards which are truly 'inderogable' is quite limited in most systems. Where legislation sets basic substantive standards on such matters as working hours which govern a whole economy or a particular industry, it is often possible for the collective parties at plan or enterprise level to derogate from such standards in the interests of flexibility (Wedderburn and Sciarra, 1988; Mundlak, Chapter 3, this volume). In this way labour law effectively sets procedural standards, thereby creating a space for collective bargaining. Except in some isolated instances (such as under the US National Labor Relations Act, which in this respect is highly unusual) neither collective bargaining nor legislation prevent individual bargaining improving upon the basic terms laid down by a collective agreement, although individual derogation downwards is rarely permitted (Wedderburn, 1992). Even where a nominally inderogable standard is fixed, such as a minimum wage which has the effect that employers cannot seek to reduce costs by depressing pay, the standard in question does not rule out other options for cost reduction, such as enhancing productivity by improved training and utilization of labour. By ruling out one option, others are encouraged. In all these respects, then, labour standards may *guide or channel* contractual outcomes, but rarely predetermine them in a rigid way.

Standards which *are* rigidly binding, in such areas as health and safety or equality of treatment, normally indicate a very high policy priority in favour of obviating particular forms of private cost to employees. However, many of these standards also have economic purposes. In particular, they may function to limit divergences between social and private costs which arise from high transaction costs or externalities (see further below).

The mere fact that most labour standards guide or redirect competition, rather than restricting it altogether, does not mean that the resulting outcomes are efficient. Welfare economics sees market exchange as the principal means by which resources are allocated to their most efficient use, and the wealth of society thereby maximized. From one point of view, anything which interferes with free market exchange could be seen as harmful to efficiency. Many labour law interventions are plainly motivated by considerations of equity, broadly understood, and not by arguments drawn from economic efficiency (although, as we shall see, this is by no means always the case). There may well be, as a result, short-run conflicts between equity and efficiency; however, the same forms of labour market regulation may provide a basis for long-run dynamic efficiency (Boyer, 1994). These are described in more detail in the text below. The essential point is that in unregulated labour markets, market failures of various kinds limit the scope for efficient resource allocation through private ordering.

1.4 LABOUR LAW AND THE COASE THEOREM

The economic analysis of legal rules typically starts with the proposition known as the 'Coase Theorem' (Coase, 1960). This can be stated as follows:

> the allocation of legal rights makes no difference to efficiency in a world of zero transaction costs, since agents are able to recontract until the resources in question reach their most efficient use.

In such a world, the legal decision to allocate a property right to one agent or another, or to impose a private cost in the form of a liability rule on one agent or another, clearly has *distributional* consequences: one side is left better off than the other. However, in a world characterized by pure competition, perfect rationality and foresight and perfect information, there are (by definition) no impediments to the set of exchanges needed to ensure a Pareto-optimal outcome: efficiency, and hence the overall wealth of society, are maximized, regardless of the initial allocation of rights.

The world of zero transaction costs is such an unusual place that one might think that the Coase Theorem has little or no relevance to practical policy-making. A world in which economic actors have perfect knowledge of all future contingencies is one in which, as Coase has remarked (1988, p. 15), 'eternity can be experienced in a split second'. The practical policy significance of the Coase Theorem can only lie in its application to a *real* world in which transaction costs are not negligible. The term 'transaction costs' may be understood to mean, in a narrow sense, the costs of writing, monitoring and enforcing contracts, but in a broader sense it may be taken to embrace all costs arising from the scarcity of information, the possibility of opportunism or strategic action, and the bounded rationality of economic agents (see Dahlman, 1979).

Three separate (and potentially contradictory) interpretations have been offered for the Coase Theorem (see Cooter, 1990; Deakin and Michie, 1997). The first interpretation suggests that:

> where markets are either competitive or contestable to some significant degree, the efficiency implications of legal norms are limited, leaving policy-makers free to pursue distributional goals.

This approach assumes that the Coase theorem has a potentially broad application in the real world of positive transaction costs. The necessary preconditions for the theorem may be met, in practice, as long as markets are competitive in the sense of achieving a broadly acceptable level of effective rivalry among competing sellers and competing buyers. Alternatively, it may be enough that the market in question is contestable, in the sense that entry and exit costs are close to zero, thereby facilitating the entry of new competitors into the market to compete with incumbents.

This strong assertion of the real-world *existence* of competitive or contestable markets is, curiously, quite compatible with an extensive system of labour law regulation designed to redistribute power and resources in favour of employees at the potential expense of other groups (such as managers and shareholders). This is because the presence of a labour law regulation (such as a minimum wage law) or a liability rule (such as a rule of employer's liability for certain work-related accidents) with a redistributional effect would not, in itself, prevent recontracting to ensure Pareto-efficient outcomes. The end result would still favour certain groups over others; but the Pareto principle, in itself, has nothing to say about the justice of particular distributional configurations.

Consider a law mandating maternity leave entitlements for employees. This does not, in itself, rule out recontracting which might result in a Pareto-efficient allocation. Employers might seek compensation for the imposition of such a rule, either by reducing wages or other benefits for all employees (assuming such reductions cannot lawfully be targeted on to women employees, by virtue of laws outlawing sex discrimination), or by reducing their employment of women of child-bearing age, or by increasing the value of the employment package at the expense of dividends paid to shareholders (see Gruber, 1994). The effect would be a series of wealth transfers between various groups: women employees who become pregnant would gain at the expense of employees as a whole; or at the expense of women employees who cannot find jobs; or at the expense of shareholders. However, it is not clear *a priori* that the outcome would be *inefficient*; nor is it clear on what *economic* grounds society should be prevented from making a political choice to protect maternity in this way. The actual judgement can only be based on empirical research.

The generally prevailing view is that labour law regulations probably *do* make a difference to efficiency, since the market for labour is not *so* competitive that agents can easily contract around regulations of this kind. Regulations themselves can be seen as an exogenous source of transaction costs. This gives rise to the second of the three interpretations of the Coase Theorem referred to above:

> since efficiency depends above all on the capacity of agents to contract at low cost, the law should seek to reduce barriers to exchange and to give as wide an ambit as possible to unqualified property rights and to freedom of contract.

This implies a legal regime of minimal regulation, since any constraint on freedom of disposition and on freedom of contract can be seen as reducing competitive intensity and hence as creating rigidities. This view is consonant with a position taken by public choice theory, to the effect that the regulatory state is the origin of the most significant market inefficiencies.

Public regulation is seen as the outcome of rent-seeking activities by organized private groups (Heldman, Bennett and Johnson, 1981; Rowley, 1985). Implicit in this position is the (questionable) view that private markets, if left alone, work reasonably effectively, but that the market for political goods (of which legal regulation is one) is irredeemably flawed by sectional interests.

The third interpretation, conversely, stresses the role of legal intervention in overcoming private market failures:

> unregulated markets are characterised by high transaction costs which derive from limited information and the bounded rationality of economic agents, and which produce mismatches between effort and reward. The law has a role to play in underpinning institutions of various kinds (not just markets) in order to facilitate effective coordination of economic resources.

At one level, the legal allocation of property rights serves to overcome basic transaction costs, leaving the parties free to make their own exchanges; at another level, liability rules of tort and contract may be needed to 'mimic' the market by allocating rights to the agent who values them most highly and who would, therefore, have purchased them in the absence of barriers to exchange. But these private law solutions may not be enough. Certain contracting problems may have to be resolved through vertical integration (Coase, 1937) or through public regulation. As Coase has repeatedly acknowledged (1960, p. 119; 1996, p. 106), there is nothing in his approach to the analysis of legal rules which rules out state intervention on *a priori* grounds.

It is often claimed by both critics and supporters of Coase (e.g. Stiglitz, 1994, p. 11, and Easterbrook and Fischel, 1990, p. 17, respectively) that the normative meaning of the Coase theorem is that the law should do what it can to promote free exchange, in particular by establishing property rights which can be the subject of transfer between economic agents. As a result, the most usual reading of Coase is that the law should avoid placing limits on freedom of disposition and freedom of contract. But this seems to be based on a misunderstanding or misreading of 'The Problem of Social Cost'; at best, as we have just seen, it is only one plausible interpretation of the Coase theorem. A better view is that the Coase theorem does not dictate any particular position with regard to the efficiency of labour law regulation. It certainly does not point with any clarity to deregulation as the preferred option. That option can only be completely compatible with efficiency if deregulation results in a zero- or low-transaction cost world, in which private ordering can generate efficient outcomes. A broader analysis of the origins of structural inefficiencies in labour markets, together with a consideration of the preconditions for effective regulatory design, would suggest that this is an implausible position. In the context of the labour market, regulation is often necessary on grounds related to economic efficiency, as opposed to the social justice considerations which are most often adduced. But to make this argument, we first have to examine the bases of the economic critique of labour legislation which has been so influential in directing public policy since the late 1970s.

1.5 LABOUR COMPETITION AND WAGE INEQUALITY

The case made by orthodox free market economists against the establishment of centrally coordinated labour standards is that both equity and efficiency are best secured by allowing the labour market to operate freely. It is argued that competition among workers for jobs and employers for workers ensures that the overall level of pay is determined by the available techniques of production and by the scarcity of labour relative to capital. The resulting wage differentials reflect variations between workers in skill and work effort, and hence differences in their value contribution. The persistence of very low levels of pay in many advanced industrial economies, even in periods of labour scarcity (see Deakin and Wilkinson, 1991), and the widespread evidence of wide wage variations, even within narrowly defined occupational, industrial or geographical groups (see Rubery and Wilkinson, 1994), would appear to confound these predictions. But these apparent anomalies are accounted for by free market theory in a variety of ways which leaves intact the central core of that theory. These explanations can be divided into differences between jobs (other than in the skill and effort they require); differences between individuals; the presence of costs of hiring, training and acquiring information; and other, 'artificial' obstacles to the free working of the labour market.

1.5.1 Differences between jobs

Jobs vary, it is argued, in amongst other things, by the degree of risks they involve, the conditions under which they are undertaken, their intrinsic interest, and the degree of responsibility which they require; these attributes result in compensating wage differentials (Smith, 1986, chapter 10). Notwithstanding overwhelming evidence to the contrary – empirical studies find little evidence of compensation for poor and dangerous working conditions unless there is high risk to life (Duncan and Leigh, 1980) – this theory predicts that boring, risky jobs undertaken in unpleasant working conditions will be paid more than interesting, safe jobs in pleasant surroundings.

1.5.2 Differences between individuals

It is also argued that individuals vary in earning power because of differences in the investments which they make in acquiring skill (their human capital) and in their ability to work hard and effectively (Becker, 1964). Skills require training and experience which incur cost and are undertaken only if a rate of return on this investment, in the form of an increment over the wage for unskilled work, can be expected. As individuals differ in innate ability, degrees of risk aversion, and preferences for consumption today rather than tomorrow, the amounts of human capital which they acquire also varies widely. At the same time, because individuals differ in their 'exertion of ability and efficiency' (Marshall, 1947, p. 456), it is 'efficiency-earnings' – that is, earnings per 'efficiency unit' – which the market tends to equalize. Therefore, wage variations among workers in similar jobs are also explained by differences in how hard and effectively they work.

1.5.3 Information costs

The costs of acquiring information also provide explanations for wage variations which are not directly attributable to the characteristics of workers or of jobs. Labour mobility may be deterred unless the expected wage increase defrays the cost of search. Similarly, the absence of full information about potential recruits leads to the use by firms of social and other characteristics – such as age, sex, race, qualifications, dress, and deportment – as *signals* of labour quality (Spence, 1973). Firms may lack information about workers' productivity, and even about the jobs which they do: since workers' skills and efficiencies are enhanced by the interaction between learning by doing and the technical, organizational and economic progress of the firm, there is no reason to believe that management has full information concerning job content and performance.[1] Therefore, the absence of perfect information about the full potential of recruits and of job content may result in a range of *different* earnings for workers of *comparable* skill and efficiencies.

1.5.4 'Artificial' obstacles

Finally, orthodox theory explains wage differentials by the operations of trade unions and other institutions which 'impede' the 'free' workings of the labour market. On the supply side, trade unions organize in order to monopolize access to routes into advantaged jobs and to shut down the supply of labour through strikes and other forms of industrial action, thereby raising barriers to entry on the part of both firms and workers. The support of the state through labour legislation is seen as essential in propping up collective labour organization, which would otherwise be undermined by the threat of competitive entry in the manner of other cartels (Posner, 1984). The result is a distortion of the wage structure, which results in the expulsion of workers from sectors of the labour market where wages and conditions of work have been raised above the market clearing level, and their crowding into unemployment or into more competitive sectors where pay and working conditions are consequently depressed. The victims of labour legislation, then, are the low paid and the unemployed.

In seeking to explain the structuring of labour markets, even some of the more sophisticated institutionalist economists have also tended to fall back upon one or more of the traditional arguments to account for intersectoral wage inequalities. For Doeringer and Piore (1971), advanced technology, specific skills, on-the-job learning, labour quality, secure product markets and effective trade union organization explain the relatively high pay of workers in the primary sector or internal labour market. By contrast, workers in the low-paid secondary sector are said to be characterized by low levels of skill, and as having a low degree of work commitment. Hicks adopted a similar quality categorization when differentiating between regular and casual trades, and noted that 'casual labour is often badly paid, not because it gets less than it is worth, but because it is worth so appallingly little' (Hicks, 1962, p. 82).

So from Adam Smith onwards, economists have found theoretical explanations for the persistence of apparently anomalous wage inequalities, without departing too far from their central contention that the market provides an effective valuation of labour. It is market competition and the market clearing effects of price which establish what Marshall described as a 'true' standardization of work and wages (1947, p. 588). Obstacles to market forces, described by Adam Smith as those 'not leaving things at perfect liberty' (Smith, 1986, p. 222), produce 'false' standardizations of work and wages (Marshall, op. cit.). Where social discrimination arises in the form of employers' 'tastes' for employing members of one gender or ethnic group in preference to another, the market responds in the form of competition from employers who do not suffer from these forms of prejudice (Becker, 1957). Contemporary critics of labour law have theorized that it is, above all, the activity of powerfully placed groups, with their ability to limit entry and to exercise control over specialized skills to raise their wages above the market clearing rate, which are responsible for producing distortions in the labour market. The result of their activities is that the less fortunate outsiders are crowded into unemployment or into sectors where competition is unrestricted, and where wages are low and conditions of employment poor. Hence the outcomes of 'false' labour standards include greater inequality and allocative inefficiency.

1.6 THE ECONOMIC NATURE OF THE CONTRACT OF EMPLOYMENT

The orthodox position has been challenged by theoretical perspectives which question any automatic tendency towards efficiency in a 'free' or unregulated labour market. The starting point for this alternative point of view is to be found in analyses that analyse the distinctive properties of the contract of employment, and in particular its 'incompleteness'. Labour lawyers tend to justify protective regulation of the employment relationship on the grounds of the inequality of power and resources between employer and employee; the classic exposition of this theme is by Otto Kahn-Freund in Chapter One of *Labour and the Law* (1983). Economists tend to reject the blanket application of the notion of power in this context as being too imprecise (see Williamson, 1985, Chapter 9). However, most branches of economic theory now accept the idea that the employment relationship has distinctive and particular characteristics that set it apart from other transactions, and that render inapplicable certain aspects of orthodox free market analysis.

The classical economists, Adam Smith included, recognized that labour cannot be alienated from the person of the worker, and that, as a result, the distribution of risk within the employment relationship was not symmetrical: labour power cannot be stored and is perishable, so that the capacity of the worker to hold out for better terms is limited; and there are fewer employers than there are prospective employees. As a result,

> It is not... difficult to foresee which of the two parties must, upon all ordinary occasions, have the advantage in the dispute and force the other into a compliance with their terms... Many workmen could not subsist a week, few could subsist a month, and scarce any a year, without employment. In the long run, the workman may be as necessary to his master as his master is to him; but the necessity is not so immediate (Smith 1986, p. 169).

The same idea underlies the Marxian distinction between labour and labour power: the form of the employment contract is such that the employee undertakes not to supply a given quantity of work, but, rather, to labour under the directions of the employer for a certain period of time (Marx, 1976, Chapter 7). Marx's analysis is notable for the sharp distinction it draws between the realm of the market, in which the contracting parties negotiate under conditions of juridical equality, and the realm of production, within which the hierarchical relation of 'master and servant' holds sway.

The asymmetrical quality of the employment relationship does not necessarily mean that the risk, or conversely the 'power', is all on one side. Modern contract theory abstracts from the broader legal and social background to the exchange of wages for labour power, and sees the employment relationship as raising problems of monitoring, information and strategic behaviour which are common to many contractual settings and do not necessarily call for specific regulation aimed at protecting the employee. This is the area of principal-agent theory and game theory. From this perspective, it is often assumed that it is the *employee* just as much as the employer in whom economic power is vested. As 'agent', he or she has the opportunity for 'shirking' or underperforming at the expense of the employer. This arises because of the presence of 'limited or hidden information' – the employer (principal) cannot effectively 'screen' potential employees (agents) for their skills and aptitude for work prior to entering into the contract, and, once performance has begun, cannot fully monitor what the employee is doing. The problem is intensified where both parties make relation-specific investments (Williamson, 1985). This means that the value of the assets that each brings to the exchange cannot be fully realized except within the context of that relationship; redeploying them elsewhere is costly. To that extent, each of the parties (and not just the employee) is subject to the threat of 'hold up'.

The solution to opportunism is seen to lie, in part, in the use of incentive structures which may be arrived at through private contractual ordering. In this context, Epstein (1984) stresses the importance of both parties to the contract having the option of costless or low cost exit from the relationship, so as to be able to deploy an effective sanction – dismissal or quitting – in response to the other's opportunism. It is argued that an employer which acts in breach of undertakings or understandings towards its employees will be penalized by loss of reputation in the market, and that this makes a legal remedy of damages or reinstatement unnecessary. Such remedies, in so far as they make employers reluctant to dismiss underperforming workers, or give rise to speculative and costly litigation, may be efficiency-reducing. Employment at will – which allows either side to exit from the relationship without the obligation to give notice or to give reasons for termination – should therefore be the courts' preferred default option when construing the contract of employment (Epstein, 1984).

But other contributions to this debate are sceptical about the use of exit as an effective sanction for opportunism in the context of the employment relationship. Where the parties make relation-specific investments, then recourse to the market or to reputation as disciplining devices is, by definition, costly (Williamson, 1985). Examples include investments by employees in firm-specific skills, know-how and expertise, which are of limited value in other organizational settings, or which are expensive to acquire anew in another employment. The problem is particularly acute where exit costs are higher for one party than for the other. There is no necessary reason to assume that it is only the employer which can exercise credible threats; it seems plausible to assume that, from time to time, changing circumstances may give the employee the chance to do so. But the question of which of the two parties tends to be the more powerful is less important, in the present context, than the idea that the parties are locked into a relationship that is insulated from the market for a certain time and space, and that under these circumstances a specialized governance structure is required to ensure optimal contractual performance.

In the case of the employment contract, elements of a governance structure are often made explicit. Employers frequently make express and detailed promises to employees concerning seniority rights and pension entitlements which reward long-term performance (see generally Lazear, 1995). Transaction cost analysis recognizes that it is often in employers' self-interest to introduce many of these benefits in order to elicit long-term cooperation (Williamson, Wachter and Harris, 1975).

The commitments made also need to be made 'credible' (Williamson, 1983) if the employee is not to withhold cooperation. If they are not, either the employee would not enter into the contract in question, or extra transaction costs would be incurred in providing the employee with contractual compensation for the additional risk. Where such undertakings are broken, the opportunity costs to the employee may well be considerable. An extreme, but not unknown case, is the dismissal of employees a matter of days or hours before the vesting of pension or other occupational benefits; corporate 'downsizing' following restructuring is a more common one.

Whether employers are effectively deterred from opportunistic action by a market sanction – the harm done to their reputation – is, in our present state of knowledge, a matter for speculation. A more specific loss can be inflicted on the employer if the parties agree, in advance, for the provision of 'hostages', such as collateral or security interests, which raise the costs of exit (Kronman, 1985). But these analyses are not able, in themselves, to show that legal enforcement of contractual promises is of no economic importance. After all, many commitments given by employees – such as promises made under 'restrictive covenants' not to compete with their employer – are routinely enforced by courts even after the contract of employment has come to an end, with only limited grounds for invalidating such agreements for being in restraint of trade. This type of enforcement is not compatible with the argument that reputational effects suffice to penalize opportunism.

The wider issue in this debate is whether legal regulation which is specific to the employment contract, in the form of implied contract terms and mandated benefits, is justifiable on efficiency grounds. One possibility is that these forms of intervention play an important role in protecting *implicit* elements of contractual governance. 'Implicit' contracts arise in circumstances where formal or explicit agreements are incomplete; they can be thought of as understandings about cooperation which, because of uncertainty about the future and the costs of making such understandings explicit, are too costly to formalize and to enforce as contract terms in the normal way (Cornell and Shapiro, 1987).

The 'incompleteness' of the contract of employment is widely recognized to be the consequence of its long-term orientation and the extreme degree of uncertainty over future performance which this induces (Mückenberger and Deakin, 1989; Brown and Rea, 1995; Jeammaud, Kirat and Villeval, 1996). In the case of most contracts of employment, it is unclear when the employment relationship is to end; the precise content of the employee's obligation to work is rarely specified; and the intensity of work effort is also left unstated. These elements are normally left to be worked out as the relationship proceeds; but they are also subject to normative influences which range from implicit understandings to workplace rules ('custom and practice') and more formal, third party regulation. It is not simply a matter of fairness, but it is also economically efficient for private ordering to be supplemented by labour law regulation in this way. The normative framework supplied by labour law may therefore be not just an important means of reducing transaction costs, but also of promoting cooperation based on *trust*.

The vast majority of contemporary labour law systems have either never applied the concept of the contract at will to the employment relationship, or have fundamentally departed from that model at some point in the past 100 years. So, far from the 'ubiquity' of the rule of employment at will indicating its 'survival' value, it is in fact a highly exceptional approach to the legal regulation of the employment relationship which persists only in particular jurisdictions of the United States.[2] Rather than regarding the employment relationship as the juridical equivalent of a black hole, which is the effect of the default rule of employment at will, most systems of labour law supply to the employment relationship a set of standardized terms, some of which are optional in nature of default rules and others of which are mandatory; these in turn generally supplement a body of formal terms which are most often laid down in an external source, such as a collective agreement or, exceptionally, agreed by the individual parties themselves. At some risk of over-generalization, we may define the distinctive features of this regulatory framework as twofold: the employment contract (1) underpins the employer's power of direction, the 'managerial prerogative', while at the same time (2) granting the employee certain expectations of continuing employment and income security.

1.6.1 Managerial prerogative

Most juridical conceptualizations of the contract of employment recognize an area in respect of which the employee implicitly cedes to the employer a degree of authority over the pace and organization of the work which he or she undertakes to do, in common with the theoretical models of Coase (1937) and Simon (1951). To this extent, it is not simply the distribution of property rights between employer and employee prior to the contract which is normally unequal, but the terms of the contract itself which are asymmetrical and which engender economic power. The effect is that the employer does not need to gain the employee's consent to any and every change in the way the job is carried out; 'functional' or internal flexibility is built into the legal definition of the relationship, in the form of the employee's implied obligations of obedience, cooperation and care (Deakin and Morris, 1995, p. 296 *et seq.*). This residual power which is vested in the employer can be seen as a layer of status 'beyond contract', or at least beyond the explicit terms of the parties' agreement (Fox, 1974).

The essential institutional feature of the contract of employment, then, is that the employer has a *unilateral*, residual right of control which, while ill-defined, distinguishes the contract of employment from others (such as sale or rent) in which a unilateral right of this kind is not present (see Masten, 1988; Marginson, 1993). To speak of employment as a continuous process of 'renegotiation' or renewal of contracts between parties to a continuing relationship (Alchian and Demsetz, 1972) is to ignore this essential feature: the employer's implicit rights enable the employer, up to a point, to dispense with the need for regular renegotiation.

1.6.2 Protection of employee expectations

The open-endedness of the employee's commitment can be seen as providing the basis for the flexibility needed to ensure cooperation between a large number of agents in the productive process. In Coasean terms, this would account for the efficiency of the firm as against the decentralized market; it is, in part, because continuous renegotiation between large numbers of agents would be highly costly that the firm comes into being at all (Coase, 1988; chapter 2). But the question then is how the employment contract can persist despite this fundamental inequality within exchange. Why would it be in the employee's interests to enter into such a contract? One explanation might be that lack of access to capital gives most prospective employees little choice over the matter. But there may also be more positive aspects to the employment relationship.

From the point of view of a rational choice analysis, the employee might be expected to demand from the employer some compensation for granting the employer an area of discretion in directing the way in which the work is to be carried out (see Simon, 1951). Equally, from an institutional and historical perspective, it is plausible to suggest that the persistence of the employment relationship is attributable to norms which create a second layer of status to add to that provided by the employer's implicit powers of direction, namely norms of employment and income protection deriving from labour legislation and collective bargaining between trade unions and employers (Mückenberger and Deakin, 1989; Streeck, 1992). Within the firm, bureaucratic rules which determine the position of employees within the system of ranks and identify the holders of managerial and supervisory posts serve to regulate the exercise of power. The internal norms of the organization are supported, in turn, by those external norms which grant legal force (up to a point) to employees' expectations of job and income security and underpin their right to collective representation at the workplace.

Rules of this kind, by institutionalizing power, seek to render its exercise less personal and hence more predictable and legitimate; by doing so, they offer an important basis for long-term cooperation which enhances the productive potential of the employment relationship (Ménard, 1994). As Coase recognized, the power of the employer to direct the employee is a power which only operates 'within certain limits' (1988, p. 39). These limits are necessary not just because continual renegotiation is highly costly, but also because, in a relationship characterized by asymmetries of information and power, the ever-present possibility of renegotiation may undermine cooperation. Conversely, the establishment of external controls over managerial prerogative may help to foster trust.

From this point of view, certain characteristic features of labour law (as found in virtually all systems other than those of the United States), which include the legal imposition of mandatory minimum labour standards, statutory support for collective workplace representation, and a high level of standardization of terms and conditions of employment, can be seen as performing an important economic role. For example, an employer's agreement to enter into a relationship of collective bargaining with an independent trade union, precisely because it is costly, can be an important signal to its workforce of a 'credible commitment' to the maintenance of cooperative relations. Equally, statutory support for employee representation may in certain circumstances help to overcome the divergence between the private gains which employers can make by resisting collectivism and the loss to society in terms of wasted opportunities for cooperation (Rogers and Streeck, 1994). The 'just cause' standard in dismissal law, because it creates an area of protection for the employee which cannot be renegotiated during the life of the contract, may assist the employer in making 'credible' promises of fair treatment in the course of the employment relationship (Büchtemann, 1993).

The employment relationship offers many other similar illustrations of the idea that formal legal restraints on private contract may be justified on efficiency grounds. The essential point is that in a world characterized by radical uncertainty, gains from cooperation between economic agents may not be attainable through private ordering alone. Collective restrictions on freedom of contract *may* therefore be efficient. In particular, the presence of asymmetric information – one party having greater access to relevant information than the other – increases the risk of strategic behaviour, that is to say, behaviour designed to enhance the position of one party directly at the other's expense (Aghion and Hermalin, 1990; Ayres and Gertner, 1992).

This is a slightly different way of expressing the labour lawyer's traditional concern for 'abuse of power'. The concepts used by economists do not have the effect of taking us full circle, back to the position that all labour law interventions can be justified simply by designating the employee as the 'weaker party'. The approach taken is more discriminating than that, and notes that if cooperation is mutual, so is the possibility of 'defection'. But at the same time, we have come a long way from the position that free exchange *must* be efficiency-enhancing, and external regulation efficiency-reducing.

1.7 EFFICIENCY WAGES, INSIDER POWER, AND LABOUR REGULATION

The insights of contractual analyses have been extensively developed in recent years within efficiency wage theory and insider–outsider theory. These approaches seek to explain why wages in internal labour markets are relatively rigid, in the sense that they are slow to respond to external shifts in supply and demand, if they respond at all. There are two aspects to this phenomenon: firstly, employers are slow to cut wages in respond to a fall in the demand for labour; and, secondly, workers are reluctant to undercut generally prevailing notions of the 'fair' or 'going' wage, even at the cost of remaining unemployed. The starting-point is the observation that wages tend to be set not solely or even predominantly by reference to external conditions in the labour market, but as part of a process of bargaining over the 'rent' or surplus which is realized through cooperation within the firm. The idea is to be found in the writings of Marshall, who used the term 'quasi rent' to refer to 'the income derived from machines and other manufactured appliances for production made by man' (1947, p. 74). The amount of the quasi rent is determined by market conditions at the time the asset is operating, and not by the cost of producing that asset; however, bargaining over the division of quasi rents between labour and capital is influenced in part by firm-specific factors, since the 'workmen would lose a great deal of their wages by going away, and at the same time injure the firm seriously' (Marshall, 1947, p. 626, fn. 2). Hence:

> in some cases, and for some purposes, nearly the whole income of a business may be regarded as a quasi rent, that is an income determined for a time by the state of the market for its wares, with but little reference to the cost of preparing for their work in it. In other words, it is a *composite quasi rent* divisible

> among the different persons in the business by bargaining, supplemented by custom and notions of fairness.

The essential point here is that there is no external market referent for the firm-specific element of earnings, since they are, *ex hypothesi*, unique to the conditions in that firm.

Within efficiency wage theory, explanations for the existence of a firm-specific element in wages include skills (Oi, 1962), privileged access to information, and difficulties in monitoring and securing performance (Akerlof and Yellen, 1986). What drives these models is, again, the 'incompleteness' of the contract of employment: the wage is now seen as a mechanism for eliciting cooperation and raising the productivity of the worker during performance beyond what was explicitly contracted for; hence, the wage rate is a *productive factor* as well as a cost to the employer (Solow, 1990, p. 34). The employer, then, has an incentive to offer a wage which is above the market clearing rate, or, put slightly differently, above the rate which the employer would be prepared to pay if the envisaged employment relationship contained no firm-specific elements.[3]

Hence the role of the external market in determining the wage paid to the worker is not eliminated, but it differs from the role that is accorded to it by the traditional orthodox account. It is suggested that a principal means by which the employer can elicit cooperation is through the threat of dismissal if the employee 'shirks' or wilfully refuses to perform. For this threat to be meaningful, however, there must be a significant gap between the wage paid to the employee and the income which he or she would receive in the event of losing that employment. Such income could be derived either from employment in a secondary sector of low paid work, or from unemployment. As a result, both the level of wages paid in the secondary sector and the level of unemployment benefits, as well as the conditions attached to those benefits, influence the rates of wages paid within primary sector firms.

More generally, the efficiency wage model offers an alternative explanation for the persistence of low pay and long-term unemployment as 'worker discipline devices'. According to this point of view, there is an equilibrium level of unemployment which is that needed to ensure an optimal level of performance from workers. It also follows that such unemployment is *involuntary*, in the sense that even if unemployed persons made themselves available for work at wages below the going rate, it would not be in the interests of employers to hire them (Bulow and Summers, 1986). One way of thinking about this phenomenon is that contractual arrangements which are *privately* efficient for the parties or agents immediately concerned – primary sector employers and their employees – may give rise to an externality or wider social cost in the form of persistent unemployment. Although the idea that private contracting can give rise to an inefficient outcome in this way goes against the grain of the traditional general equilibrium approach, it is precisely because that approach assumes full information and costless contracting that it has little relevance in this context.

Insider–outsider theory seeks to explain why workers might not offer themselves for employment at below the going (insider) rate. Here, the existence of firm-specific rents provides incumbent workers with 'insider power' which they can exploit to their own advantage. The insiders can signal to the employer their intention not to cooperate with any 'outsiders' who take jobs in breach of normal expectations governing terms and conditions of employment; this will reduce both the incentive of the outsiders to underbid the insiders, and the incentives of the employer to hire the outsiders on these terms (Lindbeck and Snower, 1988). From a slightly different perspective, the outsiders can be seen as observing social norms concerning the going rate as part of a cooperative game which they play with the insiders (Solow, 1990). Both groups wish to retain a labour market in which competition is managed or regulated, since the alternative is a market based on 'Hobbesian competition' in which life is nasty, brutish and short, where employers can enforce conditions of employment at the competitive market rate. It would be in the interest even of an unemployed 'outsider' not to deviate from the norm of recognizing the going rate, since he or she would be better off staying unemployed but with the prospect of future employment at the going rate, than taking a job at the lower, market rate in the knowledge that that rate would then prevail indefinitely.[4] This model predicts a range of equilibria, according to the extent to which the individual outsiders are indifferent to their future prospects:

> For any given rate of discounting the future, there is a range – an interval – of wage rates any one of which can be an equilibrium market wage for this game, with accompanying persistent unemployment. The higher the wage, the more unemployment there will be. Within that range there will no undercutting on the part of the unemployed, because the reversion to Hobbesian competition will be unfavorable for everyone, including them. (Solow, 1990, p. 48).

A number of consequences follow from the stories told by efficiency-wage and insider–outsider theory which place in question the conventional way of presenting the workings of the labour market (see generally Stiglitz, 1987, 1994; Solow, 1990). Firstly, competitive forces will not necessarily produce a single market-clearing price for labour. Depending on the strategies adopted by individual firms and workers it is possible to envisage a number of equilibria in which the market stabilizes around different wage levels and different levels of unemployment and unemployment duration. It also follows that there is no single 'natural' rate of unemployment for a given level of inflation.

Secondly and relatedly, there is no necessary tendency for the market to arrive at a state which is Pareto-efficient through the operation of competitive forces. The labour market is, in this sense, an illustration of the general tendency for the presence of asymmetric information and contractual incompleteness to remove the conditions under which both the first and second theorems of welfare economics can be said to hold (Stiglitz, 1994: Chapters 3 and 4): even 'slight perturbations in the standard information assumptions drastically [change] all the major results of standard neoclassical theory' (Stiglitz, 1990, x).

Thirdly, as already noted, both low pay and persistent involuntary unemployment may result from the workings of an 'unregulated' market. In other words, there is no 'natural' tendency to full employment in a free market.

In themselves, these conclusions might give cause for thought for those who advocate deregulatory solutions to the problems of contemporary labour markets. More generally, they are of interest for opening up a range of possibilities for policy which were closed off by the primacy accorded to the free market model: since 'persistent unemployment need not be voluntary or "efficient"... there is at least an opportunity for policy to improve the state of the economy' (Solow, 1990, p. 50). At the same time, it is far from clear which policy interventions might have the effect of enhancing labour market efficiency. In general, efficiency wage theorists tend to argue that legislation regulating termination of employment, for example, reduces the potency of the threat of dismissal through which the employer exercises labour discipline, thereby raising the level of the efficiency wage and so producing an increase in unemployment. Similarly, the payment of unemployment benefits based on a proportion of previous earnings can be seen as reducing the intensity of search for work by the unemployed at the same time as mitigating the effects of job loss for those in primary sector employment. By extension, the efficiency wage will also be raised by minimum wage legislation and other forms of employment protection which aim at raising the standard of terms and conditions of employment in the 'secondary' sector. Insider–outsider theory, in pointing to the need to limit the 'power' exercised by insider groups (Lindbeck and Snower, 1988), can be read as offering support for legislation limiting the right to strike and the ability of unions to organize for the purposes of collective bargaining.

But not all models suggest that social legislation increases unemployment rates. The empowerment of 'outsiders' may take numerous forms which do not involve the removal of protections for 'insiders': 'it is one thing to strengthen the hand of outsiders relative to insiders and quite another to strengthen the hand of employers relative to insiders' (Solow, 1990, p. 76). One possibility here is the *extension* of mechanisms and procedures of collective representation, so as to ensure representation for groups in the 'secondary' market as well as the unemployed (Solow, 1990, p. 77). In institutional terms, this would imply a strengthening of collective bargaining and/or consultation at sector level, as well as a role for neo-corporatist bargaining or 'social dialogue' between the state and representatives of employers and trade unions.

More generally, these analyses suggest that in the context of the labour market, transaction costs are sufficiently high to prevent optimal allocations being achieved through private contracting. This may create a space for regulation which seeks to realign incentives in such a way as to bring about 'static efficiency', in the sense of Pareto-superior allocations of resources:

> economic policy may be able to move the labor market from one possible equilibrium to another. There is a sense in which policy can create artificial initial conditions, an alternative history almost, and thus alter the equilibrium configuration without really needing to cause a change in tastes or technology... (Solow, 1990, p. 60).

For example, the impact upon firm behaviour of unjust dismissal legislation has been formally modelled by Levine from within a broad efficiency-wage perspective. His insight is that any firm offering a contract to the effect that dismissal shall only be for good cause, in a world where many other firms do not, and where workers have heterogeneous skills and aptitudes for work, might expect to attract a disproportionate number of workers whose efforts are substandard, who are attracted to the prospect of a contractually secure job. In other words, there is an externality arising from an 'adverse selection' effect. If all firms had a just-cause rule, the benefits might outweigh the costs of protecting some substandard employees; but no one firm will act to introduce such measures on its own.

The existence of multiple equilibria arising out of contractual incompleteness also means that legislators might be justified in choosing one state of the world over another on *equity-related* grounds. For example, Levine and Parkin (1995) model the effects of terminations for redundancy, in situations where one firm's decision to dismiss workers affects the costs of other firms (and hence their behaviour). Where all firms dismiss workers in a downturn, the intensity of a recession is deepened, and this increases the costs, in terms of risk, for those firms continuing to train. Firms have an incentive not to train, but to dismiss instead.

Where, by contrast, all firms adopt no-redundancy policies, recessions are less intense, and this in itself lowers the costs of training. In either case there is an equilibrium, but the implications are very different in terms of society's overall goals. The view taken of efficiency cannot, in this approach, be divorced from consideration of the fundamental political choices which are made by a given system.

1.8 LABOUR STANDARDS, TRUST, AND DYNAMIC EFFICIENCY

Efficiency wage theory points the way towards regulatory intervention which largely addresses static or allocative inefficiencies. However, a broader view would focus on dynamic efficiency, and specifically on the conditions both for effective cooperation and learning within the firm (Hodgson, 1998) and for innovation and technological development at the level of the market or system as a whole (Sengenberger, 1994).

In its emphasis upon labour *discipline* as the means by which cooperation of workers is elicited, efficiency wage theory is reminiscent of Fox's seminal analysis (1974) of low-trust employment relationships. Fox identified six main features of *low trust syndrome*: workers perceive themselves as not being trusted and are closely supervised; workers obey formal rules in carrying out their tasks; the coordination of workers' tasks is seen as an exclusively managerial function; technological and managerial constraints and monetary rewards are seen as more important than self-imposed standards or internalized for determining the pace of work; failure to meet standards results in punishment, increased numbers of rules, tighter supervision or some combination of these measures; and conflicts between management and workers are handled on a group basis through bargaining processes. Within this environment, industrial relations come to be premised upon a 'behavioural acceptance of divergent purpose' (Fox, 1974, p. 29). Because workers and management are seen as having opposed ends or values, a precisely balanced exchange in the short term is required under which both sides carefully estimate the costs and benefits of concessions. Sharing of information is limited and sanctions are readily imposed in the event of any default on obligations (Fox, 1974, p. 362).

According to evolutionary game theory, a degree of cooperation may be enforced by the threat of retaliatory defection by one side against the other, even under circumstances of unrestrained self-interest (see Axelrod, 1984). Within *actual* labour law systems, low-trust employment relations tend to be the consequence of a particular history and practice of managerial organization, on the one hand, and of resistance to managerial control on the part of workers, on the other. Even from such antagonistic beginnings, collective bargaining may emerge to provide the basis for rules which fulfil a 'peace treaty' role, regulating the issuing of threats and counter-threats. The type of trust which develops under these circumstances is a form of *calculative trust* which arises from the strategic interaction of parties who only remain in the relationship as long as they regard it to be in their immediate interest to do so. In such circumstances, the primary function of collective employee representation becomes the regulation of conflict rather than the encouragement of cooperation.

Calculative trust rests on a *low-risk* strategy in the sense that each party reserves for itself the possibility of retaliation in the face of non-cooperation, but at the same time it is a *high-cost* strategy in the sense that each side has to be prepared to bear the costs of periodically meting out sanctions and in turn having them exercised against it. A further cost arises by virtue of the relative rigidity with which rules and norms are enforced: if the contracting parties are unwilling to perform beyond the letter of the agreement, flexibility is lost and potential gains from trade are sacrificed (Lorenz, 1998). Finally, there is the opportunity cost involved in forgoing the potential gains which could be achieved through innovation based on more open-ended cooperation. By contrast, a strategy based on *goodwill trust*, which involves both parties being willing to perform over and above the literal terms of their contract, can enhance productivity based on long-term productive investments in skills and technology. According to Sako (1992, p. 39), goodwill trust arises where 'someone ... is dependable and can be endowed with high discretion, as he can be entrusted to take initiatives while refraining from unfair advantage taking'. While calculative trust ensures, at best, that expectations are met within existing technical and contractual specifications, the role of goodwill trust extends, in Fox's terms, 'beyond contract', to encompass a degree of open-ended cooperation with expected returns only being realized over a long period. But although goodwill trust offers a potential solution to the problem of contract incompleteness, it also exposes each party to a high risk of opportunism – because the degree of lock-in is greater, each side has more to lose, and the opportunities for effective retaliation may well be more limited than is the case with calculative trust.

The question is, given the high-risk strategy which is implicit in the pursuit of goodwill trust, how is it achieved? While reputational effects will undoubtedly be significant (Epstein, 1984), these cannot, by definition, rest solely or even predominantly on a parity of threats or sanctions against defection, since this would undermine the flexibility or 'give and take' which is one aspect of goodwill trust. Other factors which are important in creating positive expectations of future performance may be expected to include fairness of treatment, job satisfaction, high quality of work environment and, particularly, income and job security. The scope for determining these factors depends both on the conditions within a given employment unit, and on those within the wider environment consisting of the firm, its supply chains, the markets in which the firm operates, and the wider economy of which it forms a part. From this perspective, *the issue is not simply whether regulatory intervention can cure particular market failures, but rather how successful the regulatory framework is in creating an environment which is favourable to the emergence of high-trust employment relationships.* More specifically, the question is how far labour standards, by providing the conditions for investments in labour quality, may contribute to dynamic efficiency in the sense of the capacity of a firm or other productive system to respond effectively to changes in its trading environment, and in particular in the sense of its capacity for innovation.

Here, an important insight of labour market segmentation theory is that in an unregulated or 'free' labour market without effective labour standards, wage rates are only weakly linked, at best, to the comparative productivity of workers (Craig *et al.*, 1985). Inequality is less the consequence of differences between individuals in terms of aptitude and skills, and more the result of structural factors which are inherent to both the supply side and the demand side of the labour market. On the supply side, the labour market is segmented through the effect of social norms which reproduce conventional understandings of 'fair wages' and set the conditions upon which particular groups enter (or re-enter) the active labour force, while on the demand side, firms are ranked according to their degree of access to finance and to the more advanced machines and processes.

The effect of segmentation is that workers with comparable skills and efficiencies are undervalued to varying degrees because they receive different wages per 'efficiency unit'. The persistence of structural inequality opens up the possibility of 'predatory' strategies by firms which seek to tap sources of undervalued labour. Individual employers adjust their wage costs to their ability to pay by either shifting their demand for labour to a more disadvantaged segment or because their workers, trapped in their respective segment, are unable to resist a decline in their relative wage (Wilkinson, 1991). By being in a position to increase the degree of undervaluation of the workers they employ, firms can avoid more radical remedies such as the restructuring of production, managerial reorganization and the replacing of obsolete equipment with new technology. The direct relationship between wage rates and the ability of the firm to pay in a structured labour market also has the effect of discouraging innovation by more creative entrepreneurs, who find it difficult to expand their share of the market because of the difficulties of dislodging technically and managerially inefficient firms which can remain profitable in the short term by employing undervalued labour. The overall result is a lower average level of productivity in the economy because managerial practices and obsolete equipment which should be scrapped remain in existence and because of the slow rate of introduction of new techniques. Salter's classic description remains highly apposite:

> The argument that an industry cannot 'afford' higher wages is, in the long run, very dangerous. If it were accepted and wages were based on the 'capacity to pay' employment would be perpetuated (unless labour deserted them) in industries which should properly decline to make way for more vigorous industries. Equally dangerous is the argument that industries which are prosperous because of new techniques have 'the capacity to pay high wages. (Salter, 1966, p. 153).

Price competition based on low wages also serves to reinforce economic inefficiency by fostering an obsolete product structure. The process of competition based on the development of new, and the modification of existing, products has the effect of continuously shifting product market boundaries. A firm's success in product innovation depends on the establishment of new needs amongst consumers. But once this has happened the new demands require satisfying, so that while producers may capture the market they are also captured by the market. Failure by other firms to respond to this change leaves them behind in declining market niches, and although they may remain viable by cutting labour costs and capturing a larger share of a reduced demand this can only be a short-term expediency (Rubery, Tarling and Wilkinson, 1987). The long term depends on product rather than price competition, and this requires an emphasis on research and development and product design and quality; these are strategies unlikely to be compatible with the exploitation of undervalued labour.

In a market environment in which competition is based on process and product development, a low-pay strategy designed to retain the profitability of increasingly obsolete equipment and product lines can bring only temporary respite. There is a limit to how far wages can be reduced in even the most segmented market, but there is no such limit to cost reductions from technical improvements. Similarly, at some point a product becomes so obsolete that it cannot be sold at any price. For firms and economies trapped in this downward spiral, expectations become increasingly short-term and survival is more and more dependent on cost cutting.

Labour standards are important, then, because the ability of any one firm to adopt a high-productivity route to competitive success is limited if its rivals are able to compete on the basis of low pay and poor working conditions. Basic levels of protection in such areas as wages, working time and conditions of employment aim to forestall destructive competition by setting a floor below which terms and conditions may not fall. Effective labour standards constitute a form of discipline for firms, requiring them to engage in continuous improvements to products and techniques in order to stay competitive. By contrast, the existence of a pool of undervalued labour offers a means by which firms can compensate for organizational and other managerial inadequacies.

Labour standards do not simply permit but also effectively require firms to adopt strategies based on enhancing the quality of labour inputs through improvements to health and safety protection, training and skills development. Low pay and poor working conditions and the absence of job security also have a negative impact on incentives for training. One orthodox explanation for low pay is that it is the result of a lack of training and skill, and that an increase in pay will further discourage employers from providing training. But a closer examination reveals again a quite different direction of causation. Firstly, low paying employers are the least likely to train. Inefficient low payers require undervalued labour to subsidize poor management or keep obsolete equipment in production and cannot afford to train except in the narrowest sense. Secondly, skill is to an important degree a social category and jobs with poor terms and conditions of employment are unlikely to be afforded high status whatever their skill level. Employment status as well as the content of jobs determines the willingness of individuals to acquire the necessary entry qualifications by undertaking education and training.

The theory of labour law and the labour market which we have offered here, then, turns orthodoxy on its head by suggesting that in a 'free' labour market, wages are unable to perform the allocative and incentive functions which are traditionally ascribed to them, and that labour market regulation is necessary in order to restore both equity and efficiency. Our understanding of 'efficiency' refers not just to allocative efficiency in the static sense, but rather to efficiency in the sense of a *dynamic process* of economic growth, carried on under conditions conducive to innovation and economic sustainability.

1.9 CONCLUSION

In this chapter we have traced the main lines of the orthodox economic critique of labour legislation which has played a major part in the promotion of policies of greater labour market flexibility and deregulation. We saw that orthodox law and economics analyses have relied somewhat uncritically on general equilibrium analyses of the market process. When a contractual perspective is taken, which takes into account incomplete contracting and asymmetries of information, the conclusions of general equilibrium analysis are almost immediately undermined: free markets cannot be relied on to produce full employment, nor will they allocate rewards from employment in proportion to contributions. From a theoretical perspective, a new space is created for regulatory policy, as well as a different focus on the role of social norms. Institutional and evolutionary approaches take us still further away from the standard law and economics analysis. Here, normative and institutional factors are seen as structuring economic activity. A 'free' labour market, if not simply a contradiction in terms, is one in which the absence of labour standards creates the conditions for persistent inequality and unemployment, and for productive inefficiency.

For reasons of space, we have not considered here issues of empirical evidence concerning the effects of labour standards on productivity and economic performance,[5] nor have we sought to discuss the libertarian critique which argues against social legislation *even* where it is undertaken in an attempt to cure allocative inefficiencies arising from market failures (Hayek, 1979, vol. 1, pp. 50–51; for a discussion see Mückenberger and Deakin, 1989). We have not attempted to argue that market intervention is in any sense straightforward, or cost free. We have, however, sought to cast doubt on the conventional wisdom that economic theory is necessarily hostile to labour market regulation. We would suggest that if the insights of a range of theoretical advances within economics are to be taken seriously, the focus of policy must begin to shift away from deregulation and towards the design of labour legislation with economic policy goals in mind. This would mean abandoning the sterile opposition of rights and efficiency, and exploring in greater detail the complementarities between labour law and economic development. The implications of our analysis for the study of 'law and economics' are also far reaching: nothing less than a comprehensive institutional analysis of the 'embeddedness' of economic activity in legal and social norms is needed, if this interdisciplinary endeavour is to contribute effectively to policy formation.

NOTES

1. In modern neoclassical theory, this is related to the ability of 'insiders' to block the access of 'outsiders' to this information, and so requires the firm to pay job incumbents a wage premium if it is to benefit from these forms of productivity increases. See further our discussion of insider–outsider theory, below.
2. The reasons for the persistence of employment at will in the United States beyond the point when it was abandoned, for example, in Britain, may well be political and institutional in nature rather than related to efficiency. On the British case, see Deakin, 1998.
3. It is not clear what the 'market clearing rate' would be in efficiency wage models, or even whether it makes sense to refer to that concept. For discussion of these and related difficulties with efficiency wage theory, see Wilson, 1996.
4. This assumption may be regarded as questionable: it would only be in the self-interest of an unemployed individual to refrain from wage competition if he or she thought that they had a realistic chance of obtaining the 'insider' wage, in which case the distinction between 'insiders' and 'outsiders' begins to collapse. Solow's argument is nevertheless of interest for present purposes for showing how, from rational choice assumptions, multiple equilibra are generated (with the policy implications discussed in the text) from the starting point of contractual incompleteness.
5. Suffice to say that there is empirical evidence to support both sides of the regulation vs. deregulation debate. See the essays collected in Addison and Siebert, 1997.

ACKNOWLEDGEMENTS

We are most grateful for comments received from the editors, an anonymous referee, and participants at the *Workshop on Law and Economics and the Labour Market*, held in Utrecht, 30–31 May 1997.

BIBLIOGRAPHY

Addison, J. and W.S. Siebert (eds) (1997), *Labour Markets in Europe. Issues in Harmonization and Regulation*, London: Dryden.

Aghion, P. and B. Hermalin (1990), 'Legal restrictions on private contract can enhance efficiency', *Journal of Law, Economics and Organization*, **6**, 381–409.

Akerlof, G. and J. Yellen (eds) (1986), *Efficiency-Wage Models of the Labour Market*, Cambridge: Cambridge University Press.

Alchian, A. and H. Demsetz (1972), 'Production, information costs and economic organization', *American Economic Review*, **62**, 777–95.
Axelrod, R. (1984), *The Evolution of Cooperation*, New York: Basic Books.
Ayres, I. and R. Gertner (1992), 'Strategic contractual inefficiency and the optimal choice of legal rules', *Yale Law Journal*, **101**, 729–73.
Becker, G. (1957), *The Economics of Discrimination*, Chicago: University of Chicago Press.
Becker, G. (1964), *Human Capital. A Theoretical and Empirical Analysis with Special Reference to Education*, New York: Columbia University Press.
Boyer, R. (1994), 'Labour institutions and economic growth: a survey and a 'regulationist' approach', *Labour*, **7**, 25–72.
Brown, W. and D. Rea (1995), 'The changing nature of the employment contract', *Scottish Journal of Political Economy*, **42**, 363–77.
Büchtemann, C. (1993), 'Introduction: employment security and labor markets', in C. Büchtemann (ed.), *Employment Security and Labor Market Behavior. Inter-Disciplinary Approaches and International Evidence*, Ithaca, NY: Cornell University Press.
Bulow, J. and L. Summers (1986), 'A theory of dual labor markets with application to industrial policy, discrimination and Keynesian unemployment', *Journal of Labor Economics*, **4**, 376–414.
Coase, R.H. (1937), 'The nature of the firm', *Economica* (NS), **4**, 386–405.
Coase, R.H. (1960), 'The problem of social cost', *Journal of Law and Economics*, **3**, 1–44.
Coase, R.H. (1988), *The Firm, the Market and the Law*, Chicago: University of Chicago Press.
Coase, R.H. (1996), 'Law, economics, and A.W. Brian Simpson', *Journal of Legal Studies*, **25**, 103–19.
Cooter, R. (1990), 'The Coase theorem', in J. Eatwell, M. Milgate and P. Newman (eds), *Allocation, Information and Markets*, London: Macmillan.
Cornell, B. and A. Shapiro (1987), 'Corporate stakeholders and corporate finance', *Financial Management*, **16**, 5–14.
Craig, C., J. Rubery, R. Tarling and F. Wilkinson (1985), 'Economic, social and political factors in the operation of the labour market', in B. Roberts *et al.* (eds), *New Approaches to Economic Life*, Manchester: University of Manchester Press.
Dahlman, C. (1979) 'The problem of externality', *Journal of Law and Economics*, **22**, 141–62.
Deakin, S. (1998), 'The evolution of the contract of employment, 1900–1950: the influence of the welfare state', in N. Whiteside and R. Salais (eds), *Governance, Industry and Labour Markets in Britain and France. The Modernising State in the Mid-twentieth Century*, London: Routledge.
Deakin, S. and J. Michie (1997), 'The theory and practice of contracting', in S. Deakin and J. Michie (eds), *Contracts, Cooperation and Competition: Studies in Economics, Management and Law*, Oxford: Oxford University Press.
Deakin, S. and G. Morris (1995), *Labour Law*, London: Butterworths.
Deakin, S. and F. Wilkinson (1991), 'Labour law, social security and economic inequality', *Cambridge Journal of Economics*, **15**, 125–48.
Deakin, S. and F. Wilkinson (1994), 'Rights vs. efficiency? The economic case for transnational labour standards', *Industrial Law Journal*, **23**, 289–310.

Deakin, S. and F. Wilkinson (1996), 'Contracts, cooperation and trust: the role of the institutional framework', in D. Campbell and P. Vincent-Jones (eds), *Contract and Economic Organization. Socio-Legal Initiatives*, Aldershot, Dartmouth.

Doeringer, P. and M. Piore (1971), *Internal Labour Markets and Manpower Analysis*, Lexington, Mass.: D.C. Heath and Co.

Duncan, G. M. and D.E. Leigh (1980), 'Wage determination in the union and non-union sectors: a sample selectivity approach', *International Labour Research Review*, **33**, 24–34.

Easterbrook, F. and D. Fischel (1990), *The Economic Structure of Corporate Law*, Cambridge, Mass.: Harvard University Press.

Epstein, R. (1983), 'A common law for labour relations: a critique of the New Deal labor legislation', *Yale Law Journal*, **92**, 1357–408.

Epstein, R. (1984), 'In defense of the contract at will', *University of Chicago Law Review*, **51**, 947–82.

Fox, A. (1974), *Beyond Contract. Work, Power, and Trust Relations*, London: Allen & Unwin.

Gruber, J. (1994), 'The incidence of mandated maternity benefits', *American Economic Review*, **84**, 622–41.

Hayek, F. (1979), *Law, Legislation and Liberty. A new statement of the principles of justice and political economy*, London: Routledge.

Heldman, J., J. Bennett and M. Johnson (1981), *Deregulating Labor Relations*, Dallas: Fisher Institute.

Hicks. J.R. (1962), *The Theory of Wages*, 2nd edn, London: Macmillan.

Hodgson, G. (1998), 'Competence and contract in the theory of the firm', *Journal of Economic Behaviour and Organisation*, **35**, 1779–2201.

Jeammaud, A., Th. Kirat and M.-C. Villeval (1996), 'Les règles juridiques, l'entreprise et son institutionnalisation: au croisement de l' économie et du droit', *Revue Internationale de Droit Economique*, **3**, 99–141.

Kahn-Freund, O. (1983), *Labour and the Law*, (3rd edn by P. Davies and M. Freedland), London: Stevens.

Kronman, A. (1985) 'Contract law and the state of nature', *Journal of Law, Economics and Organisation*, **1**, 3–25.

Lazear, E. (1995), *Personnel Economics*, Chicago: University of Chicago Press.

Levine, D. (1991), 'Just-cause employment policies in the presence of worker adverse selection', *Journal of Labor Economics*, **9**, 294–305.

Levine, D. and R. Parkin (1995), 'Work organisation, employment security, and macroeconomic stability', *Journal of Economic Behavior and Organization*, **24**, 251–71.

Lindbeck, A. and D. Snower (1988), 'Cooperation, harassment, and involuntary unemployment: an insider–outsider approach', *American Economic Review*, **78**, 167–88.

Lorenz, E. (1998), 'Trust, contract, and economic cooperation', *Cambridge Journal of Economics*, **22** (forthcoming).

Marginson, P. (1993), 'Power and efficiency in the firm: understanding the employment relationship', in C. Pitelis (ed.), *Transaction Costs, Markets and Hierarchies*, Oxford: Blackwell.

Marshall, A. (1947), *Principles of Economics*, 8th edn (reprinted), London: Macmillan.

Marx, K. (1976), *Capital. Volume I*, Harmondsworth: Penguin.

Masten, S. (1988), 'A legal basis for the firm', *Journal of Law, Economics and Organization*, **4**, 188–98.

Ménard, C. (1994), 'Organisations as coordinating devices', *Metroeconomica*, **45**, 224–47.

Mitchell, R. (ed.) (1995), *Redefining Labour Law*, Melbourne: Centre for Employment and Labour Relations Law.

Mückenberger, U. and S. Deakin (1989), 'From deregulation to a European floor of rights: labour law, flexibilisation and the European single market', *Zeitschrift für ausländisches und internationales Arbeits- und Sozialrecht*, **3**, 153–207.

Oi, W. (1962), 'Labour as a quasi-fixed factor', *Journal of Political Economy*, **70**, 538–55.

Posner, R. (1984), 'Some economics of labor law', *University of Chicago Law Review*, **51**, 988–1005.

Rogers, J. and W. Streeck (1994), 'Workplace representation overseas: the works council story', in R. Freeman (ed.) *Working under Different Rules*, New York: Russell Sage Foundation.

Rowley, C. (1985), 'The relationship between economics, politics and law in the formation of public policy', in R.C.O. Matthews (ed.), *Economy and Democracy*, New York: St. Martin's Press.

Rubery, J. and F. Wilkinson (eds) (1994), *Employer Strategy and the Labour Market*, Oxford: Oxford University Press.

Rubery, J., R. Tarling and F. Wilkinson (1987), 'Flexibility, marketing, and the organisation of production', *Labour and Society*, 131–51.

Sako, M. (1992), *Prices, Quality and Trust. Inter-firm Relations in Britain and Japan*, Cambridge: Cambridge University Press.

Salter, W.E.G. (1966), *Productivity and Technical Change*, Cambridge: Cambridge University Press.

Sengenberger, W. (1994), 'Labour standards: an institutional framework for restructuring and development', in W. Sengenberger and D. Campbell (eds), *Creating Economic Opportunities: The Role of Labour Standards in Industrial Restructuring*, Geneva: IILS.

Simon, H. (1951), 'A formal theory of the employment relationship', *Econometrica*, **19**, 293–305.

Smith, A. (1986), *The Wealth of Nations. Books I-III*, Harmondsworth: Penguin.

Solow, R. (1990), *The Labor Market as a Social Institution*, Oxford: Blackwell.

Spence, A. M. (1973), *Market Signalling: Information Transfer in Hiring and Related Processes*, Cambridge, Mass.: Harvard University Press.

Stiglitz, J. (1987), 'The causes and consequences of the dependence of quality on price', *Journal of Economic Literature*, **25**, 1–48.

Stiglitz, J. (1994), *Whither Socialism?*, Cambridge, Mass.: MIT Press.

Streeck, W. (1992), *Social Institutions and Economic Performance*, London: Sage.

Wedderburn, Lord (1987), 'Labour law: from here to autonomy?', *Industrial Law Journal*, **16**, 1–29.

Wedderburn, Lord (1992), 'Inderogability, collective agreements, and Community law', *Industrial Law Journal*, **21**, 245–64.

Wedderburn, Lord and S. Sciarra (1988), 'Collective bargaining as agreement and as law: neo-contractual and neo-corporatist tendencies of our age', in A. Pizzorusso (ed.), *Law in the Making*, Berlin: Springer-Verlag.

Wilkinson, F. (1991), 'Industrial organization, collective bargaining and industrial efficiency', *International Contributions to Labour Studies*, **1**, 1–25.
Williamson, O. (1983), 'Credible commitments: using hostages to support exchange', *American Economic Review*, **73**, 519–40.
Williamson, O. (1985), *The Economic Institutions of Capitalism*, New York: Free Press.
Williamson, O., M. Wachter and J. Harris (1975), 'Understanding the employment relation: the economics of idiosyncratic exchange', *Bell Journal of Economics and Management Science*, **6**, 250–78.
Wilson, M. (1996), 'Efficiency wages and unemployment', *International Contributions to Labour Studies*, **4**, 1–20.

2. The right-to-lie: new law and economics versus Dutch labour law?

Gerrit De Geest, Teun Jaspers, Jacques Siegers and Ann-Sophie Vandenberghe

2.1 INTRODUCTION

The new-law-and-economics literature on contract law focuses on *general* contract law. It deals with rules that can be found in the Anglo-American *common law*, or in the *civil codes* of continental countries.

One important question is whether this literature is also applicable to labour law. At first sight it should be: labour contracts are, after all, just contracts. But on the other hand, labour law is a series of exceptions to civil law. Maybe there exists an economic justification for a separate labour contract law.

To date, labour law has not been extensively studied by law and economics scholars. Moreover, there seems to be an enormous gap between new-law-and-economics expertise on contract law on the one hand and the background knowledge of labour lawyers on the other hand.

In this chapter we want to help to bridge the gap by applying new-law-and-economics theories to Dutch labour law. We will focus especially on information problems in the precontractual stage. The new-law-and-economics literature is well-elaborated on this point.[1] Both in the economic analysis of contract law and in the economic analysis of regulation, information production is seen as a major issue. In contrast, labour economists have hardly paid any attention to this specific aspect.

What is important is that there seems to be a far-reaching consensus among new-law-and-economics scholars. The literature has clearly reached the stage of maturity and refinement.[2]

This chapter is organized as follows. In section 2.2, the new-law-and-economics literature on information production in the precontractual stage will be briefly summarized. In section 2.3, we will apply these general principles to labour contract negotiations. In section 2.4 we will investigate whether Dutch labour law is in accordance with these recommendations.

Yet an important caveat should be made with respect to the conclusions of section 2.4. At this stage of law and economics research it would be dangerous to conclude that Dutch law is indeed inefficient should it be in conflict with the recommendations of section 2.3. It may be as well that law and economics theories do not sufficiently recognize the typical features of labour contracts.[3]

So the conclusions of section 2.4 will only be preliminary ones. The purpose of this chapter is to explore the issue and to stimulate further research.

2.2 CONCLUSIONS ON NEW-LAW-AND-ECONOMICS LITERATURE ON INFORMATION PRODUCTION IN PRECONTRACTUAL STAGE

In this section, we will briefly schedule the conclusions of the economic literature on contract law as well as on information regulation. As already mentioned, there is a striking consensus in this literature. For a synthesis, see Schäfer and Ott (1993) and De Geest (1994, pp. 167–89).

2.2.1 In principle, lying should not be allowed

This was already the starting idea of Posner (1977): fraud should be sanctioned because it is an investment in lying and lying is a socially harmful activity for obvious reasons: a lack of information hinders markets. Lying creates asymmetric information, a major source of market failure. In addition, lying creates social losses in two other respects: (a) the lie costs are a waste, and (b) the possibility of lie costs induces the other party to make verification costs (see De Geest, 1994). For instance, if consumers know that car sellers will give them biased information, they will ask the same information of many competing sellers. But this double-checking is a waste of time, for both the consumers and the sellers.

2.2.2 The least-cost information gatherer should have a duty to produce information, as long as the information costs do not exceed its value, and a duty to reveal that information as long as the communication costs do not exceed its value

Kronman (1978) introduced the idea of the *cheaper cost information gatherer*: the party who can get information at lower cost should be given an incentive to produce and communicate this information. If we allowed the cheaper costs information gatherer to lie, this would oblige the other party to gather that information himself, which would be a waste of scarce resources.

Kronman's (1978) standard example of freely obtained information is a seller knowing there is a termite problem in his house. This is obtained as a by-product of living in the house. Here the seller is clearly the cheaper cost information gatherer, since the information costs of the buyer are above zero.

The party with superior access to information should do more than pass on the information that he possesses (information which he may have obtained freely). In some cases he should also produce new information and reveal it to the other party. The underlying idea is that information costs in society can be reduced by obliging the party who can do this at lower cost to produce it.[4]

Of course one should also take the costs of communication into account. If the costs of revealing private information are higher than the value of the information to the recipient, revealing this information is a wasteful activity. Socially excessive revelation should indeed be avoided (cf. Jovanovic, 1982). Another issue is whether the owner of information knows whether the other party is actually informed (cf. Shavell, 1989 and Shavell, 1991). Revealing information that is already known by the other party is a wasteful activity too.

Therefore, there should be no duty to reveal private information if the marginal communication costs would exceed the marginal value that the revealer expects the information to have for the other party. If it is reasonably expected that the other party already knows the information, it should not be communicated. There should also be no duty to reveal relatively unimportant details.

2.2.3 No distinction should be made between explicitly lying and concealing information

Lawyers seem to have a natural tendency to consider this as an important distinction. In the eyes of legal economists and economists in general both activities are as harmful. By not saying anything, one is creating expectations in the head of the other party. This idea can already be found in the model of Akerlof (1970): in the absence of information consumers assume that products have an average quality.

A similar mechanism can be found in Grossman (1981) and Milgrom (1981) who argued that under some conditions sellers will spontaneously reveal their products' characteristics. In a first stage consumers will assume that all products are of an average quality. This gives sellers with better than average products an incentive to reveal this information. So here consumers consider the silence of a producer as evidence for the fact that the concealed information is disadvantageous to him, and that the quality of his product is below average. The irrelevance of the distinction between lying and concealing can also be shown by the following example. At the end of the negotiations one party asks the other party: 'Have you concealed any relevant information?' When the other party utters the word 'No!' every concealment becomes an explicit lie (De Geest, 1994, p. 182) .

2.2.4 There should be no duty to give information in a verbal form when non-verbal means of communication are cheaper

Under the common law (and other legal systems) the seller is obliged to reveal latent defects but no manifest defects. Kronman (1978) explained this by bringing the costs of communication into the analysis. Legal systems should also economize on this point. Obliging sellers to describe verbally what all buyers can see would be a waste of scarce resources.

A similar idea can be found in the literature on information regulation: regulation for search goods is inefficient (Rubin, forthcoming). Search goods are goods with characteristics (and defects) that can be easily discovered by consumers.

2.2.5 Lying (and other exceptions to the former principles) should not be allowed as a technique for redistributing income

This is a very fundamental principle in the law and economics literature: one should not use private law (including property law, tort law, contract law, ...) to make poor people richer and rich people poorer. If income redistribution is considered as desirable, the tax and social security system is a much better solution. The economic literature has shown for instance that rent control leads to many unintended and undesirable side-effects, like a decreasing supply of housing (for a synthesis of the economic literature on renting, see Hirsch (forthcoming)). Rent control is meant to help poor people, but is performing that task very inefficiently. In tort law, the 'deep pocket rule' (that lets the richer party lose the case) is generally regarded as undesirable. For instance, if the injurer does not have to pay because he is poorer than the victim, the injurer is made richer but at the same time society is made poorer because the injurer will no longer have an incentive to avoid externalities. Kaplow and Shavell (1994) have demonstrated that the tax and social security system in general have less inefficient side-effects (for a summary of the relevant literature, see Curran (forthcoming)).

2.2.6 First exception: there should be no duty to reveal entrepreneurial information

This idea originates from Austrian economists. Entrepreneurs are crucial for the economic system. They see new opportunities in the market. Their major problem is that most entrepreneurial ideas are costly to develop and can at the same time be 'stolen' easily. Therefore, entrepreneurs need to be protected by helping them to conceal their ideas. They should be allowed to lie if necessary. It is not so easy to define 'entrepreneurial information'. Austrian economists relate it to the concept of unexploited market opportunities. A key element of entrepreneurial information is that it is costly to acquire and there is a danger of free ridership with respect to producing it. The latter condition has to be fulfilled: lying is justified only because it prevents free ridership. Consider for example a pharmaceutical firm that has a monopoly to produce a specific drug it has developed. Information about the side-effects of the drug is costly to produce. Yet there is no danger of free ridership, because no other firm can produce that drug. So the monopolist should not be allowed to lie about the side-effects of the drug.

It was Kronman (1978) who first applied this idea to contract law remedies. He argued that information that is costly to acquire should be protected. Information that is freely acquired as a by-product of an activity should be revealed.

2.2.7 Second exception: there should be no duty to be honest with respect to non-verifiable statements

Examples of non-verifiable statements are: 'Pepsi-Cola tastes better then Coca-Cola', 'My Toyota is fantastic', 'X is a good cook'. These statements cannot be falsified because there is no generally accepted definition of the concepts, or because scientific research has not made enough progress to reach a consensus, or because the statement is a description of subjective perceptions. Of course people do not always tell the truth in these circumstances, but it is very difficult for an outsider (a judge) to know whether someone did lie or was honest. Actually, the only way to prove the lie is by the liar's confession. This makes the apprehension rate very low.

If someone were honest and openly confessed that he lied, should he not be sanctioned at that point, when there is evidence? De Geest (1994, pp. 179–80) argued that he should not, since this would not sanction lying but rather being honest after the lie. In addition, sellers with a critical and open-minded attitude towards their own products, would have a comparative disadvantage then (because they would be sanctioned more often than non-critical sellers).

2.2.8 Third exception: if some receivers misinterpret information and others don't, a prohibition to give this information might be efficient

For instance, it is possible that only a few less intelligent consumers take extreme exaggerations seriously. In the literature on information regulation, the basic idea is that one should balance the advantages of regulation (protecting some consumers) and its disadvantages (providing some other consumers with less information) (see Rubin (forthcoming)). In most cases this will lead to a majoritarian test: if and only if the majority of consumers are misled by information, transmitting this information should be prohibited.

2.2.9 Fourth exception: if receivers systematically misinterpret information, paternalistic regulation might be desirable if this is the only technique to correct their irrationality

Should these errors be corrected by regulation? To put it another way, should homosexuals be allowed to lie in order to protect irrational employers against themselves? The new-law-and-economics literature is not so clear on this point. The idea that regulation can be justified to correct uninformed consumers can be found in the literature on products liability (a form of regulation to solve a problem of asymmetric information). Since most law and economics scholars consider information-correcting measures as superior to more severe forms of regulation (like banning products from the market) one could justify allowing lying (a simple form of information regulation) this way.

In addition Fishman and Hagerty (1990) demonstrated that under certain conditions information-limiting rules can be efficient. The key element is that by forbidding some forms of information one can also forbid some forms of misleading.

Nevertheless, this is a difficult issue, because bounded rationality lies at the borderline of economic analysis. Irrationality in the sense of suboptimal decision making, even if the actor gets full information, goes one step further than bad decisions because of a lack of information. Law and economics models are still departing from the rationality assumption. Although this assumption has stronger and weaker variants, it is never relaxed in such an extreme form that hard-core short-sightedness is brought into the model. Short-sightedness is labelled as a 'preference', the desirability of which is not judged.

Although the new-law-and-economics literature is not well-articulated on this point, the idea of paternalistic regulation on pseudo-economic grounds seems to be generally accepted (see Ogus, 1994, pp. 51–3).

2.2.10 In precontractual negotiations, parties should be honest as to the chance of a successful negotiation and the amount at stake

Only a few new-law-and-economics publications focus on the liability for failed negotiations. According to Wils (1993) and De Geest (1994) there should be no liability for failed negotiations, except in two cases:

(i) one party misled the other as to the chances of successful negotiations
(ii) one party misled the other as to the amount at stake.

To put it differently: precontractual liability (*culpa in contrahendo*) is to be seen as a sanction for not having corrected an information asymmetry.

From these two general principles one can derive more specific rules. For instance, if it is common that consumers negotiate with three builders, a consumer who starts negotiations with ten builders should reveal this to all of them. A party who starts negotiations without the purpose of buying anything is liable for the other party's negotiation costs. A party who signed a contract should inform the other candidates as soon as possible that their chances are reduced to 0% (De Geest, 1994, pp. 143–4).

2.3 APPLICATION TO SPECIFIC ISSUES IN LABOUR CONTRACT NEGOTIATIONS

From these general principles (generally accepted in the new-law-and-economics literature on contract formation), we can derive some more specific rules for labour contract negotiations.

The basic idea is that the cheaper cost information gatherer should reveal all relevant information. If we apply this to labour contracts, what information can be considered as relevant for the employer? All information on aspects that may have an influence on the *productivity* of the employee or that may indicate a lower than average productivity. What is useful for the employee? All information on aspects that may have an influence on remuneration in its broadest sense (wage, working situation, appraisal, certainty, ...).

2.3.1 Pregnant women should spontaneously reveal their pregnancy

A woman should reveal her pregnancy, not only when it makes her unfit for the job (for instance a job as a photo model) but also for all other jobs since pregnancy nearly always has an influence on labour productivity (in the same line see Bouckaert (1994)).

As explained in section 2.2.5, lying should not be allowed as a technique for redistributing income. If we apply this principle to the labour market, we have to conclude that women should not be allowed to conceal the fact that they are pregnant. The tax and social security system are much better equipped to subsidize families. A right-to-lie may lead to statistical discrimination (see also Schippers and Siegers (1993)).

Should she reveal this spontaneously or only when the employer asks it? Spontaneously, since a rational employer is interested in this information and obliging the employer to ask it explicitly is a waste of scarce resources.

2.3.2 Employees should have the right-to-lie with respect to diseases that do not reduce their labour productivity in the short and medium run

For instance, employees should have the right to conceal HIV-seropositivity, for jobs where the employer does not have to invest in training (and where the employee is fully productive already in the short run).

What if the employer asks for it explicitly? If the employer wants to take this information into account when deciding whether to hire someone or not, this indicates that he is someone who misinterprets this information. There should be a right-to-lie because of rule 2.2.9. *A fortiori*, there should be no duty to reveal this information spontaneously.

2.3.3 Employees should spontaneously reveal diseases that reduce their labour productivity

Examples of such serious health problems are depression, aids or cancer. There should be a duty to reveal this information spontaneously for the same reason. There should be no duty to do this spontaneously for less severe health problems that are on the borderline of what can be considered to belong to the selection of information that is relevant given the limited amount of information costs the employer wants to make. Once there is some doubt, the employee can always argue he did not give this information while he was in good faith, and this form of bad faith cannot be proved except by confession; in other words: in that case we are dealing with non-verifiable information.

According to the same logic, employees should spontaneously reveal minor physical handicaps (e.g. speech defects) and non-obvious medical problems that may reduce labour productivity.

2.3.4 Employees should have a right-to-lie with respect to their sexual preferences

There should be no duty to reveal this information spontaneously, since this fact has normally no influence on labour productivity. What if the employer explicitly asks for it (which indicates that he is someone who misinterprets this information)? According to the same logic (rule 2.2.9), the employee should be given a right-to-lie.

Should there be a duty to reveal this information, when it has an influence on labour productivity? An example of this could be a vacant job as a singer in a pop band (theoretically it is not inconceivable that, in some markets, consumers may buy fewer records when they know the singer is a homosexual). If we depart from the basic principles behind the current law-and-economics theories, there should be a duty to be honest in this special case.

2.3.5 Employees should honestly reveal their current wage

Such a statement is verifiable. It cannot be considered as entrepreneurial information (i.e. knowledge on unknown opportunities in the market). It is a useful indication of someone's actual productivity.

2.3.6 Employees should spontaneously reveal their recent criminal record to the extent that it may be an indication of their productivity

In many cases, someone's criminal record may be an indication of his labour productivity. However, some ex-criminals who are more productive than average ex-criminals may become the victim of statistical discrimination when they are not allowed to conceal this information. But this argument applies to all forms of statistical discrimination. If the argument is considered convincing, there should no longer be a duty to be honest whenever there is a danger of the employer drawing statistically sound but, in individual cases, perhaps incorrect conclusions. Of course, to the extent that criminal facts have no influence, employees should have the right-to-lie, for the same reasons as explained in section 2.3.4.

2.3.7 Employees may lie about their past productivity, but not about verifiable facts

Although someone's past productivity is an indication of their future productivity, most statements on someone's productivity are hard to verify. Consider for instance the following examples: (a) 'My colleagues appreciated my work', (b) 'I was one of the best employees of that firm', (c) 'I have always been a hard worker'. Statements (b) and (c) are non-verifiable, because there is no generally accepted clear definition of a 'good worker' or a 'hard worker'. Statement (a) is verifiable in principle: one could ask the employee's former colleagues whether they truly did appreciate the work. But the fact that the maker of the statement lied cannot be verified: he may have been in good faith and have had another perception of the facts. Since appreciation is not always revealed directly, 'rational' but imperfectly informed employees can make this kind of error too.

2.3.8 The employer should have the right to ask former employers for information about the past productivity of employees. Former employers have the duty to be honest on facts, but not on non-verifiable statements

Non-verifiable statements in this context are for instance 'I think he is good', or 'he is talented'. *A priori*, there seems to be no reason to oblige the former employer to reply. Replying has a cost, and if there is no compensation to be paid, the current employer may overask. However, if the employer replies, and if the statement is verifiable, there is no economic justification for lying: it is a harmful activity that hinders markets.

2.3.9 The employer should give correct information about the expected wages

Employers may desire to mislead employees as to the expected wages. For instance, they may just mention the highest-possible-wages and make the employee think this is what he may expect (once the employee has entered the contractual relationship he may of course find out the truth, but at that stage he has already made reliance costs of other relation-specific investments). *A priori* there is no good economic reason why this form of asymmetric information should not be corrected.

2.3.10 The employer has the right-to-lie about the working atmosphere

Such statements are indeed non-verifiable ('it's nice working here', 'the other workers are very satisfied') since they refer to subjective impressions.

2.3.11 The employer may be vague but should not lie about future career opportunities within his firm

As long as the statements are vague, they are non-verifiable (chances are hard to quantify). Statements about certainties in the future (precise promises) on the other hand are falsifiable and thus the justification for allowing lies disappears.

2.3.12 The employer is not obliged to reveal how much other employees earn

How much they are earning is entrepreneurial information: it reflects the belief of the employer on how productive these employees can be.

2.3.13 The employer does not need to be honest about what he thinks are the future chances of the firm

Once more this is an example of non-verifiable information. Yet he should be honest about facts (for instance current losses) and should even reveal this spontaneously in case of a long-term contract, since this is the kind of information rational employees want to know and since the employer is the cheaper cost information gatherer.

2.3.14 The employee has a right to make other incorrect but non-verifiable statements

Examples are 'I am a hard worker', 'I am very social', 'My German is excellent', 'I am sportsmanlike'. Again, this does not mean that whether someone is a hard worker or whether someone's German is excellent is irrelevant information. Our point is just that these statements – the way they are put – are non-verifiable in that there is no general definition of 'hard workers' and 'excellent' German.

2.3.15 The employer should give information about the number of people that applied for the job, and about the number of them with whom he will have further negotiations; the employee should give correct information about the number of other jobs he applied for

The rule follows from the principles set out in section 2.2.10.

2.3.16 The employee and the employer have a right-to-lie about the content of alternative job offers

This rule is an application of the principles in explained in section 2.2.6. The second element is entrepreneurial information.

2.4 APPLICATION TO DUTCH LABOUR LAW

2.4.1 Under Dutch law, pregnant women have the right-to-lie about their pregnancy

While new-law-and-economics literature on contract law seems to suggest that women should be honest as to their pregnancy, and even that they should reveal this information, there is no such duty under Dutch labour law. The law on Equal Treatment (*Algemene wet gelijke behandelin*)[5] states that pregnancy may not be a criterion for an employer to select employees (the previous law which is still applicable – *Wet gelijke behandeling van mannen en vrouwen*[6] – and Article 7:646 Civil code are similar as to this point). Article 5, par.1a of the *Algemene wet gelijke behandeling* forbids discrimination on the basis of gender in the selection of employees. As a consequence, considering pregnancy as a relevant factor constitutes a form of illegal direct discrimination.[7] Exceptions to this general prohibition of direct discrimination are possible only if it is expressly stated in the law (courts cannot allow any other exceptions). However, the exceptions mentioned in article 2, par. 2 and 3 AWGB are not relevant in this case.[8]

According to Dutch legislation and case law, the general prohibition of direct discrimination implies that an employer simply may not ask whether a female candidate is pregnant. The question itself would be considered as gender discrimination, therefore unlawful.[9] Consequently, a woman should not spontaneously reveal this information. The rule also implies that a woman has the right-to-lie should the employer ask for it.[10] If an employer discovers the lie after the labour contract has been signed, he may not terminate the contract on this ground.[11]

In summary, Dutch law seems to be in conflict with economic analysis with regard to this issue. Even if the law's aim is optimal redistribution rather than economic optimality, economic analysis suggests that redistribution could better be achieved via the tax and social security system.

2.4.2 Under Dutch law, employees have the right-to-lie with respect to diseases that do not reduce their labour productivity in the short and medium run

The Law on Medical Examinations (*Wet op de medische keuringen, WMK*) limits the number and the extent of medical examinations.[12] Medical examinations include questions (oral questions and questionnaires) and examinations aimed at getting to know the physical health condition (art. 1a *WMK*). The purpose of the medical examination is to judge if the applicant is medically fit to perform a certain job. As a consequence, medical examinations are only allowed if the performance of a certain function demands special requirements as to the medical fitness (art. 4, par. 1 *WMK*). But no medical examination may be done if it is so burdensome for the applicant that it is not in proportion with the purpose of the examination (art. 3 *WMK*).

As a general principle, examinations and questions about the health condition of potential employees are not allowed and there is no obligation for negotiating employees to spontaneously reveal the existence and seriousness of diseases. Questions about state of health are unlawful and the employee does not have to answer them truthfully; he has the right-to-lie. The general principle does not hold when there are special requirements as to the state of health for the performance of a certain job.

2.4.3 Under Dutch law, employees have no right to conceal information on diseases that make them unfit for the job

The general principle mentioned in 2.4.2 does not apply when the employee knows or should know that his illness will make him unfit for the job. If the employee knew or should have known that the disease made him unfit for the job for which he applied, concealing the disease may be a reason for the termination of the employment contract as an urgent cause.

Medical examinations of applicants are allowed when it is necessary to judge if the applicant is medically fit for the job. However, in order to protect the employee's privacy, a medical board plays a central role in this respect. The candidate has no right-to-lie to the doctor, according to the *Wet op de medische keuringen (WMK)*. But the medical board's role is limited to determining whether the employee is fit for the job. The very fact of a medical problem is insufficient for not hiring the employee. The medical board may not give away specific information on the employee's medical condition to the employer, but may only say whether the candidate is fit or not (art. 10, par. 3 *WMK*).

2.4.4 Under Dutch law, employees have a right-to-lie with respect to their sexual preferences

The *Algemene wet gelijke behandeling* explicitly forbids discrimination on the basis of hetero- or homosexuality (art. 1, par. 3 *AWGB*). This implies that the employee has the right both to conceal his/her sexual preference and to lie about it. Also with respect to the protection of the privacy of the employee, the processing of information about someone's sexual preferences is limited.[14] Dutch law is in accordance with economic theory here.

2.4.5 Under Dutch law employees have no direct obligation to reveal honestly their current wage

The employee has no legal obligation to give this information, either spontaneously or upon the employer's request. He may refuse to give this information. However, if the employee is not hired as a consequence of his refusal, then this is the employee's risk. If the employee gave wrong information, this can be no ground for dismissal, *except* for when trustworthiness is an important condition for the job and this lying can be considered as an indication that the employee is not trustworthy.[15]

So Dutch law is somewhat ambiguous on this point. Although the employee has no direct obligation to reveal his current wage (as he should be obliged to, according to economic theory on contract law), the Dutch legal system only directly creates some incentives to do so.

2.4.6 Under Dutch law employees who lied about their criminal record may be dismissed under some conditions

In principle, the employee is not obliged to spontaneously reveal his criminal record. Another question is whether he may lie about it. This depends on the nature of the job. If trustworthiness is an essential feature, the employer may dismiss the employee when he learns about his past record. In that case the employer will have to prove that his interests are harmed by that criminal record. Technically, this is an issue of dismissal law.[16]

So Dutch law is not in contradiction with economic analysis of contract law here. Indirectly employees are given an incentive to reveal their criminal record if this has an influence on their labour productivity.

2.4.7 Under Dutch law employees are not obliged to honestly reveal facts about their past productivity

According to current Dutch law there is neither a duty to spontaneously reveal these facts, nor a duty to give an honest reply to the employer's explicit questions in this respect.

2.4.8 Under Dutch law the employer has a right to ask former employers for information about the past productivity of employees. A former employer indirectly has the duty to be factually honest, in that he can be held liable for the new employer's losses that result from his incorrect information. There is no such duty to be honest on non-verifiable statements, in that the former employer's lying cannot be proven in that case

Non-falsifiable statements in this context are for instance 'I think he is good', or 'he is talented'.

From a legal point of view, the first issue is whether the employer has a right to ask this of the past employer, without prior consent of the employee. Generally speaking, the employer is indeed allowed to ask the past employer for information. His right, however, is limited when it would violate the employee's privacy.[17] In addition it is limited by so-called 'solicitation codes'.

There is no direct obligation for the former employer to be honest on facts about the past productivity of the employee. If however, the new employer would incur losses as a consequence of his reliance on incorrect information, then he could claim damages on the basis of Dutch tort law (art. 6: 162 C.C.).

Though there is no explicit rule in Dutch law, in reality there is no legal duty to be honest on non-verifiable statements, such as for instance 'I think he is good', or 'he is talented', for the simple reason that in reality the new employer will not be able to prove that the former employer lied.

2.4.9 Under Dutch law the employer who seriously misleads the employee as to the expected wages may be held liable

There is no direct legal duty to provide correct information as to the expected wages.[18] Yet misleading may be considered as a violation of the duty to negotiate in good faith (art. 7.611 B.W.). When this misleading is serious (grave misleading), compensation can be awarded under Dutch tort law (art. 6.612 B.W.)

2.4.10 Although under Dutch law the employer has no right-to-lie about the working atmosphere, the insurmountable burden of proof is allocated to the employee

Though strictly speaking the employee may claim compensation, the burden of proof is fully on his side.[19]

As long as the employer does not openly admit to deliberately having misled the employee in this respect, there will be no sanction.

2.4.11 Under Dutch law the employer may be vague but should not lie about future career opportunities within his firm

Only if the employer makes precise commitments can he be held liable because of a violation of the norm of 'good employership' (art. 7.611 BW).[20] The sanction is specific performance, eventually combined with damages.

2.4.12 Under Dutch law the employer is not obliged to reveal how much other employees earn

There is no legal duty as to this point.

2.4.13 Under Dutch law the employer has no obligation to be honest about what he thinks are the future chances of the firm

In principle there is no duty to be honest in this respect. Nevertheless, in rather exceptional cases, when the employee can prove (a) he incurred losses because (b) the employer lied, the employee may successfully claim compensation.

2.4.14 Under Dutch law the employer is not obliged to give correct information about the number of people that applied for the job, and about the number of them with whom he will have further negotiations. Under Dutch law the employee does not have to give correct information about his applications for other jobs

Such a duty may exist only when the employer has signed a solicitation code that contains such a rule. There is indeed no explicit legal rule nor case law that sanctions dishonesty.[21] The same applies to the employee.

Dutch law is in conflict with the economic recommendations of section 2.4.15 at this point.

2.4.15 Under Dutch law, the employee has a right-to-lie about the content of alternative job offers

Dutch law is here in line with section 2.3.16.

2.5 CONCLUSIONS

In this short chapter, we have tried critically to discuss (from an economic viewpoint) the Dutch law on labour contract negotiations.

Starting from the principles that seems to be generally accepted in economic analysis of contract law (section 2.2), we have first tried to determine to what policy recommendations the current economic literature on contract law would lead with respect to labour law (section 2.3).

Dutch law is largely in accordance with the principles derived in section 2.3:

- (2.4.2) Under Dutch law, employees have the right-to-lie with respect to diseases that do not reduce their labour productivity in the short and medium run
- (2.4.3) Under Dutch law, employees have no right to conceal information on diseases that make them unfit for the job
- (2.4.4) Under Dutch law, employees have a right-to-lie with respect to their sexual preferences
- (2.4.5) Under Dutch law employees have no direct obligation to honestly reveal their current wage
- (2.4.6) Under Dutch law employees who lied about their criminal record may be dismissed under some conditions
- (2.4.7) Under Dutch law employees are not obliged to honestly reveal facts about their past productivity
- (2.4.8) Under Dutch law the employer has a right to ask former employers information about the past productivity of employees. A former employer indirectly has the duty to be factually honest, in that he can be held liable for the new employer's losses that result from his incorrect information. There is no such duty to be honest on non-verifiable statements, in that the former employer's lying cannot be proven in that case
- (2.4.9) Under Dutch law the employer who seriously misleads the employee as to the expected wages may be held liable

- (2.4.10) Although under Dutch law the employer has no right-to-lie about the working atmosphere, the insurmountable burden of proof is allocated to the employee
- (2.4.11) Under Dutch law the employer may be vague but should not lie about future career opportunities within his firm
- (2.4.12) Under Dutch law the employer is not obliged to reveal how much other employees earn
- (2.4.13) Under Dutch law the employer does not have to be honest about what he thinks are the future chances of the firm
- (2.4.15) Under Dutch law, the employee has a right-to-lie about the content of alternative job offers.

However, two principles of Dutch labour law seem to be in conflict with the new-law-and-economics literature on general contract law:

- 2.4.1 Under Dutch law, pregnant women have the right-to-lie about their pregnancy
- 2.4.14 Under Dutch law the employer is not obliged to give correct information about the number of people that applied for the job, and about the number of them with whom he will have further negotiations. Under Dutch law the employee does not have to give correct information about his applications for other jobs.

Of course this should be considered as no more than a first exploration of the issue. At this stage of the literature it would be dangerous to make policy recommendations. The analysis is too premature to conclude that the problem lies with Dutch law, and not with incomplete economic theories.

NOTES

1. For a bibliography, see Bouckaert, Boudewijn and Gerrit De Geest (eds), Encyclopedia of Law and Economics, Edward Elgar (forthcoming), nr. 4300 and nr. 5510.
2. Yet the economics literature on contract law is relatively young, starting with Posner (1977) and Kronman (1978). Most research was done in the 1980s, influenced by insights from information economics and consumer theory outside law and economics (like Akerlof (1970)). These insights were very quickly integrated into the new-law-and-economics theories..
3. For instance, De Geest, Siegers and Vandenberghe (1998) have argued that the expectation measure – the normal sanction in general contract law – should not apply to labour contracts, because of its typical feature: the discretion of the employee to decide *ex post* how hard he will work. Since expectation damages are higher the harder the employee works, the expectation measure may undermine the employee's incentives to work hard.

4. A similar idea dominates the economic literature on tort law: the least-cost avoider of an accident should be given an incentive to do so (Calabresi, 1970).
5. Act of 2 March 1994 with regard to equal treatment, Stb. 1994, 230.
6. Law of 1 March 1980 with regard to equal treatment of men and women, Stb. 1980, 86.
7. CoJ EC, 8 November 1990, NJ 1992, 224; HR 13 September 1991, NJ 1992, 225.
8. The prohibition of discrimination on the basis of gender does not hold in the cases where the gender is determinate and in the cases concerning the protection of women (art. 2, par. 2 AWGB). A different treatment is also allowed to favour women in order to reduce actual inequalities (art. 2, par. 3 AWGB).
9. Also the protection of privacy prohibits asking questions about pregnancy. The Draft of the Law on the Protection of Personal Data (TK, 1997–1998, 25892) which will replace the current law on the Registration of Personal Data of 1988, includes the prohibition to process information about the pregnancy of potential employees. As the processing of information about pregnancy will not be allowed, the employer may also not ask about it. See Reeskamp and Sanders (1998), p. 26.
10. Asser-de Leede (1994, p. 283); The Committee of Equal Treatment also allows women to answer questions about pregnancy untruthfully.
11. Ktg.'s Gravenhage 25 March 1992, Prg. 1992, 3731.
12. Law of 5 July 1997 with regard to medical examinations, Stb. 1997, 365.
13. Cases in which the concealing of the disease was considered to be an urgent cause for dismissal: HR 20 March 1981, NJ 1981, 507 (an electric welder concealed his asthmatic bronchitis); HR 2 November 1984, NJ 1985, 192 (an employee hired for paintwork concealed a knee injury); Case in which the concealing of the disease was not urgent cause for dismissal: ArRb. Maastricht, 1 April 1982, Prg. 1982, 212 (a hairdresser concealed a collarbone fracture).
14. The processing of special data – these are personal data such as race, religion, health, sexual preference and criminal history data – is limited in the Draft of the Law on the Protection of Personal Data.
15. A party to an employment agreement may be confronted with situations in which he cannot reasonably be expected to continue the employment relationship (see article 7: 678 Civil code). If this situation is caused by the employee, the employer is entitled to terminate the agreement for urgent cause. The termination takes place without notice and with immediate effect (article 7: 677 Civil code).
16. The law sets forth as an example of an urgent cause, which may justify immediate termination of the employment contract by the employer: theft, fraud, or other crimes involving a breach of trust (see article 7: 678, d C.c).
17. See the Law on the Registration of Personal Data of 1988 and the Draft of the Law on the Protection of Personal Data. The former employer is bound by absolute secrecy when it comes down to medical data. He is not allowed to give out medical information to third parties without the employee's consent. Under the Law on the Medical Examination (WMK), the potential employer is not allowed to ask questions (only the medical board is) nor may he make inquiries in another way about the actual condition of health of the potential employee or about his past record of absenteeism (see art. 4, par. 2 WMK).
18. When an employment agreement is made, a duty to provide correct information as to the expected wage does exist. According to article 7:655. par. 1 C.C. the employer is obliged to give a written statement providing information on certain aspects of the employment relating to the employee. In this statement, the employee must be informed about his wage (art. 7:655, par. 1 h C.C.). The employer must give the written statement within one month after the beginning of the activities of the employment agreement (art. 655, par. 3 C. C.). Non-compliance with this rule makes the employer liable for the damages caused to the employee (art. 655, par. 5 C.C.)
19. Also in labour cases, the evidence rules of article 177 RV are applicable: the party who claims, has to provide the evidence.

20. Article 7:611 C.C. is an application of the general principle of fairness and reasonableness in the performance of obligations given in article 6:248 C.C. On the requirement of 'good employership', see Bakels (1997, pp. 80–82); Van der Grinten (1997, pp. 40–44).
21. According to case law, however, parties can be held liable for failed negotiations if the negotiations are not conducted in good faith. When negotiations are in a far advanced stage and both parties could reasonably assume that they would result in 'a contract of some kind', a party is not allowed to break off the negotiations, since this would be against good faith. Violations of this obligation give rise to compensation of the other party's expenses and also, if appropriate, of the profits that would have been made by that party. See Plas v. Valburg, HR 18 June 1982, NJ 1983, 723.

ACKNOWLEDGEMENTS

The authors would like to thank Peter Jost and three anonymous referees for helpful comments on earlier drafts.

REFERENCES

Akerlof, George A. (1970), 'The market for "lemons": qualitative uncertainty and the market mechanism', *Quarterly Journal of Economics*, **84**, 488–500.
Asser-de Leede, L. (1994), *Bijzondere overeenkomsten, Arbeidsovereenkomst*, Zwolle: Tjeenk Willink.
Bakels, H. (1997), *Schets van het Nederlands arbeidsrecht*, Deventer: Kluwer.
Bouckaert, Boudewijn (1994), 'Liegen over de moederbuik: een zonde of een recht?', *Vlaamse jurist vandaag*, **3**, 2–3.
Bouckaert, Boudewijn and Gerrit De Geest (eds) (forthcoming), *Encyclopedia of Law and Economics*, Cheltenham: Edward Elgar.
Calabresi, Guido (1970), *The Costs of Accidents: A Legal and Economic Analysis*, New Haven: Yale University Press.
Curran, Christopher (forthcoming), '6110 optimal techniques of redistribution', in Boudewijn Bouckaert and Gerrit De Geest (eds), *Encyclopedia of Law and Economics*, Aldershot: Edward Elgar.
De Geest, Gerrit, Jacques Siegers and Ann-Sophie Vandenberghe (1998), 'The expectation measure, labour contracts, and the incentive to work hard', Universiteit Utrecht, Economisch Instituut/CIAV, Working Paper.
De Geest, Gerrit (1994), *Economische analyse van het contracten- en quasi-contractenrecht. Een onderzoek naar de wetenschappelijke waarde van de rechtseconomie*, Antwerp: Maklu.
Fishman, M.J. and K.M. Hagerty (1990), 'The optimal amount of discretion to allow in disclosure', *Quarterly Journal of Economics*, **104**, 427–44.
Grossman, S.J. (1981), 'The informational role of warranties and private disclosure about product quality', *Journal of Law and Economics*, **24**, 461–83.
Hirsch, Werner Z. (forthcoming), '5840 Renting', in Boudewijn Bouckaert and Gerrit De Geest (eds), *Encyclopedia of Law and Economics*, Aldershot: Edward Elgar.
Jovanic, B. (1982), 'Truthful Disclosure of Information', *Bell Journal of Economics*, **13**, 36–44.

Kaplow, Louis and Steven Shavell, (1994), 'Why the legal system is less efficient than the income tax in redistributing income', *Journal of Legal Studies*, **23**, 667–81.

Kronman, Anthony T. (1978), 'Mistake, disclosure, information, and the law of contracts', *Journal of Legal Studies*, **7**, 1–34.

Milgrom, P.R. (1981), 'Good news and bad news: representation theorems and applications', *Bell Journal of Economics*, **12**, 380–91.

Ogus, Anthony I. (1994), *Regulation: Legal Form and Economic Theory*, Oxford: Clarendon.

Posner, Richard A. (1977), *Economic Analysis of Law* (*2nd edn*), Boston: Little Brown.

Reeskamp, P. and P. Sanders (1998), 'Bescherming van de privacy van werknemers', *ArbeidsRecht*.

Rubin, Paul H. (forthcoming), '5110 Information Regulation (incl. Advertising)', in Boudewijn Bouckaert and Gerrit De Geest, (eds.), *Encyclopedia of Law and Economics*, Aldershot: Edward Elgar.

Schäfer, Hans-Bernd and Claus Ott (1993), *Lehrbuch der Ökonomischen Analyse des Zivilrechts* (2nd edn), Berlin: Springer-Verlag.

Schippers, Joop and Jacques Siegers (1993), 'Racial, sexual and age discrimination in the labour market: similarities and differences', in Han Entzinger, Jacques Siegers and Frits Tazelaar (eds), *Immigrant Ethnic Minorities in the Dutch Labour Market*, Amsterdam: Thesis, 1994, 115–34.

Shavell, Steven (1989), 'Sharing of information prior to settlement or litigation', *Rand Journal of Economics*, **20**, 183–95.

Shavell, Steven (1991), 'Acquisition and disclosure of information prior to economic exchange', unpublished manuscript, Harvard University Law School.'

Van der Grinten, W. (1997), *Arbeidsovereenkomstenrecht*, Alphen aan den Rijn: Tjeenk Willink.

Wils, Wouter P.J. (1993), 'Who should bear the costs of failed negotiations? A functional inquiry into precontractual liability', *Journal des Economistes et des Etudes Humaines*, **4**, 93–134.

3. Information-forcing and cooperation-inducing rules: rethinking the building blocks of labour law

Guy Mundlak[1]

3.1 INTRODUCTION

Israeli industrial relations are currently in social, legal, and economic disarray. The purpose of this chapter is to observe a segment of the debate that flows from this situation – devising the background rules for dismissals for employees who are not protected by collective agreements. Yet this need not be read as a local policy paper. Not only are the Israeli policy debates well connected to those of other countries, but the thrust of the chapter is in fact theoretical. My effort here is to overcome the traditional distinction in labour law, regarding its basic 'building blocks', commonly thought to include three distinct instruments: *statutory standard setting*, *collective labour law*, and the *law of contracts*. The clear distinction among these mechanisms is rooted in ideology rather than in practice. The current breakdown of the premises underlying the Israeli system is, in part, an ideological collapse, and I find it a crucial time to assess whether restructuring the system can overcome the political rhetoric that clouds some of the issues.

The focus of the chapter will be on the analysis of the optimal (second-best) choice for the rule governing dismissals for the growing share of the workforce not covered by collective agreements. The discussion will be structured as follows. In the next section (3.2) I provide a short account of the Israeli system's collapse, and the mismatch between the 'old' premises and 'new' reality. I demonstrate how the Israeli system provides an idiosyncratic combination of continental-Europe labour market institutions, without adopting its dual representation system, and Anglo-American institutions of contract law. Recent changes have severely affected the highly centralized collective bargaining regime, and have led to an *hourglass effect*, where issues that were previously regulated by peak level collective bargaining are gradually moving to statutory standard-setting mechanisms and to the domain of unfettered contractual transactions. While collective bargaining is yet to disappear, the parties find themselves with a highly centralized tradition, but a reality of growing decentralization, and a mismatch between the old premises and new practice. An intensifying debate exists between the neo-liberal strand, which, drawing on the rhetoric of efficiency, calls for deregulation of the Israeli labour market, and the social lobby, which seeks to renew the current system by adding more regulatory schemes under the justification of distributive justice. The pressures are thus focused on what will replace the realm of collective bargaining, although little attention is paid to the need for new modes of representation. I translate this political controversy into a legal competition between the three instruments for labour market regulation.

Section 3.3 critically assesses the simplistic correlation between the ideological rhetoric and the legal means, referring to the debate on the rules governing dismissals in the non-union sector. While the efficiency side to the debate argues in favour of a simple employment-at-will rule (i.e., the employer can dismiss the employee for a good reason, a bad reason, or no reason at all) that reflects what most employers want, the social lobby claims the need for extending the just-cause standard (i.e., the employer must show good cause for dismissals) that prevails in collective agreements to all workers. My efforts here are limited to the perspective of economic efficiency, although I argue that the distributive question cannot be avoided. I demonstrate that correlating efficiency to the at-will rule is an oversimplification. Yet, the alternative need not be an across-the-board just-cause rule, and there are some shades of grey in between the two extremes. I argue in favour of two such shades. At a minimum, just-cause must be set as a penalty default rule (section 3.4). A more ambitious agenda must try to set just-cause as a constrained-penalty-default rule, that is, an immutable rule that could be derogated by structuring internal dispute resolution procedures (sections 3.5–3.6). Unlike the two extremes (at-will default or immutable just-cause rules), just-cause as a penalty-default rule is an information-forcing mechanism; just-cause as a constrained-penalty-default rule is also a cooperation-inducing mechanism.

What starts as a simple dichotomy between two background rules evolves into a complex set of choices that raises considerations too broad for a focused analysis. My objective here is limited to introducing the idea of legislating information-forcing and cooperation-inducing rules. Despite the fact that these proposals do not seek to deregulate the Israeli labour market, they can be efficient. The rules proposed are those that seek to help the parties to the employment contract to overcome inherent problems that pervade the employment contract: information asymmetry, simultaneous reliance and conflict among the parties, and the public-good nature of some of the employment relationship's attributes. At the deeper level of analysis, the objective is to deconstruct the argument that statutory standards are for the Marxists and simple contractual rules are for the efficiency oriented. In fact, the suggested rules expand the menu of legal responses and blur the dichotomy between immutable and default rules, placing them as two ends of a continuum.

3.2 THE BUILDING BLOCKS OF LABOUR LAW AND THE ISRAELI CONFIGURATION

It is common to distinguish the 'building blocks' of labour and employment law into three distinct categories: statutory law, the autonomous collective labour law, and contract law (Weiler, 1990). Other areas of law play some part in the employment relationship, but their role is generally marginal.[2] The three building blocks are often correlated with distinct political theories. Utilitarian and libertarian theories are generally attached to a preference for the law of contracts, neo-Marxist theory is assumed to justify statutory standard setting, and the middle tier of autonomous labour law is premised on the ideology of industrial pluralism. Contract doctrines are favoured by the free-marketeers, holding the employment contract as similar to other contracts. In spite of some obvious differences, the transactional nature of the contract dominates and requires the application of the conventional law of transactions. At the other extreme, statutory regulation provides employees with immutable entitlements that confiscate various dimensions of the employment relationship from the contractual apparatus.[3] Statutory regulation implies that selected aspects of the employment relationship are non-commodifiable and cannot be subject to the pressures of supply and demand. In the midst of the two extremes is the autonomous collective labour law. This category borrows from the logic of the other two. Autonomous labour law preserves regulation by markets. Unions and employers face market constraints and market pressures, and outcomes reflect the parties' relative bargaining strength. Like the law of contracts, collective labour law merely establishes the rules of the game, but not the game's outcome. At the same time, the output of the contractual negotiations serve in most countries as a quasi-statutory provision, and like statutory standards it provides individuals governed by the collective bargaining agreement with an immutable entitlement.

When viewed as such, the different building blocks regulating the employment relationship embody a meta-ideological debate about the employment relationship. Since all three building blocks appear in all democratic regimes, the balance between them provides some understanding of these countries' political climate. For example, a high level of regulation and standardization implies neo-Marxist foundations, translated mostly into social-democratic politics, while low levels suggest a more utilitarian or libertarian emphasis characterizing neo-liberal or conservative politics. Consequently, much of the debate on labour law reform suffers from a highly ideological pitch. I do not refute the need to identify a coherent ideological justification for configuring the various building blocks, but I do reject the strong link suggested between one political theory and one type of legal building block. I seek to adhere from here on to the utilitarian perspective of efficiency, although for reasons that will be made clear I do not view this perspective as detached from competing theories that observe distributional effects.

The Israeli configuration of these building blocks is probably idiosyncratic, and can be explained only as an outcome of a historical evolution.[4] The Israeli industrial relations system, dominated by only one major union, the *Histadrut*, predated the establishment of the state by more than twenty years. When the state was founded, many social services were already provided by the Histadrut, most notably health care. The political regime that was closely allied with the Histadrut entrusted the union with the power to continue the provision of social services, and thus the Histadrut became a paradigmatic 'state within a state' or, alternatively, a fourth branch of government. The industrial relations system took on a corporatist approach, according to which the regulation of the labour market was conducted first and foremost at peak-level bargaining between the Histadrut and the well organized employers' associations. The state, being the biggest employer, joined these bargaining sessions wearing the hat of both the sovereign and the biggest employer. The second biggest employer, ironically, was the Histadrut itself, thus contributing to the overriding importance of collective bargaining to the economy as a whole.

The 1950s saw the drafting of an elaborate set of statutory standards governing worktime, vacations, health and safety, and at later stages also anti-discrimination law. While these standards exceed those prevailing, for example, in the United States, there was a strong objection to further legislation of more standards, owing to the fear of confiscating the centrality of autonomous labour law and collective bargaining. The rules governing collective bargaining were developed at later stages. These laws were partial in scope, placing the juridification of Israeli collective bargaining under the British principle of voluntarism and the North American approach of clear and legally enforceable rights. The legal framework was, however, secondary in importance to industrial reality. The Histadrut was the major, almost the sole, union in Israel. It was strong in that it represented over 80 per cent of the workforce, it had no competition from rival unions, and it acted for the most part in a highly centralized fashion. It drew its strength from its monopolist position in the administration of social services, most notably health care and pensions. To the extent that its hegemonic position was challenged, the labour court took an active stance to reassert it.

The Histadrut's overreaching control of the labour market and the dominant role of collective bargaining left almost no room for governance of the labour market by the law of contracts. In the past this law had been based on the common law tradition, but the 1973 legislation introduced a continental approach to the codification of Israeli private law. Despite the new direction, the minor importance of contract law in the area of employment has surrendered employment contract doctrines to the old common law tradition. As discussed at length in the next section, one of the major implications is that Israel still holds the rule of dismissals to be that of employment-at-will.

During the 1990s Israel has experienced challenges familiar to all other western countries. Changing world and local markets have affected Israeli industry, inducing a need for greater levels of flexibility and adaptation. At the same time changes in the Israeli system have been anything but incremental. The 1995 legislation on national health care insurance 'privatized' health care services, taking them away from the Histadrut, and at the same time nationalized health care insurance. A good proxy for the sudden shock is that the 1995 reform caused a sudden decrease of almost 50 per cent in union density, measured by membership rates. Despite the strong link between labour relations and social services, the health-care reform was instituted without any attention being given to its implications for labour relations. That the industrial relations system had to be rethought and changed had been appreciated for some time, but health care reform brought what I believe to be total collapse down on labour relations. Thus reform in the industrial relations system could not have been carefully conceived, and the system is currently struggling to identify future paths.

From the late 1980s one observes significant changes in the configuration of the building blocks structuring the Israeli system. These can be summarized as follows:

- *Statutory standard setting*: Growing use of statutory mechanisms to regulate the labour market. Two major examples are the Minimum Wage law enacted in 1988, which took over the regulation of minimum wage from the collective bargaining regime, and the newly enacted law on the regulation of staffing companies.
- *Autonomous labour law*: The recent changes have brought about a decentralization of collective bargaining and a potential influx of new unions. While centralized bargaining is confronting some difficulties, there are no clear guidelines, nor is much thought given to the potentially desirable role of enterprise-based representative entities. Israel has not adopted the European dual-representation system, where there are both institutionalized unions negotiating collective agreements and enterprise-based works councils (Rogers and Streeck, 1995). Workers' committees in enterprises are constituted by the Histadrut's by-laws, and the case law on these committees aids the Histadrut in denying them any power to strike or to engage in collective bargaining. Owing to the legislature's silence on the status of workers' committees, they are almost unknown in establishments where there is no collective bargaining. The number of such establishments is rapidly growing.
- *The law of contracts*: The application of contracts law to employment contracts is slowly moving to the top of the labour court's docket, as a growing number of workers find themselves in the sphere of individual contractual relationships, with no backing of the familiar collective bargaining agreement. The labour court is seeking to define a clear jurisprudence regarding the applicability of contracts law to the employment relationship, engaging in areas such as the enforceability of covenants not to compete, the rules governing dismissals, and the applicability of constitutional principles and rights, including the principle of equal treatment, in the private sphere of employment contracts.

Together these changes reflect a growing reliance on statutory standard setting on the one hand, and on contract law on the other. These two trends seek to substitute the uncertain state of collective bargaining.

In this state of uncertainty, one of the advantages is that almost everything is 'up for grabs'. While the political climate is leaning toward the neo-liberal North American approach, there is no clear decision, and the existence of a strong tripartite culture can advance alternative visions for reforming the law of the workplace. The neo-liberal approach at first seems attractive because it matches the rather simplistic idea that avoiding all labour market regulation is efficient. It is also the most convenient political platform. It does not even require the erasure of existing statutes from the law books. Because current law is partially inapplicable to the new reality, the legislature can simply relax and allow it to gradually become irrelevant, leaving the old common law contract doctrines in place, paying lip service by enacting some more statutes that seemingly provide workers with a social safety net, and leaving the market to deregulate itself. Here is where I suggest that deregulation, like some of the new regulatory schemes, may be inefficient. What the system must seek is legal means that encourage cooperative relationships and induce information sharing between workers and employers, thereby leading to efficient contractual relationships.

3.3 THE RULE OF DISMISSALS – OVERVIEW

3.3.1 The Israeli Debate

A fundamental assumption in Israeli employment law is the employment-at-will doctrine (i.e., the employer can dismiss a worker with a contract of employment for an indefinite term for a good reason, a bad reason, or no reason at all). However, the scope of the doctrine and its applicability has rarely been tested. The idea that workers can be dismissed for any reason probably also sounds quite strange to the local ear. The strong penetration of collective bargaining agreements, with their elaborate constraints on dismissals, lead many to believe that these agreements reflect the rule rather than the exception.

In 1985 there was a legislative effort to enact the law of employment contracts. Section 12 of the proposed law prescribed a mandatory just-cause rule. This was not the first effort to draft such a law, or the last. But the 1985 effort failed precisely because of the just-cause provision. The employers associations' objection to this provision was not based on a concern for the inefficiency of the rule or its constraint on managerial flexibility. As described earlier, in 1985 Israeli industrial reality was strongly coloured by the excessive scope of collective bargaining agreements, most providing for a just-cause standard and enforcement mechanisms. The employers' argument was that the just-cause standard in collective bargaining agreements was their concession to the Histadrut. If the proposed law expropriated this issue from collective agreements, they would have to provide further concessions instead. The employers' opposition was thus presented in terms of bargaining power.

Current reality raises new concerns because a growing number of workers are not governed by collective agreements. The background conditions have changed, but the policy options have remained the same: mandatory just-cause or default at-will. From here on, the discussion in this chapter will utilize mostly the American literature owing to its sophistication and rigorous analysis. For the reasons stated above, Israeli literature on the topic is almost non-existent. Israeli case-law provides little insight regarding the applicability of the rule in the non-union sector, and in fact, the first cases that challenge the at-will assumption have been given during the last few years.[5]

3.3.2 The Terms of the At-will v. Just-cause Debate

The strongest defence of the at-will rule is in fact libertarian (Epstein, 1984), but I will leave the critique of deontological property-based accounts aside. Economic analysis provides an alternative explanation that views the at-will rule as an efficient bargaining outcome. The voluminous literature in the United States, which used to be a major stronghold for this rule, confronts the growing limitations that state courts impose on its applicability. However, economic considerations are used by both sides to the debate, as justifications for imposing a just-cause rule (whether immutable or default will be discussed later), usually relying on arguments of efficiency as well.

From the economic point of view, the major argument in favour of replacing employment-at-will with a just-cause rule is based on delayed-compensation models.[6] According to these models, the problem of dismissals is deemed most acute for 'career workers' (Schwab, 1993; Issacharof, 1996). These are workers who, together with the employer, make a shared firm-specific investment upon entering the firm and thereafter. According to human-capital theory, entry-level workers and the employer share the costs of firm-specific training. The entry-level worker receives wages lower than her opportunity wage, but higher than her productivity, the difference being split between the worker and the employer. After the initial training period, the worker receives a wage that is lower than her productivity, thus ensuring the employer the worker's lock-in and encouraging the worker to work hard, with the promise of higher wages in the future. Wages constantly rise with seniority, until at some advanced stage of the worker's career her wages exceed productivity. This arrangement hinges on an implicit contract between the career workers and the employer. It provides the employer a mechanism that induces high levels of effort from the employee and her loyalty to the firm. It further allows the employer a long time period in which she can spot and weed out shirkers. It provides the career-worker job security and, assuming workers are risk-averse, it also assures the worker escalating wages throughout her career. The described arrangement is an implicit contract (Charny, 1991). Devising an explicit employment contract to reflect this arrangement is difficult, owing to the assumption of bounded rationality (Williamson, 1985). Courts must therefore mirror the implicit promise by using just-cause background rules that match the worker's stage in her career. This mode of intervention is not anti-contractarian but modelled on the contractual premise that courts must accommodate the parties' agreement at the time of formation.

The proponents of the employment-at-will rule provide a rather simplistic response to these arguments. To a large extent their argument is purely Darwinist (Verkerke, 1995; Morriss, 1994). They claim that most non-union employers prefer the at-will rule, and where state courts have imposed just-cause limitations, employers tend to contract around the default, thus indicating the default was inefficient to begin with. The Darwinist argument further holds that the prevalence of employers' preferences for at-will at the time the employment contract is signed indicates that justification must be provided by those seeking alternative rules and the burden of proof lies with them. There are therefore only limited efforts at explaining the efficiency of the at-will rule.

An exception to the Darwinist stance is provided by Edward Rock and Michael Wachter (1996), who argue that from the efficiency point of view, the at-will rule can be portrayed as a response to the shirking problem. Their argument accepts the delayed compensation model as the starting point. They hold that in firms where there are mutual firm-specific investments, there is a risk for opportunistic behaviour, caused by 'the combination of match specific investments, risk aversion, information asymmetry and transaction costs'. The danger of mutual opportunistic behaviour leads employers (in the non-union sector) to voluntarily adopt a just-cause dismissals policy. Together with other measures, such as severance pay, and a monitoring policy that responds to shirking with the sole sanction of dismissals, the common pattern found in the non-union sector indicates the efficiency of these solutions, which the authors identify as self-enforcing contractual provisions. Their viewpoint is thus coloured by an empirical perception of non-union reality. While most opponents of the new just-cause trend highlight employers' response to the new common law as limited to contracting around the new default in favour of the at-will principle, Rock and Wachter emphasize that many employers *de facto* adopt just-cause policies. There is no contradiction between the two observations. It may very well be that many employers adopt a dual approach – on the one hand insuring themselves by inserting an explicit at-will clause into the employment contract, and on the other hand developing internal measures to ensure that dismissals will only be with cause. They thus desire and are concerned to prevent unjust (or inefficient) dismissals, but at the same time they want to be the sole judge of their own actions' propriety, constrained only by market forces and not by third parties.

Rock and Wachter describe dismissal as an effective, and efficient, sanction against shirking, given the high costs of the monitoring process itself. Any alternative sanction, such as reduction in wages, will only give the employer an incentive to overstate the degree of shirking and thus reduce labour costs. This arrangement is thus in the best interest of both parties. Similarly, the voluntary adoption of a just-cause dismissals policy allows the parties to make *ex ante* efficient investments. This policy is self-enforcing because if the employer discharges without cause he will not be able to induce workers to make a shared investment in firm-specific skills. This assumption rests on the reputational effect of the employer's decisions on dismissals. Dismissing senior workers damages the employer's reputation in both external and internal labour markets.[7]

The two sides of the debate seek the optimal rule for internal labour markets in non-union firms. Setting aside the Darwinist approach, both positions assume that internal labour markets can enhance efficiency by providing for mutual investment in firm-specific learning. Furthermore, both views emphasize only well developed internal labour markets, and thus do not deal with issues such as staffing companies, peripheral workers, or highly turbulent sectors characterized by intensive entrepreneurial activity. The focus of the controversy is not the alleged efficiency of internal labour markets. Instead, there are two distinct controversies. The first is about the choice of background rules at the time the parties enter the employment relationship. Some argue in favour of an immutable rule of just cause that replicates the implicit promise and distinguishes between the various stages in the worker's life cycle. At the other extreme are those who hold that the default rule should be employment-at-will. Thus, parties who wish to contract around the default must provide explicitly for a just-cause or any other rule of dismissals.

The second debate is about the enforcement of the implicit contract. Rock and Wachter hold that there are sufficient market incentives for employers to avoid reneging on their implicit promise to the career worker. Dismissing a trained worker requires investing from scratch in a new one. To the extent that mistakes are made by agents at various levels of the firm's hierarchy, the employer can reduce the costs of mistakes by establishing procedural safeguards to prevent abusive dismissals. While reputation may not always be perfect, Rock and Wachter hold the alternative to be far worse. Because the proof of a just-cause for dismissals requires an understanding of the internal labour market and the norms developed within the firm, a third party, such as a judge, is at an information disadvantage, and litigation requires ascertaining the internal norms that are hard to verify and prove. The detection costs are likely to be high, and render the solution both *ex ante* and *ex post* inefficient. I will treat each of these debates separately (sections 3.4 and 3.5–3.6, respectively).

3.4 CHOOSING THE BACKGROUND RULE: MAJORITARIAN STANDARDS OR PENALTY-DEFAULT RULES?

The debate between just-cause and at-will background rules seems to be a dichotomous choice between two symmetric options that mirror one another. There are, however, important differences that dispel their symmetric quality. First, at-will is a *rule*-type option, while just-cause is a *standard*-type option.[8] When courts confront the need to decide whether dismissals are a violation of the employer's contractual duty, their task is quite simple under the at-will rule as dismissals are categorically not a breach of contract. Enforcing a just-cause norm requires imparting content to the vague idea of contractual justice. Moreover, at-will and just-cause present two sides of a continuum, where all options between the two ends are standard-type options. Just-cause can be interpreted as a rather encompassing rule prohibiting any dismissal in which the employer cannot prove a bona fide rationale relating to the worker's quality of work. It can be constructed more narrowly so as to apply to situations in which the employer dismisses the worker to avoid paying the worker a promised benefit.[9] Just-cause can also be applied to situations that are deemed morally wrong, for example, the discharge of whistleblowers. Some contrast just-cause to 'with good cause', the latter indicating that economic needs of the employer provide a good justification for dismissals (St. Antoine 1992, p. 371).[10] These options, among others, can be aligned on a continuum, but only the at-will end of the continuum provides for a rule-type option.

Not only are the two basic options asymmetric, they can also be collapsed into a broader range of options. Each option may be presented in the form of an immutable or default rule. Thus, just cause may be an immutable rule that the parties are not allowed to contract around. As such it belongs to the category of statutory standards, similar to the regulation of worktime, minimum wage and maternity leave. This was the legislature's choice in the failed effort to pass the law of employment contracts in Israel. Alternatively, it can also be viewed as a contractual default rule which the parties are permitted to contract around. The same can be said for the at-will rule, although again the discussion is not symmetrical. I am not aware of anyone who suggests that it is not possible to contract around the at-will rule. Even if the at-will is presented as an immutable rule, it is generally correct that statutory employment standards provide minimum terms and can be improved in a contract, but not derogated (I will touch on this point later in the analysis). I will assume at this stage that just-cause is a default rather than an immutable rule, and thus the choice between just-cause and at-will is a choice between two default rules. I will return later to the second assumption according to which just-cause is an immutable rule.

In the choice of the appropriate default rule, the traditional rationale holds that the default must be set to equal what most contracting parties would have wanted. This rationale is often labelled as the *majoritarian approach* to default rules (Goetz and Scott, 1983). If this is the appropriate guideline for choosing a default rule, then the Darwinist methodology described earlier seems most appropriate. In fact, many employers do not voluntarily restrict their prerogative to dismiss in individual contracts (rather than in collective bargaining agreements). It is therefore conceivable that the parties do not want to negotiate a just-cause rule. Like wages, the rules of dismissals are negotiable. Like wages, many employees cannot negotiate their wages and are 'contract-takers' rather than 'contract-makers'.[11] For the same reason that the Darwinist approach is not concerned about employees being contract-takers with regard to wages, they are not concerned about them being contract-takers with regard to the rule of dismissals.

Stronger support can be provided for the at-will default rule if we observe employers' behaviour in states where courts have started to impose just-cause restrictions. In these states there is a growing number of employers who opt out of the courts' default and explicitly provide for an at-will covenant in the employment contract or employees' manual (Verkerke, 1995).[12] The majoritarian argument holds that the default should lower transaction costs by providing what most parties want. If the majority prefers to contract around the just-cause default, then that default is misguided.

Even on majoritarian terms this argument is incomplete. At a minimum, when designing the majoritarian default (what most parties want) it is not sufficient to count the number of parties who want one default rule rather than the other. The majoritarian approach must also multiply the number of parties who want to opt out of the default by the costs of contracting around it (Ayres and Gertner, 1989; Johnston, 1990, p. 627). As noted, the at-will rule is the only rule-type option. All others are standards. The costs of specifying a standard in detail are generally high, unless the parties are willing to provide the standard in vague terms and leave its enforcement and interpretation to a third party (i.e., the courts). To the extent the parties want to give some 'local' content to what just-cause means, then contracting around the at-will default is significantly more costly than contracting around the developing common law of just-cause. By contrast, in order to reach the rule-type at-will option, it is sufficient to provide a disclaimer in the contract that under all circumstances the employee has no protection against discharge.

The suggested critique, drawing on majoritarian terms, opens the door to a more extensive critique of whether the majoritarian approach, at least when based on Darwinist empiricism, is at all founded. The process through which employees are selected and according to which the employment contract is signed cannot be tested by simple empiricism. Two major problems with the contractual process over dismissals arise at the initial stage: information asymmetry and strategic bargaining over the share of the joint surplus.

3.4.1 One-sided Information Asymmetry

There are several causes for concern about information asymmetry at the stage when the employment contract is bargained. For most employees, the search for employment is a process in which the employee gives all requested information, while the employer can easily withhold or obscure information. It is common today to see employment ads in which the employer does not even publish the name of the firm or specify the exact nature of the position she seeks to fill. The employer advertises only the necessary qualifications required from the applicant, and requires the applicant to send a résumé, recommendations, and a handwritten letter which is then submitted to a graphologist. There is no case-law, nor are there statutes, governing the process of selection, and aside from the general provision of privacy in the developing Israeli constitutional law, no identifiable standard seems to exist that limits the applicant's transparency or the employer's veil of secrecy. At this initial stage the employer is an observer and the employee is being observed. During the interview the applicant receives more information, although she is generally the one being questioned and not the inquiring party. Anecdotal evidence suggests that most employers in Israel do not provide applicants with detailed information regarding the firm's human-resource practices.

The contractual outcome is therefore vulnerable to the problem of unilateral mistakes that cast doubt on its efficiency (Trebilcock, 1993, pp. 102–26). While this is a general problem regarding the bargaining process of the employment contract, there are further problems that are unique to the negotiation of the dismissal rule.

In the process of bargaining the employment contract, the employer is often the repeat-player, thus at an information advantage and with a higher level of sophistication than the applicant. As noted, the prevailing belief among the Israeli workforce is that employees have protection against dismissals, and a strong sense that there is such a thing as 'unfair dismissal'. Few are aware that the rule is in fact the opposite and that applicants for work in firms that are not a party to a collective agreement must bargain some form of just-cause protection if they so desire. On the other hand, any employer relying on legal advice must know about the at-will rule that is so fundamental (although not commonly disputed) to the system.

Even if the applicant is familiar with the law of dismissals and its implications, she is denied the true opportunity to ask many relevant questions. An applicant cannot seriously hope to gain employment if she inquires about the employer's dismissals policy, or about the employer's policy regarding the enforcement of non-competition clauses.[13] Thus the worker's acceptance of the contract-maker's rule for dismissals or non-competition clauses is not really similar to acceptance of the employer's wages. Any effort to bargain over these rules provides adverse signalling on the employee's suitability to the employer.[14] The flip side is that if an employer emphasizes that she provides an enforceable just-cause protection, given the fact that most employers do not, she runs the risk of adverse selection. High visibility of the just-cause standard may attract employees with a shirking disposition (Levine, 1991).The problem can be mitigated if most employers offer just-cause protection, thus indicating that the single employer's choice of rule in the non-organized sector runs into the general problem of collective action, and cannot be detached from the choices made by competing employers.[15]

Despite these problems, asymmetric information may not be troubling if we assume that the formation of an internal labour market is of mutual benefit to both employer and employee. This is in fact the assumption that underlies both arguments for and against just-cause rules. Given that the employer is interested in establishing an internal labour market, she will voluntarily provide employees with the optimal level of security. The emphasis is on the shared interests that bond the parties in the internal labour market. The following argument, however, holds that this underlying assumption may be inaccurate as well.

3.4.2 Strategic Bargaining

In the process of negotiating the employment contract the parties seek two objectives: both seek to maximize their joint surplus, and at the same time each seeks to maximize her share of the surplus. This view of dual objectives must be distinguished from two alternative views. Unlike the Marxist approach which sees the employment relationship as a zero-sum-game, or the unitary perspective of the firm, which holds the employment relationship to be a win-win situation, the proposed view holds that the employment relationship embodies both. Employees rely on the employer's profitability to increase their share of the gains, yet the distribution of gains is conflictual in nature. They thus share the employer's interest to increase the total gains, and at the same time the employer and employees play a strategic game where each seeks to increase her share of the total gains.

There is reason to suspect that the employer will not unilaterally establish the optimal level of security against unjust dismissals. Providing the employee with the most efficient level of job security also provides her with a standard-type level of protection that increases her share of the joint surplus the parties can gain. The employer gives up her ability to dismiss workers whose productivity is lower than the wages the implicit contract assigns. The employer is denied making an *ad hoc* cost-benefit calculation regarding each and every dismissal, in which she compares the value added from the dismissal to the costs in reputation. The employer thus loses what she deems to be her (rather than the parties') optimal level of control.

The employer's dilemma is augmented by two factors. First, while it may be beneficial for the employer to identify an Archimedean point along the continuum of at-will and just-cause, any search for such a point is a search for a sensitive standard-type norm. Owing to the parties' bounded rationality, this point cannot be defined explicitly *ex ante*. Because of the standard-type nature of all rules but the at-will rule, all norms that can be contracted are inherently ambiguous. Consequently, they can later be strategically exploited by the other party (i.e., expropriating quasi rents). Given that any rule of dismissals but at-will is standard-type, the employer is also reluctant to move from the certainty of the rule-type at-will. It is the only rule whereby she can roughly calculate her expected gains.[16]

Second, if the rule of dismissals could have been substituted with wages, then the employer could negotiate with each worker more optimal levels of security.[17] Yet no clear indication exists that there is a substitution effect, as a simple theory of compensating differentials would predict, according to which a just-cause dismissals policy entails lower wages. The fact that workers not governed by collective agreements generally receive higher wages than their union counterparts in the same establishment cannot be attributed solely to the absence of just-cause. Instead, higher wages mostly compensate for the lack of fringe payments that are common in the union sector, and for the lack of relative future uncertainty when renegotiating the contract.[18] The various factors accounting for higher wages of at-will employees compared with their union counterparts must be controlled before a clear substitution effect is established. Indications exist that substitution is limited. Workers who were removed from the collective bargaining regime received higher wages at first, but these often evened off with the union wages after a number of years because of lack of adjustment. The initial higher wages were therefore a function of a buy-out price, not of a substitution for the just-cause protection.[19] Moreover, rarely does one see in a non-union enterprise some career-workers enjoying just-cause while others are governed by at-will.[20] This indicates that there is no cafeteria-type bundle of contracts from which the parties to the employment contract can negotiate a contract well-tailored to the mutual preferences of both parties.[21]

3.4.3 From Majoritarian- to Penalty-default Rules

The problem of information asymmetry that inhibits the parties' capacity to bargain efficiently, and the employer's incentive to determine a rule that maximizes her share of the surplus, rather than the parties' joint surplus, necessitates dropping the majoritarian approach for designing default rules. Darwinist evidence regarding the prevalence of at-will clauses, or failure to contract around the at-will rules, is at most an approximation of what *employers*, but not most *parties*, really desire. Rather than a majoritarian convention we must seek for an alternative method for designing the default rule. One such option is to use the theory of penalty-default rules.

The idea of penalty-default rules is attributed to the relatively recent work of Ayres and Gertner (Ayres and Gertner, 1989; Ayres & Gertner, 1992). While most theoretical work has been conducted accounting for the use of either immutable or default rules, no systematic theory has been put forward for the efficient design of default rules.[22] Ayres and Gertner object to the interpretation given so far to default rules, according to which default rules always mirror what most parties want. While some rules indeed reflect what most parties want, others do just the opposite. They impose a penalty on parties who fail to negotiate around the default. The function of penalty-default rules is to provide the contracting parties with an incentive to engage in an explicit formulation of their mutual preferences. Conventional default rules are appropriate when the legislature seeks to aid the contracting parties by reducing their transaction costs. Penalty-default rules are appropriate when the bargaining parties engage in inefficient strategic behaviour during the pre-contractual negotiations. Thus, penalty-default rules can be designed so as to force both parties to reveal information. Alternatively, when one party with an information advantage prefers not to reveal her information for strategic and inefficient reasons, the penalty can be administered one-sidedly on the non-cooperative party.

These guidelines for designing default rules are especially instructive for the employment relationship at the time the contract is negotiated. The problem of information asymmetry and the employer's reluctance to contract for an optimal dismissals norm maximizing the parties' joint surplus, require penalizing the parties for not negotiating a suitable dismissals rule. The employer's information advantage at the time of bargaining demands that the penalty be directed unilaterally at the employer. The choice of just-cause as a penalty-default rule has the further advantage of acting as a *separating* mechanism. It requires employers to explicitly reveal that they do not bind themselves to any just-cause standard, and so assume the consequences (damaged reputation and the difficulty of motivating workers to invest in firm-specific human capital) of their policy. An at-will default rule may have a *pooling* effect, where employers may choose, for strategic reasons, to develop some form of just-cause dismissals policy but to leave the at-will default intact.[23]

In sum, a general just-cause requirement is a preferred default rule that serves as an information-forcing mechanism. It ensures that despite the parties' asymmetric relationship at the time the employment contract is negotiated, the parties to it act under full information. Nevertheless, the utility of an information-forcing default rule is limited if we believe that the fact that workers are usually 'contract-takers' renders the employment contract inherently inefficient. But according to traditional economic analysis the terms of the contract need not be bargained for but governed by pressures of a competitive market. Generally, economic rationales would be satisfied with the propriety of the contractual outcome, given full information.

3.5 THE IMPLICIT CONTRACT AND THE PROBLEM OF ESTABLISHING NORMS

The assumption thus far has been that the problem of the dismissals rule is rooted in the bargaining process. If the problem is merely one of asymmetric information during the contract negotiations it is sufficient to view just-cause as a penalty-default rule. But this may not be enough. The time when the parties signed the contract may not be a relevant point of reference, especially when examining the relationship between an employer and a career-worker. This is generally true of employment contracts owing to their relational nature.[24] The employment contract is dynamically revised by the parties. Israeli law acknowledges that one party's repeated behaviour or silent consent to the other party's change in behaviour entitles the other party to rely on the change, thus revising the terms of the contract. For the same reason, a unilateral change in the terms of the contract is prohibited unless the other party consents. Consequently, interpretation and construction of relational contracts in general, and of the employment contract in particular, refrains from a strict observance of the terms determined by the parties at the time the original contract was signed.[25]

Law's treatment of the employment contract as a relational contract that is dynamically revised indicates that the original bargain must not be overemphasized. For the proponents of just-cause, the duration of employment at the time of dismissals is indicative of the worker's career stage, and the scope of just-cause protection must be tailored accordingly. For the proponents of at-will, the argument is that developing an internal labour market with protection from abusive dismissals is indeed efficient, but reputation is the optimal police. The debate is therefore not about information asymmetries at the initial stage of bargaining. The fact that there are idiosyncratic norms that develop dynamically within the firm as the employment relationship progresses is not disputed. Instead, the dispute is about who will enforce these norms. This view of the debate merits further examination of what *norms* are.

Because the internal labour market is a contractual device, it is assumed to be to the benefit of both parties to the employment contract. For both sides of the debate, the implicit contract is only a very general frame for a fuller and dense set of norms. While just-cause is the *rule*, it relies on *norms* that determine expected performance, levels of effort, pace and quality of work, moral conduct, loyalty, and interpersonal behavioural standards. Every workplace embodies its own particular set of norms that provide the parties with a shared understanding of what conduct amounts to a just cause for dismissal. These norms are firm-specific. They are developed incrementally through experience, and are tested and refined with each and every decision on dismissals. They are hard to define *ex ante*, and difficult to verify *ex post*. They are complex, contingent on dynamic events, and generally unwritten. Neither position provides a detailed account of how these norms are established. Both positions assume the existence of such norms, but treat them as exogenous to the model itself.

Norms are intersubjective attitudes commonly shared and developed. Norms shape individuals' preferences and thus shape rational choices, but are not necessarily rational themselves (Sunstein, 1996). As such, norms are similar to public goods that have evolved over time. An effort to change them requires collective action and runs into the common difficulties of maintaining a public good. However, once norms are stable they are sustained by common conviction, and may not need continuous enforcement. Norms are not spontaneously created. Norms are nurtured through a process of mutual interaction between those affected by the norms developed.

The emphasis on reputation attributes narrow significance to norms. Their particular content and how it came about need not concern any model based on rationality. Reputation can be used simply as a label for full information available to future contractees with the subject of information (Kreps, 1990). But at the empirical level one may question whether reputation is an adequate source of monitoring compliance with vague and mostly unwritten norms. Owing to the parties' bounded rationality, and the resulting fact that norms are never perfectly defined, the price of signalling by reputation may be too high, and the margin of error concerning the information available may be too wide. An employer's reputation cannot be measured in the number of dismissals per year or the number of law suits the employer entertains. Reputation is an imperfect governance device. 'Young job entrants cannot easily assess an employer's reputation for how it handles senior workers. Great problems arise in passing on knowledge of a firm's opportunistic firings between generations of workers. These problems are particularly acute in small or new firms where much of the workers work' (Schwab, 1993).

An additional problem with the prescribed role for reputation is that it is of no use in the 'end-game'.[26] When workers face mass dismissals, employer's relocation abroad, or mergers, the employer can erase its reputational history. Because workers know they cannot trust the employer in the 'end-game' they will reject the cooperative (norms-based) solution in the next-to-last game, and thus workers will, *ex ante*, reject structuring their employment relationship on unenforceable norms. This suggests that the existence of shared norms cannot be explained merely by total reliance on reputation or market signalling in general. Norms are sustained *in spite* of the end-game problem (and imperfect information), which can considerably weaken the effect of reputation. There are further indications that cooperative norms can be sustained even though each party has the opportunity to exploit the other.[27] The fact that in some establishments there are higher levels of cooperation indicates that these establishments have stable cooperative norms. Why these and not others?

More generally, reputation functions as a deterrent against reneging on promises, not because it directly persuades the parties to the implicit contract to observe it but because the parties are aware that market signalling, in the form of lost reputation, will lead the reneging party to internalize the costs of its behaviour.[28] The strength of internal norms, measured in their legitimacy and clarity from the viewpoint of those who shape them, is thus dependent mostly on the perfection of the invisible hand (namely complete information) and not on the visible relationship within the firm. The narrow view thus assumes the existence of norms and their stability in light of the reputational effect. It is not interested in how norms are created and what induces the creation of norms to begin with. Internal labour markets and reputation come into effect once the appropriate norms are established. Why some firms succeed in establishing the required norms for cooperative functioning and mutual investment in firm-specific human capital is exogenous to the analysis.

An alternative view of norms holds that they provide a context and meaning for individual choices (a broad meaning of norms). Individual choices cannot be comprehended without an observation of the norms that make their behaviour rational. Working faster, even at the price of poorer quality, may be rational in one establishment and irrational in another. An aggressive conflictual approach may be an expected behavioural pattern in one place and a justified cause for dismissals elsewhere. Why has a worker learned to be aggressive in one place as a rational strategy to avoid dismissals? How has she learned the corporate culture? Is she part of the process that has made a conflictual attitude the dominant strategy? How do the worker and manager learn to draw the red line that distinguishes norms-guided behaviour from disloyalty and disruption (themselves a just cause for dismissals)? The norms that shape the worker's preferences and behaviour must be treated as endogenous to a descriptive model that seeks to explain their stability. They cannot be taken as given.[29] This alternative view holds that a governance scheme must observe both the *process* of governance and its *outcomes*. Governance by reputational effects is inadequate to form a set of shared norms. On this account the implicit contract has never been spelled out. While its broad contours can be vaguely defined, its detailed arrangements must be established starting from the shop-floor, up the hierarchy's ladder and down again.

What kind of norms are necessary to sustain the implicit promise and permit a high level of firm-specific human capital investment? While the substantive answer varies from one firm to the other, the broad view of norms holds that these norms, by definition, must be jointly established by all parties to the contract, and constantly tested. This view emphasizes the process through which norms are defined. It is a process of establishing shared meaning, or meaning-making. This view of norms holds that some form of collective action is required in order to change and shape norms. This accounts for the detailed norms that are found in unionized settings. Where employees are not represented by a union, rarely does an institutionalized venue exist for collective determination of norms. Nevertheless, the fact that the employer can unilaterally mobilize change may seem to resolve the problems associated with collective action. However, it is then obvious that norms are structured by employers, and workers are generally passive receptors of the norms.[30] In terms of previous arguments, the employee is not only a *contract-taker* but also a *norms-receiver*. The employer must therefore take special measures to assure workers that these norms reflect a real bargain and match the interests of all sides to the contract. Negotiated rule-making, joint labour-management committees, cross-departmental cooperation, and internal dispute resolution systems, for example, make the process of establishing and developing norms visible. Workers' presence and active involvement in such proceedings allows the parties to prescribe shared meaning to local norms.[31] Norms are not a by-product of market signalling but of active involvement in the process of meaning-making.

If process matters, the belief in market signalling by conveying information on the firm's reputation is inadequate. Yet what about courts? Rock and Wachter (1996) view courts as generally inefficient where local norms are concerned. I would generally agree. Just-cause proponents, by contrast, view courts as the sole executors of the implicit contract. Yet courts are remote from the local setting of norms. Courts are accessible mostly to the high waged workers and not to all workers. Courts are slow. Courts intervene only when the employment relationship fails completely. Taking the matter to court and litigating it for years distances the problem from the firm. Courts are adversarial, and are generally counterproductive to the establishment of cooperative norms back in at the local arena, where norms continue to affect the parties' behaviour. A lack of collective representation on the workers' side prevents a dependable flow of information into the court's decisions and its processing. Where there are juries, their verdicts tend to be erratic and, unlike prices, often fail to convey useful information. However, if they are taken seriously, as if containing some meaning, they can induce irrational uncooperative norms. Courts tear apart the parties to the implicit contract and let those who remain patch themselves up.

Neither markets nor courts are suitable agents of meaning-making. Consequently, neither the at-will default nor the just-cause immutable rules are adequate to induce internal cooperation. The former entrenches managerial monopoly in the making of meaning. The latter is simply naive, thinking that courts are conducive to the structuring of norms. Instead, one should seek how to utilize legal rules to encourage parties to bargain over real meaning, and allow workers and management in the non-union setting to incrementally shape norms and structure them. The role of law should be to motivate the parties in the internal labour market to jointly develop their own set of norms rather than to follow stringent norms determined by the legislature and the courts. *Ceteris paribus*, internal norms are always preferable to externally coerced norms. This is true from both a moral and an efficiency point of view. The question therefore is, what legal rule would be most conducive to such a task. What rule could motivate the agents to engage in the establishment of norms? If earlier we searched for information-forcing rules, we now search for cooperation-inducing rules.

3.6 INTERNAL DISPUTE RESOLUTION, WORKS COUNCILS AND CONSTRAINED-PENALTY-DEFAULT RULES

The assumption underlying the view holding just-cause to be simply a penalty-default rule is that many parties do not want to negotiate a just-cause provision, but the choice of default rule need only ensure that the parties be well informed. No barriers to contracting around it should exist. The evidence indicates that in the United States many employers do contract around just-cause where courts enforce the just cause. Yet it was also noted that many employers continue to provide workers with ongoing assurances, explicit or implicit, that they will not be dismissed without just cause.[32] If both empirical claims are true, they merely indicate a gap between the formal contractual terms and the ongoing practice governing the employment relationship.

What are we to make of this gap? Hoult Verkerke (1995, p. 127) comments that 'some employers strategically offer just-cause protection in unsigned writings in order to deceive employees into thinking that they have legally enforceable protection when in fact they don't'. This seems to me a defeating form of human resource management, and one that Israeli law has already established to be in bad faith, applying the doctrine of estoppel to preclude a party to a contract from making such an argument in court.[33] Yet even if no malicious intent underlies such practice, further rationales are argued to justify the gap. In the United States the courts have established the argument that employers' internal grievance systems seek to rationalize the employer's behaviour given the agency problem.

Bureaucratic policies are intended to constrain front-line managers from making erroneous termination decisions, but are not intended to provide workers with a legally recognized reliance interest against unjust dismissals.[34] I find it difficult to perceive how parties aiming at expanding the joint surplus by establishing shared norms can manage this gap. Furthermore, breaking the just-cause practice into two separate dimensions, one that governs the employment relationship and one that governs the bureaucratic relationship, is difficult to justify. Just-cause practice is a single phenomenon that creates a shared understanding among all those affected.

The distinction between formal (written rules in the original contract) and informal (unwritten, or rules of practice) norms, or between norms that seek to rationalize the employer's bureaucracy and norms that provide employees with enforceable rights, seems to poorly translate into a policy of cooperative mutual investment in human capital. If the only safeguard against artificial sorting of norms is reputation it is not adequate. If we emphasize how norms are established, and why the parties provide these norms with the required legitimacy to sustain them, despite the imperfect nature of reputation as a governance mechanism, the distinction between law and norms must be abandoned. If default rules, whether majoritarian-default or penalty-default, as well as mandatory just cause coupled with third party intervention, are inappropriate cooperation-inducing mechanisms, what other options are available? I suggest that between the immutable and the default we can insert an additional rule, which I will designate as a constrained-penalty-default rule.

3.6.1 Derogatory Arrangements as a Constrained-penalty-default Rule

It has been assumed so far that just-cause is a possible default rule rather than a mandatory statutory standard. According to the conventional typology of labour law's building blocks, this assumption relegates the just-cause rule to the law of contracts, where most statutory terms are default terms, rather than to the statutory standards that provide employees with a safety net that cannot be bargained. It was argued that this distinction is not applicable to the at-will rule. Even if we conceive of the at-will as a statutory standard outside the law of contracts, then the rule is generally that standards that improve the employees' gains above and beyond what the law provides may be contracted for.

Contract law's default rules and statutory standards are not diametrically opposed. One of the recent trends in employment law is to provide for the possibility of derogating statutory standards. Unlike conventional default rules, the possibility of derogating these standards is constrained and requires more than an explicit provision in the employee's contract of employment. Derogating a statutory provision requires a collective bargaining agreement, or an enterprise-based agreement with a works council, or paying a tax for non-compliance.

Israeli labour law allows derogation in a limited number of cases. The statutory provision prohibiting paying lump-sum wages that compensate for overtime can be derogated in a collective bargaining agreement. The statutory definition of the standard work-week (43 hours a week or 8 hours a day) can be derogated by collective bargaining agreements that are ratified by the Minister of Labour and Welfare. The law establishing free export trade zones allows derogation of some statutory standards in a collective bargaining agreement. The recent law on staffing companies requires these companies to provide a security to ensure that their workers will be compensated. The security required can be derogated by 10 per cent if the staffing company engages in collective bargaining with a union. Moreover, once an employee of a staffing company is engaged by a different employer for more than three years, that employer's collective bargaining agreements apply to the staffing company's employee as well. This arrangement can be derogated if the staffing company has a collective bargaining agreement with a union, in which case only that agreement applies to the staffing company's employee.

The use of derogatory arrangements currently prevails in industrial systems where there is heavy use of statutory standards, such as Italy, Germany, and France (Biagi, 1995; Sciarra, 1988; Treu, 1986). It is common to allow derogation on condition that it is negotiated through collective bargaining or with a works council. The use of derogation clauses is most suitable in cases where statutory standards are justified only on the basis of correcting bargaining inequality, but not in cases that are justified by the need to correct a negative externality of the employment contract. For example, anti-discrimination law is not appropriate for derogation clauses. By contrast, if the rules governing dismissals are attributed to statutory standards rather than to contractual default rules, I believe that they can be appropriately derogated. In fact, many of the traditional justifications favouring just-cause entitlements rest on the problem of unequal bargaining power.[35] Because of the particular measures required in order to derogate statutory standards, I designate these rules *constrained-penalty-default rules*.

It is possible to draw on the mechanism of derogatory arrangements and hold that any dismissal of a long-term employee will be litigated according to the developing common law of just-cause, but the court must defer to intra-firm dispute resolution institutions unless the employee proves she was denied fair justice. Thus, where the rule has been appropriately derogated, courts will be granted only limited power of review, similar to their power in reviewing arbitration rulings. According to the proposed rule, if Rock and Wachter (1996) are correct in emphasizing the costs of third-party intervention, the derogatory arrangement allows resistance to external intervention, but only upon proof that the employer has established an internal safeguard to ensure against unjust dismissals, where the idea of 'justice' is defined locally through joint meaning-making.

The Darwinist may justly wonder. If the theoretical argument is correct, and the establishment of local norms for dismissals, combined with an internal dispute resolution mechanism that ensures due-process justice, is efficient, why don't we see explicit contracts providing for such an arrangement? The easy answer is that the parties have little incentive to do so. If the at-will rule prevails, then the employer can set up internal dispute-resolution procedures at-will, and dismiss at-will. As noted, some employers have in fact willingly adopted such schemes, and the proposed scheme only seeks to further encourage such efforts. As long as employers know that all internal dispute-resolution outcomes are vulnerable to judicial intervention they have a limited incentive to develop such schemes. By contrast, the possibility to derogate statutory standards and third-party enforcement provides an incentive for employers to rationalize the process of dismissals.[36] Furthermore, providing default guidelines for the development of such schemes can considerably lower the transaction costs required to establish them. Thus a derogation clause, accompanied by a model dispute resolution code, can lower the costs of establishing internal schemes, and also change the base-line by which the employer measures the utility gained.

The Darwinist can be provided with an additional explanation. The proposed constrained-penalty-default rule in fact suggests some version of a works councils legislation. The justification for this type of legislation is very similar to that provided for switching to the penalty-default rule at the initial bargaining stage. Freeman and Lazear (1995, pp. 29–33) justify statutory establishment of works councils in light of an inherent market failure where the parties try to increase the joint surplus, while at the same time trying to expand their share of the surplus. The authors demonstrate that while limited joint management may be to the benefit of both parties (enlarging the pie), they cannot agree on the degree of power that workers should have. The employer would be willing to provide workers with sub-optimal levels of power in order to enlarge her share of the pie. Similarly, workers would be interested in obtaining more power than efficiency prescribes in order to enlarge their share. Moreover, when the power struggle over the share of the pie is complicated by the fixed costs of establishing the works council to begin with, the parties may withdraw from the effort in spite of the final outcome, which could improve the lot of all parties. Freeman and Lazear hold that the law on works councils prescribes an approximate power balance that is conducive to intra-firm cooperation. Furthermore, the law can also reduce the fixed costs of establishing the council. Finally, works councils legislation does not mandate works councils in all firms, and, similarly, the proposed idea of derogation does not mandate adopting an internal dispute resolution mechanism. The employer may prefer to rely on the default just-cause entitlement with judicial enforcement.

3.6.2 The General Framework for Derogation

The structuring of a constrained-penalty-default rule is complex. The variations are endless and require a much finer analysis than I can provide here. Moreover, my intention is to reflect on the need to seek cooperation-inducing rules rather than to draw specific policy proposals. Several sources may be instructive for such efforts, although none can be adopted *in toto*. The prevalence of grievance procedures in the organized sector in Israel provides one model. Voluntary internal dispute-resolution systems that have been developed in non-union establishments provide another, more heterogeneous, model. Lacking any systematic study on such practices in Israeli non-union enterprises, one may turn to the experience of some American non-union firms that have been experimenting with these forms of internal grievance systems, including those with systems where workers are given a true voice in the process (Edwards, 1993, pp. 141–8, 203–17). European measures in line with the idea of designing a dismissals procedure avoiding the at-will-default/just-cause-immutable dichotomy can provide yet a third model. For example, the German works councils legislation on the councils' involvement in dismissals (Weiss, 1995, pp. 94–5), or the French legislation requiring consultation with the works councils for certain types of terminations and pre-conciliation hearings (Despax and Rojot, 1987, p. 228–31).

Derogation of just-cause requires considering whether the parties can only bypass judicial intervention and litigate just-cause internally, or whether the just-cause standard itself could be derogated as well. The objective of the derogation scheme is to encourage the parties to develop an internal set of norms that give meaning to just-cause. An internal grievance system requires developing a 'local common law' that clarifies the local norms regarding expected levels of work and conduct. If the local common law applies a strict at-will policy, holding that dismissals are categorically permitted regardless of years of service, the circumstances surrounding the dismissal, reliance, and implicit understandings that have evolved with the employment relationship over the years, then the objective of derogation is lost. Nevertheless, there should be quite considerable leeway for developing different rules and different norms in various workplaces. One would expect a very different meaning to be given to just-cause in a highly volatile high-tech establishment and in a stable insurance company.

Distinguishing between legitimate experimentation and the unreasonable is a familiar task for Israeli courts. For example, the judicial interpretation of covenants not to compete upon termination of employment has instituted the rule that unreasonable restrictions on the employee's future career will be struck out. The courts do not render the covenants void altogether, but provide the parties with a standard 'off-the-rack' covenant.[37] Similarly, unreasonable developments of just-cause rules within enterprises may bring the parties back to the judicial default interpretation of just-cause. Thus, courts' intervention can be restricted unless internal norms are unreasonable. Alternatively, courts' intervention can be limited only to those situations where due process is not observed. The two alternatives cannot be wholly separated because proof of due process reflects the reasonableness of outcomes, and the reasonableness of outcomes reflects the observation of due process.[38] In sum, it would be fair to say that the just-cause rule must be sustained, but the establishment of norms that provide meaning to local justice must be permitted within a very broad range. If just cause and at-will have been painted as two ends of a continuum, I would suggest that most of the continuum is available for the parties to design. What must be denied is the categorical holding that all dismissals are just and thus do not merit individual attention. The categorical at-will obviates the need to develop an internal dispute resolution mechanism.

As to the process, a model code for internal dispute resolution can serve as a default structure as long as some fundamental premises are held to be mandatory.[39] Lacking the active involvement of a union, a model code cannot simply replicate the common grievance arbitration that developed in collective agreements. A minimal version would require establishing fundamental due process conditions. However, because the major objective for providing the possibility to derogate the statutory standards is to encourage joint meaning-making, a more ambitious scheme must opt for employees' involvement in the process. Such a scheme can draw on the vast experimentation with works councils and joint labour-management committees in Western European countries.

The main argument against allowing derogation in the non-union sector is that workers will be trapped into unbalanced arbitration schemes that will place them at a disadvantage (Stone, 1996). The argument may be correct only if the employee's rights are compared to those of employees with an immutable entitlement that they can litigate in court. At the same time, I argued earlier that courts are not conducive agents to the establishment of internal meaning-making. Moreover, there are some inherent advantages to the internal grievance procedure. These proceedings are generally speedier and less expensive than litigation; they are more informal in terms of procedure and rules of evidence, and when structured correctly they also have a 'therapeutic force' over the parties to the process and the workplace community in general (Gorman, 1995, p. 647–8). Even if one party may feel itself on the losing side at the end of the process (and arbitrators have more leeway to advance compromises that avoid such outcomes), the arbitration of each and every case has a spillover effect on the internal climate of the establishment.

Many variables must be considered, and an explicit consideration of each is outside the scope of this paper. Just to point to some, it is possible to consider whether med-arb forms that emphasize joint decision making rather than replicating the court's final decision-making power may be preferable to simple arbitration.[40] Arbitration itself can be structured in different ways. It can rely on external *ad hoc* arbitrators or on internal joint committees that closely resemble the operations of works councils. The stated objectives – inducing cooperation and joint meaning-making – can aid in selecting among the various options. Thus, mediation may be preferred to arbitration, and internal councils may be preferred to external arbitrators. At the same time, joint meaning-making must bring the parties together as equals, and given the fact that the possibility of derogation was endorsed because the problem is mostly one of power imbalance, some recourse to external intervention and conclusive decisions may be needed.

A unique feature which may be needed to fulfil the underlying objective of meaning-making is to require publicizing the internal proceeding's final decision. Although there are reasons against making public an arbitrator's decision, including the interest of the grieving employee's privacy, there is a need to provide both the workforce and managers with a guideline on the application and creation of norms. Modern human-resource approaches could utilize such decisions as part of the learning process within the firm. They can be abstracted (to protect the direct parties' interests), codified, and made accessible to all workers. More generally, internal proceedings cannot be viewed as merely a private affair, and they must be held to be semi-public.

Opting for a process-based, rather than standard-based, option in non-unionized establishments has its risks. Let us bear in mind the evidence brought in the United States by the ACLU before the Commission on the Future of Worker-Management Relations (the Dunlop Commission), stating that

> We have seen ADR systems in which the employee is not permitted to be present when the employer presents its case. We have seen systems in which the employee is not permitted access to relevant documents. We have seen systems which do not even use a neutral arbitrator, but instead have one company manager rule on the conduct of another, both knowing that their roles may be reversed tomorrow.[41]

Stone (1996) further notes that following a recent Supreme Court decision in the United States that upheld contractual clauses requiring internal arbitration that precludes employees from asserting their statutory rights in court, employers frequently require their employees to sign such arbitration clauses as a condition of employment. The internal processes are, however, heavily biased against the employees and rarely provide the necessary level of due process. The highly unbalanced American experience with such internal processes is instructive for a design of a model code, but should not be viewed as a conclusive argument against the derogatory approach. Process-based protection for workers is indeed precarious, but not impossible. Moreover, its potential for abusing employees' rights and the implicit norms that govern the employment relationship must also be compared with the disadvantages of enforcing statutory standards by means of judicial intervention. The quest is for the second-best alternative, not for the theoretical optimum.

Devising a model dispute resolution code and a derogatory scheme is about finding the approximate balance that will encourage the parties to expand their joint surplus rather than allow one party to appropriate power and inefficiently expand her share of the pie. Naturally, it is more convenient for the Israeli legislature to avoid such experimentation for lack of experience in providing non-union workers with process-based rights. Indeed, the middle ground between the immutable just-cause and the majoritarian default of at-will must be carefully devised. Its implementation, however, can create a new mechanism that abstains from the drawbacks of both conventional responses.

3.7 CONCLUSION: MAJORITARIAN-DEFAULT RULES, PENALTY-DEFAULT RULES, CONSTRAINED-PENALTY-DEFAULT RULES, AND THE RECONFIGURATION OF LABOUR LAW'S BUILDING BLOCKS.

The current debate in Israel is framed around the hourglass effect and limited to binary options: add more statutory standards or deregulate and allow managers to use their prerogative with no intervention. Justifying the first argument is the need for legislative empowerment of workers, given their inferior bargaining power. Justifying the second argument is the trickle-down theory that workers will benefit if employers can act with no external interference on their prerogative. The former justification is based on the assumption of a zero-sum game, the latter on the assumption of a win-win game. The one calls for immutable rules that grant workers judicial protection, the other holds that employees must bargain for whatever they want in the employment contract. This dichotomous framing of the debate is not conducive to either party in the employment relationship.

Between the just-cause immutable rule and the at-will default I inserted two alternative options. The minimal option holds just-cause as a penalty-default rule that serves as an information-forcing institution. It can apply to other debates, and recently has been applied to another dimension of the employment relationship – covenants not to compete.[42] The more encompassing option holds that just-cause must be set as a constrained-penalty-default rule that allows derogation of the just-cause statutory standard, contingent on developing an internal dispute resolution mechanism modelled on the premises of European works councils legislation. This option serves also as a cooperation-inducing mechanism for it encourages the establishment of internal norms by providing for joint meaning-making.

The two options added to the debate also raise questions about the conventional distinction between default and immutable rules. If we apply a majoritarian-default rule of at-will, the standard-type nature of just-cause raises the costs of contracting around the default, making it prohibitive. Furthermore, asymmetric information and problems of strategic bargaining may render the effort to contract around it extremely difficult to achieve. At-will is thus majoritarian in the sense that it reflects what most employers, being the contract-makers, want, but not what most parties want. Moreover, owing to the strategic dilemma the parties face at the time of bargaining, the majoritarian default can translate, in practice, into an immutable rule that is not in the best interest of both parties. By contrast, the possibility to derogate statutory standards transforms the immutable into a default rule. Under this arrangement, the costs of contracting around the just-cause standard are not negligible, but once the start-up costs are invested, the parties have an incentive to cooperate in order to capture the fruits of investment. As the Freeman and Lazear model reflects, the arrangement may be viewed by both parties as giving them too little, but it expands their joint surplus. The fact that each party wants more leverage in the process, together with the public-good nature of such internal grievance systems, accounts for the parties' failure to establish these institutions voluntarily.

What started as a debate between expanding statutory protection or unfettered markets also brings the middle tier of collective labour law back into the policy arena. There are some inherent shortcomings in the total deregulation of the labour market, as well as in the juridification of the employment relationship by means of judicial imperialism. The Israeli system of collective bargaining was designed on the basis of the 'old rules of competition'. Changes in these rules have led some to bury the idea that the workers' collective voice could be used to the benefit of all parties involved. Politically, there is a counter-reaction to the Histadrut's past hegemonic reign over the Israeli labour market. In the process of racing to the ultimate protection of workers by statutory standards, or, alternatively, by market signalling, the possibility of changing the assumptions and rules governing collective labour law have remained outside the political, judicial, and academic debate. It is not surprising that opting for new means that avoid the drawbacks of immutable just-cause standards and the at-will contractual default has brought back the need to rethink the middle tier of the workers' collective voice, even if that voice falls short of unionization.

ENDNOTES

1. Lecturer, Haifa University, Faculty of Law.
2. In the United States, for example, the law of torts plays an important role especially in the developing law on dismissals, as well as on issues of libel and slander. The law of torts has not penetrated labour law in Israel and I thus omit it from the analysis. It is noteworthy that much of what the law of torts provides in American litigation can be achieved under the umbrella of the vast contractual doctrine of good-faith in Israeli law.
3. Arguably, statutory standards can also be justified in utilitarian terms, as means to correct for various market failures. Indeed, I argue in the following sections that statutory standards are not inherently inefficient. Nevertheless, it is noteworthy that many of the statutory standards are viewed as objectionable by those who draw strictly on neo-classical analysis.

4. The literature on the Israeli industrial relations system and labour law in English is scarce. Moreover, in the last few years dramatic changes have taken place, and I dare say that labour law is changing by the month. The discussion of the Israeli system in the text is sketchy at best, and lacking much needed nuance and subtlety. It is provided in order to give the necessary background and justification for the theoretical analysis. For a more thorough analysis of Israeli labour law and industrial relations, although somewhat outdated, see Ben-Israel (1992); Shalev (1992); Grinberg (1991). I avoid providing references to the more rigorous materials available in Hebrew, assuming that these are not accessible to most readers.
5. 'The Histradrut's local authority at Rehovot – Weitzmann Institute' (not yet published, 1997). The case is in fact about dismissals in the organized sector. In a nutshell, the worker was a biology researcher at the Weitzmann Institute. She was hired as part of a funded project and her employment was contingent on the availability of funds for the project. Her contract was extended from time to time. Her contract was terminated after 14 years of almost continuous employment because funding for the particular project had been terminated. There was no dispute about the good quality of her work. The majority interpreted the collective bargaining agreement and concluded that the worker had no protection from dismissal. The two dissenting opinions argued that the collective bargaining agreement must be interpreted in a manner that provides security not only to employees with an indefinite term contract but also to a worker who invested so much of her research career in the Institute. The dissenting opinions further emphasized her reliance on the job, her firm-specific human capital investment, and her low opportunity wage if she is to seek work elsewhere.

   Other cases that have utilized the good-faith rationale to hold dismissals as a breach of the employment contract are scarce: The International Association of the Jewish Reform Movement – Ary Ben-Shahar, 25 PDA 3 (1994) [dismissal of an employee five days after he was accepted for work]; B.G. Polimers – Zehava Shtul, 28 PDA 421 (1996) [dismissing a worker because she refused to work on the Sabbath, although that was not required by her employment contract]; Ahmad Abu Romi – The Jerusalem District Electric Company (not yet published, 1997) [dismissing a worker who was ill when employees were offered the opportunity to retire with high severance pay].
6. The literature on delayed compensation models is voluminous and encompasses several competing models. One of the major strands of this literature is the *efficiency wage* model. For an overview of the literature on this topic see Akerlof and Yellen (1986); Hutchens (1989). Selected landmarks in the development of these models include Becker and Stigler (1974); Lazear (1981); Medoff and Abraham (1981); Raff and Summers (1987).

   For other delayed compensation models that account for rising wages with seniority, see Lazear (1995).
7. For a similar argument in favour of reputation as the optimal monitoring device see Carmichael (1989); that the implicit contract is not self enforcing, in spite of the reputational effect can be derived from the analysis by Klein and Leffler (1981).
8. On the distinction between standards and rules, see Ayres (1993). Ayres utilizes the distinction of Posner and Ehrlich, according to which 'A rule withdraws from the decision maker's consideration one or more of the circumstances that would be relevant to decision according to a standard.... The difference between a rule and a standard is a matter of degree – the degree of precision.'

   I agree with Ayres' observation that default rules may be either rules or standards. An awkward implication of this observation is that the term 'rule' carries too many meanings. I will therefore denote the distinction between rules and standards by adding the suffix '-type', and use the term 'rule' as a standalone when making a general claim about default rules. For example: at-will is a rule-type rule.

9. In this situation we need to distinguish between a contractual (or restitution-based) claim the worker can make for the promised benefit, and the more encompassing claim holding the dismissal to be a breach of contract, thus granting the worker not only the recovery of the promised benefit, but also foreseeability damages.
10. I assume throughout the article that just-cause does not deter dismissals based on the employer's economic difficulty. Yet even when the employer needs to lay off a large number of employees, an employee can make an individual claim that her inclusion in the list of those who are fired is not warranted by just-cause.
11. The terms here draw on Gandy (1993), but the concept underlies much of the literature on uniform contracts (or contracts of adhesion).
12. No comparable data exist for Israel, but based on anecdotal evidence I can assume that employers in the non-union sector do not insert just-cause provisions into individual contracts, thus leaving the at-will default rule in place. Much of the literature in the United States deals with the enforceability of employees' manuals that provide a just-cause statement. The institution of employees' manuals is however not as common in Israel and can be found only in a limited number of establishments.
13. The problem of dismissals and covenants not to compete are strongly linked and raise partially similar concerns. Discharging a worker sends her out to the external labour market and denies her a job, while covenants not to compete augment the worker's vulnerability because they restrict her future ability to obtain employment.
14. Samuel Issacharof aptly compares the application process to a first date 'between a polygamist and a monogamist' (Issacharof, 1996, pp. 1794–6).
15. On the relationship between the single employer's human resource strategy and the choices made by other employers see generally Levine and Tyson (1990).
16. Future uncertainty regarding the scope of the legal rule and its application can often lead to a chilling effect on the employer and to overcompliance. See generally Polinsky and Shavell (1989).
17. This follows from the Coase theorem. Verkerke (1994, p. 874) argues that '[I]f employees were fully informed they might well be less likely to work for these employers, and the employers would be forced either to raise wages or to offer legally enforceable just cause protection'.
18. The comparison is among similarly situated jobs, as the unionized 'core' in a large enterprise often earns more than the non-union 'periphery'.
19. This argument is based on anecdotal evidence in Israel (personal communications with Prof. Amira Galin, Graduate School of Business, Tel Aviv University, who studied the strike of employees who exchanged collective bargaining for individual contracts in the Israeli Aeronautics Industry).
20. There is evidence of this in the United States: see Verkerke (1994, p. 866). No comparable data are available for Israeli enterprises, but based on anecdotal observations the situation is similar.
21. Even in the United States, where cafeteria-plans are more common, the menu of options usually allows employees to tailor their compensation by deciding whether they want more long-term saving (e.g., pensions) or short-term compensation (i.e., higher wages). The cafeteria-nature of the compensation schemes is thus limited to the monetary aspects of the employment relationship, not to the expected level of effort, working conditions or the rule of dismissals.
22. Trebilcock (1993, p. 126) aptly notes that 'the choice of default rules in incomplete contracts, especially in the case of asymmetric information, poses one of the most daunting challenges for theories of contract law... For the moment, "muddling through" may define our aspirational limits'.
23. Ayres and Gertner (1989, p. 95) define *pooling* and *separating* equilibria: In 'separating' equilibria, the different types of contracting parties, by bearing the costs of contracting around unwanted defaults, separate themselves into distinct contractual relationships. In 'pooling' equilibria, different types of contracting parties fail to contract around defaults, thus avoiding transaction costs but bearing the inefficiencies of the substantive default provisions'.

24. The classic statement on relational contracts is Macneil (1980). On the economic controversy surrounding the relational-contract analysis see Richard Craswell (1993).
25. For the developing Israeli doctrine on relational contracts in general, and employment contracts in particular, many of the observations are provided by scholars of relational contracts. See Milfalder v. National Labour Court PD 41(2) 210 (1983) (the Supreme Court denied the employer's prerogative to make a unilateral change in the employment contract with the employee's consent); Miriam Zohar–Habima National Theatre, PDA 6 309 (1975) (the National Labour Court established the principle of revision in employment contracts). On the interpretation of relational contracts see Tadmor v. Yishpar, PD 47(2) 517 (1995) (the Supreme Court held that when interpreting relational contracts the court must observe the parties' behaviour after the contract was signed).

    In this respect the Israeli approach is different from the North American. Courts. in the United States tend to deny interpretation of the relational contract according to the parties' behaviour, and return to the parties' agreement at the time of contract formation. There are court rulings upholding an employer's unilateral modification of the employment rule from just-cause to at-will. See, for example, Bankey v. Storer Broadcasting Co. 443 NW2d 11 (Mich. 1989). Moreover, courts distinguish between explicit written terms of the contract and the employer's behaviour, and do not acknowledge the employee's reliance on repeated patterns of behaviour. See Edwards (1993, p. 139, 179–80)
26. On the end game problem, or the backward induction paradox, see Ordeshook (1986, pp. 442–8).
27. For an interesting demonstration of this claim see Ostrom (1991).
28. It is assumed here that the damage to the employer's reputation entails two different costs. In the internal labour market the cost is likely to be tit-for-tat uncooperative behaviour by the employees. Incumbent employees are however not likely to respond to abusive dismissals by means of quitting their job in protest. From an efficiency point of view the individual employee is likely to lose income when moving from a job in which she has worked for many years, and the costs of protest against the employer's behaviour are rather high for each employee to assume. This will matter for the most part when recruiting new employees. In the external labour market, assuming that there is sufficient information to convey the employer's reputation to new job applicants, the cost incurred by an employer for abusive behaviour is their inability to draw new career workers.
29. For the distinction between the two meanings of norms draw on Sunstein (1996, pp. 24–8).
30. This is obviously an oversimplification, because even when unions do not represent employees some norms are developed by the employees or through informal co-management. A good example of an employee's response to a management-initiated norm can be observed in the case study conducted by Whyte (1977) on the implementation of a piece-rate incentive system. Nevertheless, overcoming the problem of collective action in non-institutionalized settings is much more difficult than in settings where there is a union or alternative means for collective representation.
31. The thrust of the argument here, while not provided in a purely economic analysis, is consistent with the work, among others, of Leibenstein (1987) and Akerlof (1983). Both theorists emphasize the process of structuring cooperation. Leibenstein's theory of x-inefficiency emphasizes that the efficiency of intra-firm institutions is a factor of concrete interactions within the firm. The entry of a worker into the firm is not enough to bring the parties to a high level of cooperation ('the golden rule'). There must be a process that brings the parties into a state of trust and cooperation. The endogeneity of the *process* is necessary because in 'completely ahistorical situations there would be no basis for trust' (p. 46). In a similar vein, Akerlof holds that certain processes allow individuals to test and assess their values and loyalties. These he holds as 'loyalty filters'. Certain experiences, but not others, serve as loyalty-enhancing filters and aid in establishing a culture of trust.

32. Rock and Wachter provide a general observation to that extent. Also see Edwards (1993, pp. 142–9).
33. Kalmar v. Guy (not yet published, 1995).
34. See, for example, Edwards (1993, pp. 179–80), who describes the US Court of Appeals' decision in Aiello v. United Airlines holding that in spite of the employees' manual that provides a clear procedure for grievance arbitration, these procedures are 'not controlling' owing to the clear disclaimer holding employment is at-will.
35. See, for example, Weiler (1990).
36. An important incentive for the development of internal grievance systems in the United States has been the civil liberties legislation there. See Sutton (1994).

    Employers' responses to these statutory provisions suggests that laws can have a transformative effect on internal managerial practices. Although these laws did not require establishing internal dispute resolutions systems, the authors note that '[f]aced with an apparently hostile legal environment, employers adopted due-process governance to out potentially litigious employees and demonstrate good-faith compliance with government mandates'.
37. Drawing on the distinction made by Ayres and Gertner (1989), this is a court non-enforcement penalty-default rule.
38. This is a private-law adaptation of John Rawls' reflective equilibrium, where outcomes reflect the design of the process, and observation of process ensures just outcomes.
39. An example in this spirit can be observed in the European directive establishing works councils in multinational enterprises. The directive proposed a set of rules for establishing a multinational works council, but also allows negotiation around the default. See Council Directive 94/45/EC of 22 September 1994 on the establishment of a European Works Council, Articles 5, 6.
40. There are quite a few differences between arbitration and mediation. These include not only the different decision-making powers the mediator/arbitrator has, but also differences in the process itself. For an economic analysis of mediation's advantages see Brown and Ayres (1994).
41. Citied in Gorman, (1995 at fn. 56).
42. In a recent decision, Egged v. Mashiach, PD 48(2) 66 (1994), the Supreme Court held that unless the parties provide explicitly for a covenant not to compete in the contract, the court will hold the parties' silence against the employer. The rationale provided for this decision is based on a vague application of the constitutional right of freedom of occupation. Regardless of the explicit rhetoric of the court, I believe that the analysis provided here reinforces the doctrinal outcome.

REFERENCES

Akerlof, G. (1983), 'Loyalty filters', *American Economic Review*, **73**, 54.

Akerlof, George and Janet L. Yellen (1986), 'Introduction' in George Akerlof and Janet Yellen (eds), *Efficiency Wage Models of the Labor Market*, *NY*, NY: Cambridge University Press, pp. 1–19.

Ayres, I. (1993), 'Preliminary thoughts on optimal tailoring of contractual rules', *Southern California Interdisciplinary Law Journal*, **3**, 1.

Ayres, I. and R. Gertner (1989), 'Filling gaps in incomplete contracts: an economic theory of default rules', *Yale Law Journal*, **99**, 87.

Ayres, I. and R. Gertner (1992), 'Strategic contractual inefficiency and the optimal choice of legal rules', *Yale Law Journal*, **100**, 720.

Becker, G. and G. Stigler (1974), 'Law enforcement, malfeasance and the compensation of enforcers', *Journal of Legal Studies*, **3**, 1.

Ben-Israel, Ruth (1992), 'Israel' (monograph), in Roger Blanpain (ed.), *International Encyclopaedia Labor Law & Industrial Relations*, Deventer: Kluwer.
Biagi, M. (1995), 'Labour law in small and medium-sized enterprises: flexibility or adjustment', *Comparative Labor Law Journal*, **16**, 439.
Brown, G. J. and I. Ayres (1994), 'Economic rationales for mediation', *Virginia Law Review*, **80**, 323.
Carmichael, L. (1989), 'Self enforcing contracts, shirking and life cycle incentives', *Journal of Economic Perspectives*, **3**, 65.
Charny, D. (1991), 'Hypothetical bargains: the normative structure of contract interpretation', *Michigan Law Review* **89**, 1815.
Croswell, R. (1993), 'The relational move: some questions from law and economics', *Southern California Interdisciplinary Law Journal*, **3**, 289.
Despax, M. and J. Rojot (1987), *Labour Law and Industrial Relations in France*, France: Kluwer.
Edwards, Richard (1993), *Rights at Work: Employment Relations in the Post-Union Era*, Washington D.C.: Brookings Institution.
Epstein, R. (1984), 'In defense of the contract at will', *University of Chicago Law Review*, **51**, 947.
Freeman, Richard B. and Edward P. Lazear (1995), 'An economic analysis of works councils', in Joel Rogers & Wolfgang Streeck (eds), *Works Councils*, Chicago: Chicago University Press, NBER series, 27.
Gandy, Oscar (1993), *The Panoptic Sort: A Political Economy of Personal Information*, Boulder, Col.: Westview Press.
Goetz, C. and R. Scott (1983), 'The mitigation principle: toward a general theory of contractual obligation', *Virginia Law Review*, **69**, 967.
Gorman, R. (1995), 'The Gilmer decision and the private arbitration of public law disputes', *University of Illinois Law Review*, (1995), 635.
Grinberg, Lev Louis (1991), *Split Corporatism in Israel*, Albany, NY: SUNY Press.
Hutchens, R. (1989) 'Seniority, wages and productivity: a turbulent decade', *Journal of Economic Perspectives*, **3**, 49.
Issacharof, S. (1996), 'Contracting for employment: the limited return of the common law', Texas Law Review, **74**, 1783.
Johnston, J. (1990), 'Strategic bargaining and the economic theory of contract default rules', *Yale Law Journal*, **100**, 615.
Klein, B. and K. Leffler (1981), 'The role of market forces in assuring contractual performance', *Journal of Political Economics*, **89**, 615.
Kreps, David M. (1990), 'Corporate culture and economic theory', in James E. Alt and Kenneth A. Shepsle (eds), *Perspectives on Positive Political Economy*, NY: Cambridge University Press.
Lazear, E. (1981), 'Agency, earnings profiles, productivity and hours restrictions', *American Economic Review*, **71**, 606.
Lazear, E. (1995), *Personnel Economics*, Cambridge, Mass.: MIT University Press.
Leibenstein, Harvey (1987), *Inside the Firm: The Inefficiencies of Hierarchy*, Cambridge, Mass.: Harvard University Press.
Levine, D. (1991), 'Just cause employment policies in the presence of worker adverse selection', *Journal of Labor Economics*, **9**, 294.
Levine, David I. and Laura D'Andrea Tyson (1990), 'Participation, productivity and the firm's environment', in Alan Blinder (ed.), *Paying for Productivity*, pp. 183–230.
Macneil, Ian R. (1980), *The New Social Contract: An Inquiry Into Modern Contractual Relations*, New Haven, CT: Yale University Press.

Medoff, J. and K. Abraham (1981), 'Are those paid more really more productive? The case of experience', *Journal of Human Resources*, **16**, 186.

Morriss, A. (1994) 'Exploding myths: an empirical and economic reassessment of the rise of employment at will', *Montana Law Review*, **59**, 679.

Ordeshook, Peter C. (1986), *Game Theory and Political Theory*, NY: Cambridge University Press.

Ostrom, Elinor (1991), *Governing the Commons*, NY: Cambridge University Press.

Polinsky, M. and S. Shavell (1989), 'Legal error, litigation and the incentive to obey the law', *Journal of Law, Economics and Organizations*, **5**, 99.

Raff, D. and L. Summers (1987), 'Did Henry Ford pay efficiency wage?' *Journal of Labor Economics*, **5**, S57-D86.

Rock, E. and M. Wachter (1996), 'The enforceability of norms and the employment relationship', *Pennsylvania Law Review*, **144**, 1.

Rogers, Joel & Wolfgang Streeck (eds) (1995), *Works Councils*, Chicago: Chicago University Press.

Schwab, C. (1993), 'Life-cycle justice: accommodating just case and employment at will', *Michigan Law Review*, **92**, 8.

Sciarra, S. (1988), 'Plant bargaining: the impact of juridification on current deregulative trends in Italy', *Comparative Labor Law Journal*, **8**, 123.

Shalev, Michael (1992), *Labour and the Political Economy in Israel*, Oxford: Oxford University Press.

St. Antoine, T. (1992), 'The making of the Model Employment Termination Act', *Washington Law Review* **69**, 361.

Stone, K. (1996), 'Labor/employment law: mandatory arbitration of individual employment rights: the Yellow Dog Contract of the 1990s', *Denver University Law Review*, **73**, 1017.

Sutton, J., F. Dobbin, J.W. Meyer and W.R. Scott (1994), 'The legalization of the workplace', *American Journal of Sociology*, **99**, 944–71.

Suustein, C. (1996), 'Social Norms and Social Roles', *Columbia Law Review*, **3** (97), 903.

Trebilcock, Michael (1993), *The Limits of Freedom of Contract*, Cambridge, Mass.: Harvard University Press.

Treu, T. (1986), 'General report: procedures and structures of collective bargaining at the enterprise and plant levels', *Comparative Labor Law Journal*, **7**, 219, 251.

Verkerke, J. Hoult (1995), 'An empirical perspective on indefinite term employment contracts: resolving the just cause debate', *Wisconsin Law Review*, (1995), 83.

Weiler, Paul (1990), *Governing the Workplace: The Future of Labor and Employment Law*, Cambridge, Mass.: Harvard University Press.

Weiss, Manfred (1995), *Labour Law and Industrial Relations in Germany*, Deventer: Kluwer.

Whyte, William Foote (1977), *Money and Motivation: An Analysis of Incentives in Industry*, Westport, CT: Greenwood Press.

Williamson, Oliver (1985), *The Economic Institutions of Capitalism*, NY: Free Press.

4. The law and economics of dismissal regulation: a comparative analysis of the US and UK systems

Matthias Beck*

> The flexibility of the common law consists not in the change of great and essential principles, but in the application of old principles to new cases, and in the modification of the rules flowing from them, to such cases as may arise; so as to preserve the reason of the rule and the spirit of the law.
>
> (*Rensselaer Glass Factory v. Reid*, 5 Cow., N.Y.)

> The inexhaustible and ever changing complications of human affairs are constantly presenting new questions and new conditions which the law must provide for, as they arise; and the law has expansive and adaptive force enough to respond to the demands thus made of it, not by subverting but by forming new combinations and making new applications out of its already established principles.
>
> (*Woodman v. Pitman*, 79 Me.)

4.1 INTRODUCTION: DISMISSING EMPLOYEES IN THE UK AND US[1]

For the majority of all employees their job is one of their most important assets. Jobs provide not only a principal source of wealth, but are also a key source of social status and individual psychological well-being.[2] In most Western countries, public sector employees enjoy substantial statutory and constitutional job-protection, which typically limits dismissal to well-defined categories of 'just cause'.[3] The provision of such protection is based on a wide variety of rationales, including concerns for the loyalty, integrity, or autonomy of public sector employees, or the fact that these employees have made substantial job-specific human capital investments in order to perform their jobs.[4]

In the private sector, meanwhile, job protection is more tenuous. This is particularly true for the US labour market. Although US courts have introduced legal doctrine which allow private sector workers to seek redress in the case of questionable dismissals, the job security enjoyed by public sector workers has not evolved. What has emerged has been described as a 'complex web of legal theories that differs from state to state and changes with each new court opinion, which tends to destabilise employment relations and to make the current law governing employment relations unpredictable'.[5] Perhaps not surprisingly, questions about the appropriate regulation of dismissals have become a core concern in the North American management and legal literature.[6] Mendelsohn has estimated that between 1980 and 1987, inclusive, more than 150 articles on dismissal litigation appeared in the major American legal journals. My own estimate locates the number of articles on unjust dismissal appearing over the last ten years in the ten major applied management and personnel journals as being somewhere in the high 200s. In Britain, the question of employment rights has also resurfaced, both because of the influence of European legislative initiatives, and because of the expectations associated with the new Labour Government. The latter has announced a commitment to the creation of a stakeholder society; a term whose implications for labour law are, as yet, not fully clear, but have nonetheless created a forum for debate.[7]

Scholars of comparative labour law have traditionally considered the US employment regulation as inferior to the approaches taken in many of the advanced capitalist nations of Europe and the Pacific Rim.[8] This view is in line with theories of American exceptionalism, which assume that in the US, decisions on economic governance have been guided by anachronistic beliefs in the equity and efficacy of market forces.[9] Thompson's (1981) analysis of US employment law, for example, has argued that the only property rights effectively recognized in the US are those of capital.[10] In Canada, France, Germany, Italy and the UK, by contrast, laws passed in the 1950s and 1970s have established relatively comprehensive formalized systems for adjudicating dismissal related disputes.[11]

Questioning this assumption of a US-European disparity, this paper argues that, from a Law and Economics perspective, the notion of a US exceptionalism with regard to dismissal protection is unwarranted. Contrasting the US system of dismissal protection with that of the UK – which for many analysts still represents one of the prominent 'European' models of dismissal regulation – I suggest that the absence of an effective protection of job–property rights is symptomatic of both the American and the 'UK version' of the European model.[12]

This chapter is structured as follows. I start by reviewing the evolution and the key characteristics of the US and UK systems of discharge regulation. Next, I discuss some of the principal arguments which pervade the contemporary debate on dismissal protection. As an alternative, a job property rights model is introduced. The conclusion then analyses the implications of this job property rights model in the context of the US and UK dismissal regimes, and assesses its ramifications for the effective protection of employees from unjust and excessive dismissals.

4.2 THE US AND UK DISMISSAL REGIMES: A BRIEF LOOK AT THE FACTS

The regulation of private sector dismissals in the US and UK differs widely, with the US relying heavily on individual litigation, and the UK depending largely on statutory rights and enforcement mechanisms. This section briefly compares the key characteristics of both systems.

4.2.1 Dismissal Regulation in the United States

The United States has often been described as the last industrialized country without comprehensive unjust dismissal legislation.[13] Existing employee rights statutes generally protect particular groups of the workforce against certain types of dismissals, but not the workforce as a whole.[14] In addition to these statutes, most North American collective bargaining agreements include clauses that prohibit the discharge of employees except for 'good cause'. These provisions are typically enforced through contractual grievance arbitration procedures.[15]

Partly due to this lack of a comprehensive body of dismissal legislation, the US courts have faced a dramatic increase in unjust dismissal suits. Peritt, a law professor at Villanova University, has estimated that the number of wrongful discharge suits (excluding plaintiffs who claim discrimination on the basis of race, sex or age) has risen from only a handful in the 1970s, to 60 000 cases in 1982, and then to about 100 000 annually from the late 1980s onwards. A survey conducted by the American Management Society's *Committee of 500* similarly found that the incidence of unjust dismissal suits had risen dramatically, and that 53 per cent of responding managers in a sample of 295 companies stated that an unjust discharge claim had been brought against them.[16] Today, it appears that some employers may perceive these suits as a threat to their business operation, both because of high plaintiff success rates and the relatively high level of awards granted by juries. Indeed, over recent years, an industry has evolved, largely within the Human Resource Management field, which advises on the avoidance of dismissal suits and/or provides insurance schemes covering employers against potential litigation costs.

Based on data from California verdicts, the legal publishing firm Jury Verdicts Weekly reported that during the period from October 1981 to November 1987, the plaintiffs in unjust dismissal suits prevailed in almost 66 per cent of all cases. A more recent 1993 survey estimates a similar success rate of 63 per cent for the US as a whole.[17] Plaintiffs' settlement demands in the Jury Verdict Weekly Survey were as high as $5 875 000 (approx. £3 670 000); with maximum settlement offers of $760 000 (approx. £475 000); while verdicts apportioned damages to individual plaintiffs of up to $8 000 000 (approx. £5 000 000). Recently cases were recorded in which damage awards exceeded the $10 million mark, including a $10.29 million award (approx. £6.4 million) against the manufacturers of WD-40. As yet the highest recorded jury award stands at $69.5 million (approx. £43.3 million); these damages, however, were not exclusively based on civil action. The mean total award (i.e., compensatory and punitive damages) in the aforementioned California Jury Verdicts survey amounted to about $500 000 (approx. £312 000), and the median award was $60 000 (approx. £37 000); with the difference between mean and median being primarily due to a few exceptionally high awards. The aforementioned 1993 report estimated the median verdict in an unjust dismissal suit where no discrimination was alleged, for the US as a whole, at $102 000 (approx. £64 000). According to this survey punitive damages were added in 26 per cent of the cases surveyed, resulting in a median jury award of $150 000 (approx. £94 000).[18] Reinstatement, meanwhile, is rarely demanded by plaintiffs, as this could infringe on the potential awards.

For the legal profession unjust dismissal litigation has become a major source of revenue. A 1988 study by the *Rand* corporation estimated average legal fees charged by defence attorneys at $80 073 (approx £53 000) with a median of $65 000 (approx £43 000). In several instances, fees exceeded the half million dollar mark. Joel Kelly, a partner in a Los Angeles law firm has estimated the 1995 cost of legal fees to the employer at $75 000 to $100 000 (approx. £47 000 to £63 000).[19]

The exceptional size of these awards, together with the expenses created by wrongful discharge suits to court systems and employers, have prompted proposals for a reform of the current system of dismissal litigation. One of the first attempts to curb the expansion of unjust dismissal litigation came from the California Supreme Court, which had, in the past, handed down many of the pioneering judgements that expanded the scope of this type of litigation. In its judgement on *Foley v.*

Interactive Data Co. (1988), the California court limited action in tort for wrongful discharge. This step was largely ineffective, as the restrictions imposed merely made some courses of action less lucrative, and hence encouraged attorneys to focus on higher paid employees.[20] Ironically, there is now evidence that the California court's exacting analysis in *Foley* has been used to expand unjust dismissal claims in states where the law was not yet as developed.[21]

Other challenges to the common law system of wrongful discharge litigation have proven equally unsuccessful, both in California and elsewhere. In 1987 the state of Montana passed the first comprehensive statute regulating dismissals in the US. This statute extended the right of individuals to challenge their dismissal, but limited damages to a maximum of four years' lost wages. Perhaps most importantly, it required that the employee exhaust internal company appeals procedures before bringing a suit to court.[22] The example of the Montana Act prompted the National Conference of Commissioners on State Laws to draft a *Model Uniform Termination Act* with similar provisions, which was ratified by the Commission in 1991. Hitherto only one other state, South Dakota, has adopted similar legislation.[23]

Given these experiences, several observers have suggested that, for years to come, most dismissal related proceedings in the US are likely to continue taking the form of common law suits. US legislatures, sections of the bar, as well as some interest groups associated with employer organizations, appear to favour a flexible system which assigns substantial damages according to the perceived misconduct of employers, as opposed to a more formal approach which caps awards. These views may have been shaped by a preference of employers for a low-probability of high awards, versus a frequent payment of less substantial sums. Such a preference, perhaps, can be best explained on account of organizational rather than economic considerations. Historical surveys have documented a primary concern of US managers with the preservation of managerial authority.[24] Given a preference structure which favours the maintenance of managerial authority over other issues, the risk of law suits may be more acceptable to US managers than the institution of formal and accessible structures of dispute settlement. It is also possible that employers, despite some claims to the contrary, perceive the threat of dismissal suits as relatively unimportant. Today, only about 4 per cent of all dismissal suits go to trial, while the majority of disputes is resolved through settlement before judgement is made. There is moreover some evidence that employers are developing effective strategies to counter the threat of dismissal litigation, including insurance schemes, in-house arbitration provisions, and contract formats which may bar employees from litigation for discharge.[25]

4.2.2 Dismissal Regulation in the United Kingdom

Like the United States, the United Kingdom originally relied on private suits and collective bargaining agreements as a source of dismissal regulation, but, from the 1960s onwards, established a formalized system for the adjudication of dismissal related disputes.[26] Today, the UK system of dismissal legislation has two principal components; redundancy payments requirements and the right to bring a dismissal case to an industrial tribunal. The latter has the power to award reinstatement or damages.

The *Redundancy Payments Act* of 1965 provides monetary compensation for workers with two or more years of service who were dismissed for reasons of redundancy. Employees may be disqualified from this compensation if they are 'guilty' of misconduct, have been offered suitable alternative employment, worked under a fixed term contract, have waived redundancy rights, or have participated in a strike action which preceded their termination.

The *Industrial Relations Act* of 1971 gave employees the right to complain to an industrial tribunal if they perceived their termination as being unjust. These rights were extended in the 1975 *Employment Protection Act* which confirmed that 'in every employment to which this section applies, the employee shall have the right not to be unfairly dismissed by his employer'. To qualify for this remedy, employees must have two years of continuous service.[27] Initially, part-time employees were required to have five years of service in order to qualify, but this rule was suspended in 1995 as it violated European Law.[28] More recently, the constitutionality of the two year rule has been challenged by two female employees in the Court of Appeal on the basis of its alleged sex discriminatory effect. The Court of Appeals has referred the case to the European Court.

If a dismissal is judged unfair, a British industrial tribunal may order re-engagement. This remedy occurs in only 3–6 per cent of all cases, but it must be remembered that only a comparatively small number of employees request it. In the majority of all successful cases monetary compensation is provided. This compensation consists of two elements: a basic award which, being equivalent to a redundancy payment, is a function of the employee's length of service, but which must not exceed £63 000. The second component is a compensatory award which has an absolute limit of £11 300.[29] In 1991–2, the median total award was £2 616 and only about 14 per cent of all awards exceeded £9 000. Meanwhile almost a quarter fell below £1 000.[30] Unfair dismissal claims constituted the vast majority of cases heard at industrial tribunals by the Advisory Conciliation and Arbitration Service (ACAS). In 1995, for instance, 40 851 out of a total of 91 568 cases heard pertained to unjust dismissal.[31] Studies indicate that for most years only approximately 11 per cent of all cases heard were successful and resulted in the compensation or reinstatement of the employee.[32]

Despite relatively low and infrequent awards to discharged employees, the UK system of dismissal regulation has come under heavy criticism, primarily from employer interest groups. Objections by employer organizations have focused on inappropriate deterrence effects, inefficiency, and interference with employer's rights allegedly created by these regulations. As regards economic deterrence, it has been argued that the statutory protection of employees increases the costs and obligations of employing labour, and hence reduces the demand for employees. This cost-push has been said to apply irrespective of a firm's actual experience of tribunals.[33] The potential costs and delays resulting from the tribunal system have been said to discourage employers from dismissing inefficient or otherwise unsatisfactory employees. Lastly, the frequency of tribunals in the UK has been said to threaten the status and authority of employers, prompting them to adopt an overly cautious approach to restructuring and downsizing.[34]

Partly in response to these criticisms, a succession of Conservative reforms have reduced access to unjust dismissal remedies. Whereas in the early 1980s, 26 weeks of continuous service were required in order to qualify for an industrial tribunal, this was gradually increased to two years. As a result, in some industries, such as construction, virtually the entire workforce is excluded from unjust dismissal protection, as few employees remain with an employer for two years.[35] Employers with less than 20 employees, moreover, are now exempt from supplying their staff with details of disciplinary procedures, while employers with less than 5 employees need not reinstate workers after maternity leave if is impractical to do so. Lastly, the right to redundancy payment has been limited to terminations occurring before the 'normal age of retirement', with a maximum age of 65 for both sexes.[36]

Despite a host of changes, some analyses have continued to criticize UK dismissal law for imposing excessive barriers to the discharge of employees. Such criticisms are often linked to claims about the greater efficiency and equity of US labour market regulations.[37] The Stanford economist Flanagan (1987), for instance, has argued with regard to European legislation that,[38]

> ... procedural delays, severance payments, and compulsory awards all raise the labour cost per employee. This will reduce the volume of layoffs, even though

layoffs are technically feasible. It will also create incentives for employers to substitute labour for capital and uncovered workers for covered workers.

In a 1986 article published in the *British Journal of Industrial Relations*, the UK-born economist Addison similarly suggested that US job creation could be directly linked to the absence of government-imposed job security and dismissal regulation.[39] According to Addison, the lack of stringent job protection regulation provided the US labour market with a comparative advantage which allowed for faster job creation as compared to Europe.

Like Addison, most economists who view the US approach to dismissals as exemplary, have either ignored the role of unjust dismissal litigation in US courts, or emphasized the frequency and tediousness of dismissal related tribunals in Europe. Unjust dismissal litigation in US courts, meanwhile, has often, and perhaps unrealistically, been considered a short lived aberration from the country's traditional *laissez faire* approach to labour relations.[40]

4.3 THE PRACTICE OF UNJUST DISMISSAL REGULATION

During the last ten to twenty years questions have arisen, both about the formal structure of dismissal regulation and its labour market implications. This section focuses on the unintended consequences of the respective legislative arrangements of the US and UK.

4.3.1 The UK: Dismissals and the 'Economic Imperative'

The *United Kingdom's Redundancy Payments Act* (RPA) of 1965 was originally introduced and justified on the basis of economic efficiency arguments. Its proponents believed that the Act would improve the economic performance of corporations, and the functioning of the labour market, as well as providing social protection for workers.[41] Redundancy compensation was thought to encourage workers to cooperate with economic restructuring, by making it 'easier' for them 'to change their jobs in accordance with the needs of technological progress'.[42] These views were based on the assumption that employees could move freely from declining industries to what Harold Wilson had referred to as the 'white hot' industries. Improvements in labour utilization and factor productivity were expected to allow for pay rises, which would provide the capital necessary to compensate those, 'who were expected to make sacrifices in the interests of economic expansion'.[43]

Today there is evidence of the perverse effects of these provisions. Rather than providing incentives to employers to upgrade their human capital, the Act appears to have subsidized, throughout many years, the wholesale abandonment of human capital.[44] Since the introduction of the RPA around 10 million workers have received statutory severance pay. In the 1980s alone, an estimated £30 billion was spent on redundancy pay, over a quarter of this sum was used to cut the workforce of the coal industry.[45] Despite these aggregate figures, the statutory amounts typically paid out to individual employees have hardly provided adequate compensation for job loss. Today, workers aged between 18–21 receive one half a week's pay for each year of service, those aged between 22–40 receive one week's pay, and those aged between 41–64 receive one and one half week's pay for each year of service. The maximum payment under the RPA, meanwhile, is restricted to 20 years' service or the aforementioned £6 300.[46]

Even when private industry or the government provided 'voluntary' lump sum payments to redundant workers, this compensation has often remained in the low range. In the plant rationalization of the Port Talbot works (1980–81), where 55 per cent of the workforce were made redundant, the average lump sum payments amounted to £6 400. Higher payments were reported in some instances, such as the Markham Colliery pit closure (1985), and the Port Tilbury (1989) restructuring, where employees received an average of £22 500 and £35 000 respectively. In both cases, in excess of 60 per cent of the workforce were laid off, and for both cases, as in many others, there is now evidence that the Act might have encouraged excessive layoffs.[47]

Prompted by the effects of the *Redundancy Payments Act*, some of the British management publications now acknowledge the dangers of excessive dismissals. A 1995 editorial in *Management Today*, for instance, expressed concerns that, with the help of these statutory provisions, redundancy had 'become an obsession, like anorexia'.[48] The *Observer's* management page similarly suggested that following restructuring 'a number of companies resemble nothing so much as buildings blasted by a neutron bomb. The processes and structures are all there but no human life to make them productive.'[49]

If the first pillar of UK dismissal regulation was a partial failure, the second pillar, the *Employment Protection Act* (1975) and its revisions, has also been marked by major deficiencies. Apart from low success rates in tribunals and comparatively derisory awards, the enforcement of unjust dismissal statutes in the UK has suffered from substantial, perhaps deliberate, gaps in the law.[50] To give just a few examples: if an employee is dismissed because she participated in unofficial industrial action, no legal action may be brought by her. Even in the case of dismissals occurring in connection with official strike action, industrial tribunals will be excluded from jurisdiction, provided that the employer discharges all those who are on strike, and does not offer to re-engage some of them within three months after their dismissal (*Edwards v. Cardiff City Council, Marsden v. Fairey Stainless Steel*).[51]

Even more serious problems arise from the absence of a clear definition of the term 'other industrial action' within existing law. Today, it is assumed that 'other industrial action' includes a wide range of industrial techniques, such as work-to-rule, go-slow, sit-ins, and possibly 'working without enthusiasm'. In *Thompson v. Eaton Ltd.* workers who were standing around new machinery, allegedly in order to prevent employers from testing it, were dismissed.[52] The court held that they were engaged in 'other industrial action' and, in consequence, concluded that the industrial tribunal had no jurisdiction over their dismissal. In *Power Packing Casemakers v. Faust* the refusal to do overtime in protest about a wage dispute, was similarly construed as exempting the tribunal from jurisdiction.[53] In what was perhaps the most objectionable application of this rule, 2000 seafarers were sacked by P&O following a dispute. This particular incident led the International Labour Organization to condemn the limited unfair dismissal protection for strikers in Britain. In addition to asking the British government 'to amend its legislation', the ILO admonished the removal of protection from unofficial strikers under the Employment Act of 1990, as this gave too large a leeway to employers to dismiss unjustly.[54]

On the whole, UK court rulings and legislative initiatives, particularly in recent years, have shown a clear preference for the preservation of managerial prerogatives. Statutory provisions, such as the RPA, have been used to encourage workers to surrender job control, while key judgements on issues of unjust dismissals have increasingly strengthened managerial dominance in the workplace.[55] While the total legal apparatus of dismissal regulation in the UK appears extensive, it has increasingly become a paper tiger, unable to provide adequate protection of workers from unfair and unnecessary discharge.

4.3.2 The US Model of Dismissal Litigation

The structure of US dismissal regulation differs fundamentally from that of the UK regime. In the US, developments within common law itself, rather than statutory enactments, have come to form the principal barrier to the dismissal of individual workers. At its core, US dismissal litigation has evolved from the reinterpretation of the 19th century common-law principle of employment-at-will. This section will briefly review this development in order to contextualize modern unjust dismissal litigation within the traditions of US employment law.

In the late 18th century, the US adopted the English law of master and servant, which stipulated that, where there was no evidence to the contrary, an indefinite hiring was presumed to be for one year.[56] By the late 1800s, this law was in a state of confusion, with the courts disagreeing on issues of employment duration and notice requirements for indefinite-term employees. In a treatise published in 1877, Horace Gay Wood argued that since no term of employment was specified in the typical indefinite-term employment contract, none should be implied by the courts. Wood's rule concluded that the indefinite employment relationship was *at-will*, that is, that either party could terminate employment any time and for any reason.[57]

In the late 19th century, Wood's concept of employment-at-will quickly came to govern the workplace all over the United States. In economic terms, the doctrine of employment-at-will corresponded well to the demands of the growing US economy, as it allowed for a quick movement of scarce labour between jobs or industries. Legally, the establishment of employment-at-will was in line with the 'golden age of the law of contract', in 'which barriers to arms-length bargains, in a free, impersonal market, were systematically removed'.[58]

While initially limited to non-manual employees, employment-at-will came, within roughly three decades, to cover virtually every type of worker in every state of the union.[59] Typical of the unrestricted use of Wood's rule was the oft-cited case of *Payne v. Western and Atlantic Railroad* (1884, pp. 519–20), in which a Tennessee court stated that, 'All may dismiss their employee[s] at-will, be they many or few, for good cause, for no cause, or even for cause morally wrong without being guilty of legal wrong.'[60] US legal history is rife with accounts of the most blatant abuses of human rights, resulting from the unquestioning application of the at-will rights by employers. In the case of *Comerford v. International Harvester* (1932), for instance, a worker was discharged because his wife refused to sleep with the man's supervisor. The husband's challenge was rejected by the court, because the at-will status of the employee empowered the employer to discharge at any time, even for morally wrong reasons.[61]

The employment-at-will rule, more or less unaltered from the Tennessee version, remained firmly in place until the 1930s, when a series of state and federal laws were passed which protected employees who engaged in legally protected activities from dismissal. The passage of the *National Labour Relations Act* in 1935 established some dismissal protection for workers, whose termination could be linked to participation in legal organizing activity, or the pursuit of industrial action.[62] In 1938, the *Fair Labour Standards Act* prohibited the dismissal of workers on the basis of their filing a minimum wage or overtime claim.[63] Similar legislation was enacted from the 1950s onwards to protect workers who filed occupational safety complaints, and, later on, to protect those who reported environmental violations. In 1964, the passage of the *Civil Rights Act* triggered the enactment of a host of laws, which offered limited protection from termination for specific categories of employees in the private sector. Today, there are at least 22 different statutes of this type. For example, employees cannot lawfully be dismissed for reasons of race, colour, religion, national origin, age, sex, handicap, Vietnam-era veterans or citizenship status.[64]

Although the state and federal protective legislation modified the at-will relationship for some groups of employees under certain circumstances, it did not alter the employment relationship for the majority of the workforce. Grenig (1991) has estimated that, taking all prohibitions together, including those of a statutory nature and those emerging from collective bargaining agreements, about two thirds of all employees in the US can be discharged from their jobs without any justification.[65]

The application of employment-at-will to non-union employees without statutory protection, however, itself experienced restrictions from the 1970s onwards. The first exemption from employment-at-will was granted by a California court, in connection with a case which would have denied protection to an employee whose dismissal resulted from a refusal to commit a criminal act. In *Peterman v. International Brotherhood of Teamsters Local* (1959), a California state court ruled that an employee could not be discharged for refusing to perjure himself. The court found the legality of dismissals resulting from a refusal to commit an illegal act to be contrary to its 'public policy', and concluded that it would be 'obnoxious to the interests of the state' to allow an employer to fire at-will under such circumstances.[66]

The legal possibilities of the *Peterman* decision remained largely unexplored until similar decisions were made by several progressive state courts. In 1973, the Indiana Supreme Court extended the applicability of the 'public policy exemption' by ruling that, even in absence of a specific statute, it was wrongful to discharge a worker because she filed a worker's compensation claim (*Frampton v. Central Indiana Gas Co.*).[67] In 1978, a Michigan court applied the Peterman doctrine to the case of an employee who refused to falsify pollution reports (*Trombetta v. Detroit, Toledo, &*

Ironton Railroad).[68] In 1977, the Massachusetts Supreme Court concluded that it was not only contrary to public policy to allow an employer to dismiss an employee for exercising rights created by law, but also to allow employers to discharge employees for exercising a private right spelled out in a company handbook (*Fortune v. National Cash Register Co.*).[69] One year earlier, a Massachusetts court had held that, where an employer's conduct in discharging an employee was extreme and outrageous, the employee could recover damages for the employer's intentional infliction of mental distress (*Agis v. Howard Johnson Co.*).[70] In 1980, New Jersey followed earlier California doctrines, by ruling in favour of a drug company employee who objected to the submission of a drug for human testing, even though no explicit statute supported the employee's objections (*Pierce v. Orthopharmaceutical Co.*).[71]

Today, US courts recognize three exemptions from employment-at-will. First, following *Peterman*, an employee is considered exempt from the at-will rule if the employer terminated her employment in violation of *public policy*; i.e., dismissed her because she refused to commit a criminal act on behalf of the employer, or reported a violation of federal, state, or professional regulations.[72] A second possible exemption from employment-at-will has been recognized in cases where the employer's personnel policies, course of conduct, or oral promise, created an *implied contract* for continued employment.[73] A third type of claim for unfair dismissal arises from an employer's breach of the *covenant of good faith and fair dealing*, that is, from instances in which an employer's actions are aimed at depriving an employee from contractual benefits, such as a bonus or pension.[74] A 1991 survey indicated that these doctrines were widely accepted. The courts of 39 states had adopted the public policy exemption, 27 states adopted the implied contract exemption, and 7 states the good faith exemption.[75]

Wrongful dismissal suits alleging any of these three exemptions, or combinations thereof, have been successfully filed against large multinational firms, small local companies, and public employers. Typically, the plaintiffs are individual employees who are not represented by unions. Workers from all levels have filed unjust dismissal suits, but supervisory and managerial employees seem to be overrepresented. According to a 1987 survey of 323 managers at US companies, 27 per cent of all firms were accused of unfairly dismissing a worker. Of this 27 per cent, 74 per cent of the charges were filed by white collar workers, of which 34 per cent could be categorized as professionals and 25 per cent as management-level employees.[76] Plaintiffs are typically represented by private attorneys who work on a contingent fee basis; that is, on the basis of an agreement where the attorney is compensated by a percentage of the award, and remains uncompensated if the law suit fails. Since the attorney's risk in accepting contingency fee compensation is higher than in conventional law suits, the remuneration rates negotiated tend to exceed payments of conventional fee-for-service contracts. Employees, in turn, appear more willing to enter a suit as the risk of paying legal fees for an unsuccessful lawsuit is virtually eliminated.

Despite the availability of contingency contracts, court action is likely to impose financial risk and potential hardship upon dismissed employees. This has raised serious questions about fair access to justice in the context of common law dismissal suits perhaps most important of which are issues of information barriers and opportunity costs. A 1988 *Rand* study of 120 dismissal suits filed at the Los Angeles Superior Court, for instance, found that for the average unjust termination payment, the costs of litigation were about 30 per cent higher than the amount the plaintiff eventually received. In the typical settled case, the defence costs alone amounted to 80 per cent of the average post-tax amount awarded to the plaintiff.[77]

Apart from favourable institutional arrangements, the expansion of unjust dismissal litigation appears to have been helped by a combination of socio-economic factors. Mendelsohn (1990) speculates that termination litigation in the US became acceptable, in part, because the country saw a rise in litigiousness manifest itself in consumer litigation, personal injury litigation, and landlord tenant suits. These developments, Mendelsohn proposed, created spillover effects on labour issues.[78] Corporate restructuring meanwhile, resulted in greater uncertainty about employment security, particularly amongst middle-management employees, which, in turn, might have encouraged them to seek recourse from the courts.[79] Finally, the accelerated decline in unionization in the early eighties, has removed much of the framework of collective dismissal protection. This may have encouraged judges to grant exemptions from the unrestrained application of the at-will rule, as well as pushed more employees towards unjust dismissal litigation.[80]

Whatever factors are responsible for the rise in wrongful termination litigation in the US, the expansion of unjust dismissal litigation as a legal category has sharpened the debate on the expediency of different forms of dismissal regulation and protection. Most of the arguments involved – although originating primarily within the US context – are general enough to apply to the UK system of statutory protection as well. The next section will provide a brief review of the core arguments of this debate.

4.4 THE DISCOURSE ON DISMISSAL REGULATION

Initially, most discussions on dismissal regulation centred on the question of the efficient versus the equitable assignment of employment rights. More recently this discourse has started to encompass questions about employee and employer opportunism and property rights. The following section reviews this debate in a roughly chronological order.

4.4.1 Efficiency Versus Equity: First Generation Arguments

The neo-classical economic paradigm implies that markets are the most effective mechanism for the operation of the labour market. Deviations from unrestrained market processes, such as the enactment of employment regulation, are likely to result in sub-optimal outcomes. Applying this view to employment contracts and dismissals, some economists have explored the 'benefits' of at-will rights *vis-à-vis* a greater restriction of employer's prerogative, and put forth several arguments in favour of at-will dismissals.

Firstly, it has been argued that the unadulterated at-will right of employers to dismiss, and that of employees to quit, reduces monitoring costs.[81] Knowledge that each party can renounce the agreement is said to decrease the chances that a worker will not put forth the expected levels of performance, and that employers will not proffer the promised compensation. Since employee shirking can be costly, and monitoring is often impossible, the freedom of the employer to dismiss employees ultimately ensures output. An alteration of this contract format through a restriction of dismissals, may lead to a less efficient employment relationship, which may impose substantial costs on the economy as a whole, as output in existing firms is lowered and/or fewer workers are hired.[82]

A second set of efficiency arguments put forth in favour of the at-will doctrine, proposes that the ability of an employer to decide on discharges without restriction is essential to the organizational efficiency of the firm. Since restrictions on firing for redundancy reasons cannot be completely separated from restrictions on unjust dismissal, interference with the right to dismiss, and particularly the imposition of penalties, can result in excess employee capacities (i.e. adversely affect quantity decisions), as well as inflexibilities regarding the choice of the workforce (i.e. adversely affect quality decisions). An exponent of this view, the free market advocate

Gary Becker, has strongly warned against 'the courts becoming a pink slip police'.[83] Becker has suggested that court policing of dismissals erodes managerial property rights and, in the long run, reduces incentives for the creation of new firms.

Arguing along similar lines, the British right-wing philosopher Gray has stated that any interference with managerial decisions, such as the imposition of restrictions on hiring and firing, will destroy 'entrepreneurial intuition' and 'self confidence'. Successful managerial conduct, according to Gray, involves decision making in contexts where much theoretically desirable information is lacking. Entrepreneurs succeed in such uncertain environments because they possess *tacit* knowledge; that is, knowledge that cannot be articulated, that exists only in use and can be attained only by experience of its use. Gray (1993) argues that,

> Individuals are most likely to deploy their personal *tacit* knowledge when they are least constrained by collective decision-procedures in which this knowledge is diluted or lost. (This is, perhaps, especially true of that species of tacit knowledge which is expressed in entrepreneurial insight.) In order to be able to make the best use of their personal or tacit knowledge, individuals need a domain in which they may act solely on their own judgement (and, of course, at their own risk). Such a domain is provided by private property in productive assets.[84] (p. 74)

The economists Picot and Wenger (1988) have gone a step further in this line of reasoning by suggesting that,

> If employees have protective rights there is no guarantee that these rights cannot be exercised in order to expropriate the employer. Protection against dismissal, for example, may reduce work effort because the employer cannot fire 'at-will' ... The ensuing moral hazard problems are a strong argument in favour of short-term termination rights.[85] (p. 32)

In both views, the dangers of giving employees job rights are perceived as formidable, primarily because the creation of such rights creates counter-incentives to adequate contractual performance.

These efficiency arguments, on the whole, are rejected by those who favour a greater restriction of employment-at-will. Here a different line of reasoning has evolved, which focuses on the idea that the employment contract varies from other contracts in fundamental ways. Because of this variation, the application of the freedom of contract to employment as exemplified in the at-will doctrine, is deemed inadequate. Underlying these arguments is the common assumption that, rather than involving two equal partners, employment contracts involve an asymmetric relationship, where the employer is the dominant party.

If left unrestricted, this relationship is assumed to result in dramatic social and legal inequities.

The argument that employment contracts differ from other commercial contracts has a long pedigree. It had, in fact, been put forth in the US industrial relations literature as early as 1916. In their *Principles of Labor Legislation* (1916), Commons and Andrews argued that, since the abolition of slavery, the labour contract differed from other contracts in that restrictions on the sale of labour were imposed. Commons and Andrews stated that,

> Business contracts, if violated, are ground for damages... The labor contract also, if violated, is ground for damages, but for the court to order damages paid out of labor property would be to order the laborer to work out the debt. This is involuntary servitude.[86] (p. 505)

Commons and Andrews further proposed that the 'peculiar relation' between a propertyless seller of his own self and a prosperous buyer, necessitated a legal conception of the labour contract different from other contracts. The decision to dismiss a worker could not be left to the employer, but had to be regulated by a type of legislation which went 'behind the legal face of things' and looked 'at the bargaining power which precedes the contract'.[87]

While also relying on the notion of power inequalities in its opposition to the at-will doctrine, modern treatments of this issue have attempted to pinpoint specific sources of power inequalities. Two principal sources of power asymmetry have been explored in this context.[88] Firstly, it has been argued that an employer's financial resources exceed those of employees substantially. The adverse effects of resignations are therefore unlikely to endanger the financial well-being of an employer. Employees, by contrast, depend on their jobs for their financial well-being. Therefore, they cannot effectively use the threat of quitting.

Another group of arguments suggests that, since skills are not perfectly transferable, employees can face long job searches and/or incur wage losses due to inadequate job-matching. Employers, meanwhile, can recruit from a more or less extensive pool of possible future employees, thus facing short replacement gaps and/or replacement losses.

Although convincing at first sight, power asymmetry arguments have been subject to some criticism in the recent literature. Most objections are based on the assumption that, unless employers have an interest in dismissing workers beyond economic rationality, the presence of power asymmetries does not explain why an employer would take advantage of this position in a manner that would warrant legal intervention.[89]

If decisions are ruled by economic rationality on both the employer's and the employee's side, we should accordingly expect a profit-maximizing employer to limit discharges to those necessitated by economic circumstances. Such a rule of conduct should then be bolstered by the possibility of reputational damages arising from an unjust dismissal.[90]

4.4.2 Opportunism and Dismissals: Second Generation Arguments

Second generation arguments in favour of restrictions on the doctrine of employment-at-will have reversed the 'shirking' and 'opportunism' argument of earlier analyses. This reversal is based on the proposition that an important source of employer opportunism arises from rising age–wage profiles in the context of implicit employment contract.

In the traditional model of the labour market, the employer pays a worker the value of her marginal product for each pay period.[91] Modern labour market analysis assumes that any single pay period's wage is insufficient to deter shirking, and that therefore special measures must be taken to ensure output.[92] Becker and Stigler (1974) have suggested that problems of shirking can be resolved through compensation schemes where the employee pays the employer a bond upon taking a job.[93] Bond schemes of this kind, however, are impractical, because most workers are unable to borrow sufficient funds at the start of their jobs.[94]

It has been argued that the practical alternative to bonds posted at the beginning of an employment, lies in a wage structure which internalizes the 'bond effect'. Such wage structures defer a part of a worker's wage to later periods of her employment. In practical terms the resultant employment contract offers the worker a more or less steep age–wage profile, which provides wages below the worker's marginal product for the early years of her employment, and wages above the marginal product for later years. By shifting proportionally more compensation to these later years, the employer raises the cost of termination to the worker. If dismissed, the employee loses her accumulated deferred wages in escrow. The worker therefore has an incentive to put in adequate effort throughout her working life. The scheme as a whole is nevertheless preferable to the employee, as she is likely to be paid the higher wage associated with the employee's assumption of continual higher effort.[95]

From the standpoint of incentive compatibility, the difficulty with this scheme is how the total amount of deferred wages changes over time. In the early years of the job, when wages paid are below the employee's productivity level, the total amount of deferred benefits rises, reaching a maximum around the mid-period of employment. Following this reversal point [R], the amount of benefits is paid off, as wages rise above the marginal product of the worker. If the firm discharges a worker at or after the reversal point [R], that is during the second half of the job, it not only avoids paying the extra cost of the incentive payments, but also incurs the wage savings it has accumulated from the time it hired the employee.

In a world in which no market or legal constraints operate, a firm will hence have a rational incentive for the dismissal of a productive worker for no cause (see Figure 4.1).[96] In other words, implicit contracts with rising age–wage profiles result in a market failure which may require explicit regulation or legislation aimed at combating employer opportunism.

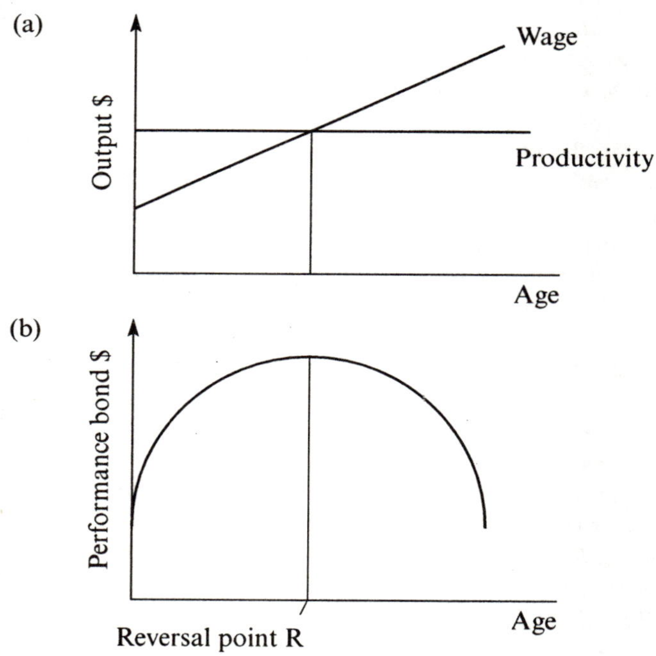

(a) Life-cycle wages and productivity
(b) Size (implicit) performance bond over life-cycle

Source: modified from Parsons (1986)

Figure 4.1 Life cycle wages and performance bond

Several economists have suggested that deferral systems with rising age–wage profiles are a standard feature of pay systems in modern industry. Indeed, a series of econometric studies has documented the prevalence of rising age–wage earnings profiles with deferred benefits, which cannot be attributed to human capital or other factors outside the implicit contract rationale. These studies confirm the existence of residual age-earnings increases over the working life, both for the US labour market, and more recently the UK context.[97] While support for the deferred benefit hypothesis appears to be strong overall, there is some disagreement as to what to include under these benefits. Medoff and Abraham (1980a, 1980b), for instance, have used work-life data in order to show that relative earnings increase with time on the job, even if relative productivity does not.[98] Edward Lazear (1979), by contrast, has argued that mandatory retirement represents the principal evidence that workers are paid more than their productivity requires at the end of their working-life, and suggests that private pension payments serve as an incentive to induce such retirements.[99]

Despite the imperative for a restriction of the doctrine of employment-at-will, which ensues from the combination of a prevalence of deferred benefit systems with the potential for employer opportunism, critics have pointed to several conceptual problems. The University of Chicago Law Professor Epstein (1984), has argued that the firm's concern with its reputation will prevent such opportunistic behaviour, even under circumstances where there are strong economic incentives to dismiss unjustly.[100] More specifically, Professor Epstein suggested that workers have access to information about opportunistic firms which will ensure that firms with a history of opportunistic conduct will go out of business in the long run. In a not untypically circular 'Chicago school' argument, Epstein concluded that, if reputation did not discipline opportunism, workers would negotiate for restrictions on dismissals; given that such clauses were rare or completely unknown, opportunism had also to be negligible.

More recently, it has been argued that these problems of 'double moral hazard' are resolvable through so called incentive-compatible contracts.[101] Examining possible contract formats which prevent opportunism, Malcomson (1984, see also McLeod and Malcomson, 1988) has suggested that the problems of employer opportunism can be overcome by specifying that a certain proportion of the workforce will be paid a higher wage than the rest, while the total wage bill of the firm is fixed.[102] Under these conditions, employees are able to verify that the firm does not act opportunistically, while at the same time an incentive for individual employees to work productively is provided. As an alternative, a firm can employ a group of workers throughout a probationary period, while paying them the going market rate, and then promote a certain portion of this workforce into permanent employment. In the case of these 'in-or-out contracts' employer opportunism is avoided, as workers do not accumulate future benefits during the probationary period.

While there is some qualitative evidence for the existence of both types of contracts, particularly 'in-or-out' contracts in the legal professions and academia, there are several practical objections to this notion of incentive compatibility. Firstly, the alleged contract formats contradict the empirical evidence in favour of increasing age–wage profiles. Secondly, within the specific incentive compatible contracts proposed, there is no apparent process which would prevent employer shirking with regard to maintaining a fixed wage bill or promoting employees. Since there is no credible mechanism which ensures that a certain wage bill will be maintained, an employer could benefit from reducing the wage sum which is distributed amongst the various employees. In the case of 'in-or-out' contracts, another form of employer opportunism can arise. Knowing that the effort put in by probationary employees is, in part, based on their expectation of continued employment, the employer will benefit from hiring and dismissing more probationers than is necessary for screening, while giving deliberately false information about the prospect of promotion. These types of opportunism, of course, would be curbed if a firm suffered reputational losses from such conduct, or if employees were able to counteract this type of behaviour collectively.

A Note in the *Harvard Law Review* (1989) has rejected arguments alleging the importance of a firm's reputational concerns, on grounds that these arguments neglected information barriers which prevented employees from acquiring necessary information about a firm's past opportunistic conduct. Reputational losses, accordingly, impose few limits on opportunistic practices, as barriers on information and transaction costs prevent prospective employees from acquiring the necessary information. Job searchers cannot easily obtain information about a firm's personnel relations, among other reasons because the applicant feels inhibited about asking a potential employer about employment practices.[103] Firms, moreover, may deliberately project a false image of job security and steady employment relations.[104]

Once the costs of enforcing any type of unjust dismissal standard are taken into account, arguments in favour of regulation, however, become less obvious. Here, problems arise from the fact that the cost of enforcement can easily outweigh potential efficiency gains. Arguing along these lines, the *HLR* Note concludes that the case for or against dismissal regulation will probably remain open. This, according to the *HLR* Note, is the case because,

> From a purely efficiency based perspective, the fact that ... employer opportunism exists does not necessarily justify a general good cause standard. Remedying opportunism does achieve efficiency gains ... Such benefits, however, come only at a cost. Where the fact finder can collect information and evaluate claims easily ... a judicial remedy may be appropriate ... Reasonable solution may thus be limited exceptions like the public policy, implied contract, and faith exception. However in the general case the employer's motive is only implicit, information for the fact finder make the remedy much more costly.[105]

The *HLR* Note suggests that the trade-off between potential gains from the enforcement of legislation which alleges to prevent opportunistic discharges and its cost is irresolvable. In practice, most attempts to quantify the gains or costs of a general just-cause standard on the basis of experiences from tribunals indeed appear to have been abandoned by researchers. This is indicative not only of the technical difficulties involved in the *a priori* assessment of regulatory effects, but also of the ethical/conceptual dilemmas raised by the possibility of employer opportunism.

The next section will explore the issue of deferred benefits and opportunistic discharges from an alternative perspective, namely the property-rights view of job protection, which offers a different line of reasoning leading to different policy conclusions. The property rights view of job protection, I will argue, permits unambiguous conclusions regarding dismissal regulation while allowing for a comparative evaluation of existing regulatory regimes. My analysis starts with a discussion of a contemporary analysis of the nature of ownership of firms.

4.4.3 Deferred Benefits, Unjust Dismissal, and Property Rights

The socio-legal origins of employment-at-will are based on the strict conceptual separation of employers and workers, which evolved as a product of historical circumstances, rather than on the basis of economic contingencies. In investigating this distinction from an economic efficiency perspective, several researchers have encountered difficulties which have prompted them to suggest alternative views on the allocation of employment rights.[106]

Property rights theory conventionally defines as a firm's owners those persons who share two rights; the right to control the firm's investment decisions, and the right to appropriate the firm's residual earnings. Most firms are owned by persons who supply to the firm some factor of production, usually capital. This is true for classical consumer and producer cooperatives in particular, but it is also true for the standard business corporation, which is frequently owned by those who lend capital to the firm.[107]

The Yale Law and Economics Professor Hansman suggests that, in legal terms, the producer cooperative and the business corporation can be regarded as structurally equivalent. In the producer cooperative, say a dairy cooperative, ownership rights are held exclusively by virtue of the fact that the farmer sells milk to the firm. Not all farmers who sell milk to the firm need to be owners, since the firm may purchase some milk from non-members who are paid a fixed price but who do not exercise control over the firm or participate in the division of residual earnings. In the business corporation, ownership is exercised not through the supply of an intermediary product, but rather through the supply of capital. In a simplified case, the members each lend the firm a given sum, for which they are paid a fixed interest low enough so that the firm can run a profit. At fixed intervals, residual profits – after deducting contractual expenses such as wages, raw material costs and interest earned – are distributed among the lender-members. As in the case of the cooperative, some lenders may not be members of the firms, i.e., may not exercise control over the firm. These lenders, typically banks or other bondholders, are paid a fixed rate which should lie at or above the market interest rate.[108]

In the typical cooperative, members engage in continuous exchanges and vary their volume of transactions with the firm. Meanwhile, the loans of investors are often perpetual and can only be retrieved upon a dissolution of the firm. Professor Hansman has shown that these differences are not fundamental. Some investor owned firms are structured so that the amount of capital invested by member-owners can be redeemed at specific intervals or, as in the case of a partnership, at will. Conversely some cooperatives, including electricity generation and distribution cooperatives, and mutual life insurance companies, require a long-term commitment from their members. For purposes of economic analysis business corporation statutes, therefore, can be regarded as specialized versions of more general cooperative statutes, which are distinguished from the latter merely on historical grounds.[109]

By contrast to the Knightian firm, where a single entrepreneur supplies capital in a risky endeavour and then reaps the benefits of her investment, ownership in the investor owned firm and cooperative is assigned to persons who are in the transactional relationship of a mere resource supplier to the firm.[110] The reason for this is that the ownership relation mitigates some of the costs that would attend these relationships if they were managed through contracting.[111] The advantages of assigning ownership to a supplier of resources extends to issues of market power, as well as *ex post* market power or lock-ins.[112] In terms of market power, ownership by resource suppliers reduces efficiency losses associated with the setting of input prices above marginal costs. *Ex post* market power benefits arise from the fact that suppliers of capital or other resources must make transaction-specific investments upon entering into the transactional relationship. Once such a transactional relationship has been entered into, exit becomes costly; a situation which can be exploited either by the firm or the employee. Partial or full ownership of the firm/cooperative by the supplier/investor can hence reduce the incentives for opportunistic behaviour.

The crucial result from the cooperative, investor-firm analogy is that ownership need not be associated with the actual investment of a lump sum of capital, or the provision of raw materials or an intermediate product. From a conceptual standpoint, it can be associated with the continued furnishing of moderate sums of capital or a goods input. In other words, the distinction of investor owners according to the amount, timing, and nature of the resource provided to the firm has no bearing on ownership rights. Conversely, property rights do not depend on the amount, timing, and nature of the resource provided. Rather, a claim to a property right arises when a resource, which had been provided consistently and upon which the firm's performance crucially depended, was not exchanged for compensation at the full market rate at the time of use. Under all of these conditions under-compensation has been accepted by the resource supplier in the expectation of some future benefit.

It can now be argued that, by supplying the input of her labour continuously to the firm, the worker may also acquire a property right in the firm. Indeed, some property rights analyses suggest that any worker, continuously employed for a given time period, has acquired such a property right. This, it has been suggested, is the case primarily because the job enables 'an employee to achieve social status, personal opportunity, and power – attributes that in the past tangible property, such as land and personal possessions, bestowed'.[113]

A second, perhaps conceptually more consistent view, qualifies the aforementioned analysis. Workers acquire a compensable property right in their job, if the compensation they receive does not account fully for the work done; or in other words, if the work input and work effort was conducted in the expectation of additional future compensation. This will typically be the case if the worker is paid on the basis of a rising age–wage contract, and dismissed before completion of her expected lifetime employment. It will also be the case if the worker has acquired, at her own cost, substantial skills, whose acquisition helped the firm to increase productivity but which cannot be transferred to other firms.[114] In this case, the employee's investment resembles a contract-specific sunk cost, which, although not resellable as prior investment, gives rise to an ethical claim to restitution.

If certain patterns of employment give rise to compensable property rights, the question is how such rights could or should be transformed into a monetary claim. There is some agreement that there is no obvious valuation mechanism for the loss of earnings due to a premature dismissal in an implicit contract situation, or losses due to the non-transferabilty of skill. Therefore an approximation rule has to be applied. One simple rule of thumb is to approximate forgone earnings of an implicit contract scheme through the payment of a sum, which increases as the number of years worked by the individual employee increases. This rule can be refined to account for the firm-specific skill of the worker, approximated by her wage and/or the period it took to find alternative employment.

Contrary to the approach adopted in the *Harvard Law Review* Note, the property rights approach implies that a discharged employee, having completed a fixed spell of employment, should be compensated irrespective of the nature of the discharge or the motives having led to it (excepting obvious and unquestionable cases of misconduct by the employee). The advantage of this approach *vis-à-vis* the current system of dismissal litigation is twofold. Firstly, by granting such a severance pay to all or to most workers who are dismissed, socially unproductive monitoring and litigation costs are reduced, as court expertise is no longer required in assigning awards. Secondly, assuming that severance costs are substantial enough, the requirement of such payments is likely to reduce employer incentives to respond opportunistically to an increasing age–wage profile, (especially as the chance of employees being discharged without such a payment is eliminated). Thirdly, given that firms discharge employees in excess of the social optimum (as they externalize costs of dismissal), a severance pay requirement would reallocate the costs of dismissals in a more efficient way.

4.4.4 Property Rights and the Courts

The record of contemporary courts in implementing job-property rights is generally insubstantial. Yet, the protection and compensation of individual property rights, in principle, is an accepted objective of both the US and UK legal systems. In the US this mandate is explicit: the oft-cited fifth amendment to the US Constitution (1791) states that 'No person shall ... be deprived of life, liberty or property, without due process of the law; nor shall private property be taken ... without just compensation.' Similar assurances as to the inviolability of private property can be found throughout English legal history. Their remit has been extended and clarified in 20th century judgements, which have endowed UK citizens with a concept of property rights akin to the protection provided in the US. In the 1933 case of *Glassbrook Bros v. Leyson*, for instance, the Court of Appeals ruled that statutes should be interpreted so as to respect individual property rights.[115]

In both countries, there also appears to be at least a rudimentary legal tradition of applying property rights to jobs. This is more explicit in the case of US judgements. American courts, on several occasions, have ruled in favour of employees who have made a property rights claim based on expected job security. In 1910, the Supreme Court of the State of Washington held that an individual's job qualified as a compensable property. According to the Washington court, this was the case because the job provided the employee with the 'wherewithal to maintain himself and his family'. The court concluded that, in order to prevent expropriation without compensation, the employee was to receive payment for his job loss.[116]

The leading contemporary court ruling involving questions about compensable job-property rights is *Perry v. Sinderman* (1974). In *Perry*, Mr Sinderman, a teacher with ten years' experience in the Texas college system, had worked under a series of one-year contracts. Without receiving an official statement of the reasons why he was dismissed, or an opportunity for a hearing, the teacher's contract was terminated for alleged insubordination. The teacher argued that the denial of a hearing violated procedural due process as required by the fourteenth amendment. The Supreme Court agreed that 'job security, whether it was express or implied, was a property right that should not be abridged without due process'.[117]

When discussing how the property right came into being, the Supreme Court limited the generality of this analysis, however. The court stated that the existence of a *de facto* tenure policy established expectations of continued employment, thereby creating the teacher's property right. With still only a handful of relevant rulings to go by, it seems that the Supreme Court follows a 'reasonableness of expectations' standard. If past practice and experience lead a public sector employee to reasonably expect continued employment, a property right is created, whose abridgement might require compensation.[118] Otherwise, the public employee is at best guaranteed a hearing which would satisfy the constitutional due process requirement.

The creation of property rights, as supported by US court decisions, today extends to constitutional guarantees that protect individuals from wrongful *state* action only. The key barrier to the general implementation of such a property rights clause against discharge, is that, in order for the taking to acquire fifth amendment compensation, the damage must originate from the public sphere. Some legal theorists have argued that federal and state interventions into the employment relationship, such as social security requirements, have become so broad that all discharges represent a *de facto* public act. As such, all dismissals would have to be subject to 5th and 14th amendment tests.[119]

Despite a strengthening of the rights of public employees in the US, however, there seems to be little movement toward the acknowledgement of property rights in private sector or even non-profit sector jobs. In the UK, meanwhile, the acknowledgement of such property rights remains limited to statutory legislation, such as the RPA. Ultimately it is questionable whether this legislation was ever more than an instrument to take dismissal and redundancy 'out of both conflict and the area of collective action and control by workers', as Fryer had already argued in 1974.[120]

4.5 EVALUATING DISCHARGE REGIMES: A PROPERTY RIGHTS PERSPECTIVE

The property rights paradigm of job protection raises serious questions concerning the equity and efficacy of the existing US and UK systems of dismissal protection. Today, there is mounting evidence that the US system of unjust dismissal litigation does not effectively address the type of employee opportunism which arises in the context of implicit contracts and rising age–wage profiles. The public policy exemption, with its focus on societal relevance for instance, is difficult to apply to unjust dismissals occurring in the context of an employer's attempt to deprive a senior worker of her earnings. The implicit nature of the increasing age–wage contract usually also precludes a cause of action based on implied contracts, or the covenant of good faith and fair dealing, both of which require explicit evidence of a prior agreement. Finally, specific Federal statutes, such as the Employee Retirement Income Security Act (ERISA) which protects workers from dismissals aimed at depriving them from pension rights, are also limited in their scope with regard to combating employer opportunism; primarily because their application requires a specific act of violation which employers may be able to circumvent through other, non-detectable or non-actionable, conduct.[121]

At first sight, the UK system of redundancy pay appears to represent a closer approximation of the property rights paradigm. Payments are available to all or most workers, and amounts paid out respond roughly to previous job tenure and wage rates. The reality, however, is less generous. Bankrupt companies often fail to make payments. Even when payments are made, they are typically derisory, representing neither an incentive for companies to retain and retrain workers, nor adequate compensation for individual employees. A recent US estimate has suggested that the real losses incurred by a worker's discharge from a manufacturing occupation amount on average to more than £50 000; a sum which is about eight times as high as the maximum statutory UK redundancy payment.[122] Existing RPA or ACAS payments also inadequately reflect the property loss incurred by employees with rising age–wage profiles. If we calculate the income-property loss of an employee earning £15 000 with a typical wage profile, dismissed at mid-career, this would amount to £26 700 in compensation forgone due to below-market wage payments during the first part of employment alone.[123]

Both the US and UK systems of discharge regulation on the whole, do not ensure the reasonable compensation of discharged employees for their loss of property. Whether there will be movements in either country to remedy this situation in the near future is questionable. For the US, the statements of the country's leading labour law expert William Gould, now chairman of the National Labor Relations Board, are revealing. Said Gould, with regard to the possibility of a general US statute protecting employees from arbitrary dismissal, 'I suspect that given the powerful forces that are hostile or ambivalent to this legislation, and the lack of effective organisation on the part of those who would benefit from it, its prospects in the short run are poor.'[124] (p. 5)

In the UK the outlook for effective dismissal regulation is perhaps more optimistic. Concepts of a stakeholder society, which have gained popularity in New Labour circles, appear to acknowledge a need for the greater protection of workers from arbitrary and excessive dismissals.[125] A paper by Labour's principal economic advisers, Kay and Silberston (1995), contrasts the old vision of the corporation – the principal agent model – with a new vision – the trusteeship model. In this trusteeship model,

> The responsibility of the trustees is to sustain the corporation's assets. This differs from the value of the corporation's shares. The difference comes not only because the stock market may value these assets incorrectly. It also arises because the assets of the corporation, for these purposes, include the skills of its employees, the expectations of customers and suppliers, and the company's reputation.[126]

While the trusteeship model implies a greater concern for the needs of employees, its implications with regard to dismissal protection are less than clear. Kay and Silberston argue,

> Thus the trusteeship model demands, as the agency model does not, the evolutionary development of the corporation around its core skills and activities because it is these skills and activities rather than a set of financial claims, which are the essence of the corporation. This does *not* preclude diversification or divestment, but it restricts operations to areas that relate in an obvious way to the firm's distinctive capabilities. Deal making becomes ... again a function of financial markets rather than management. (Kay and Silbertson (1995), p. 91 emphasis added).

As yet the stakeholder society envisaged by New Labour appears to be defined very much from the perspective of the firm, rather than from a consideration of the needs of individual workers. Ultimately, however, there may be a chance that an improved understanding of the role of the firm as employer and producer, rather than as profit maximizer, will also lead to an increased awareness for the need to protect individual workers from dismissal.

NOTES

1. It is perhaps worth noting that there are some differences with regard to the commonly used terminology in American and British articles. The US literature typically uses the terms discharge, dismissal, and termination interchangeably. The terms wrongful discharge (also wrongful termination) and unfair dismissal are also often used synonymously. In Britain, contract termination covers a much wider area than that of dismissal. This chapter largely follows the US usage of terminology, unless UK material is explicitly referred to.
2. See, for example, Glendon and Lev (1979), Gould (1986), Lee (1989) and Reich (1964).
3. In the US such protection is explicitly provided through the due-process and equal protection clauses of the Constitution.
4. For a broader discussion of sectoral differences in the legal status of US employees see Beck, (1994).
5. Lee (1989).
6. See Mendelsohn (1990), at pp. 19–20. My own estimate is based on queries conducted with the *Public Affairs Information System* (PAIS-CD ROM) in 1995.

   A large portion of these discussions were concerned with how employers can prevent lawsuits. Examples of such articles include Frierson (1990), Keppler (1990), and Jenners (1994). Jenners recommended that employers 'sanitize' the language of all written documents so that promises may not be construed from any of these documents. She also warned employers not to make any oral employment guarantees during conversations. Frierson advised that employers reduce their exposure to lawsuits through several measures, including an interviewing and hiring strategy which eliminates potentially 'troublesome' employees, explicit company policies and documents which emphasize the at-will nature of employment, and pay and promotions procedures which emphasize that company rules apply to all employees. Keppler suggested that employers adopt a proactive strategy which uses the company's employee handbook as a legal defence by identifying behaviour that will and will not result in dismissal.

Paradoxically some articles now suggest that at-will strategies adopted in light of the threat of lawsuits have had a negative impact on employment relations. See Hilgert (1988) and Schwoerer and Rosen (1989).

7. For a general overview of such theories see Blair (1995).
8. See Bellace (1983), Gould (1986) and Summers (1976).
9. The notion of such an exceptionalism has a long pedigree and is perhaps best traced to Sombart's, *Why is there no Socialism in America*? (1906). Sombart argued that the conditions of a frontier society and high social mobility moulded the American belief structure so as to reject state intervention in favour of a greater freedom of the market.
10. Thompson (1981).
11. See, for example, Estreicher (1985).
12. The UK tribunal system has been cited as a prototype for the effective adjudication of dismissals in several recent US articles. See, for example, Gould (1988), which argues in favour of the implementation of a Canadian style arbitration and tribunal system in the US, which in itself is based on the British example.

    The argument about the deficiencies of the UK systems with regard to a protection of property rights is not based on the fact that regulations often fail to be implemented; a point which has been noted earlier in, for example, Williams and Lewis (1982) and Simmons (1984). Rather I argue that the structure and premises of these systems are – from a law and economics perspective – themselves faulty and have perhaps never been aimed at providing an effective measure against unjust or excessive dismissals.
13. Peritt (1987), section 2.1.
14. Grenig (1991).
15. A 1989 study by the Bureau of National Affairs, based on a sample of 400 contracts, reported that 94 per cent of all collective bargaining contracts included provisions allowing dismissal for 'cause', 'just-cause', or specific offences only. See Bureau of National Affairs (1989).

    Such data indicate that in the US the protection of job property rights is largely a function of private ordering, whereas the state as a whole fails to encourage or provide such protection to the private labour force at large. In the US legal literature, questions have repeatedly arisen about the efficacy of union controlled 'just cause' policies in the context of union officials' failure to adequately process a dismissal related grievance.
16. Peritt's estimate was reported in Rauma (1986). The AMS survey is reported in Pilla (1985).
17. Key figures from the Jury Verdicts weekly survey were reported in Mendelsohn (1990). The 1993 survey was conducted by Jury Verdict Research Co. and is cited in Nye (1995).
18. See Mendelsohn (1990), p. 20 and Nye (1995), p. 32. The average figure reported in the Jury Verdicts Weekly survey closely matches a recent calculation by the California Employer Association, which estimated average awards at $440,000 for the years 1994 and 1995, *vide* <http://www.employers.org/seminars/96brief.html>. Approximate pound figures are based on an exchange rate of £1.6 per USD(1$).
19. See Dertouzos, Holland and Ebener (1988), at p. 37–8, table 15. The estimate by Kelly is reported in Nye (1995), p. 32.
20. See *Foley v. Interactive Data Co.*, 47 Cal. 3d 654, 254 Cal. Rptr. 211, 765 P. 2d 373 (1988). In Foley the California Supreme Court attempted to halt a further expansion of dismissal suits by taking a tougher stance on wrongful discharge claims. The court affirmed already existing causes of action then gave guidance as to what constituted a proper claim and proper remedies. Among others, the court limited action in tort in public policy matters in which no explicit public concern could be identified.

21. See Moon (1990). In a review of the impact of *Foley*, Moon concluded that despite the restrictions imposed by the courts the *Foley* case was likely to have little impact on current litigation practices. Moon suggested that some cases might become less lucrative in California, which would encourage attorneys to represent higher paid employees with projected future losses of at least $150,000. If the number of employees seeking court action continued to increase, this restriction would have no effect on aggregate case numbers.
22. The passage of this law, called the *Montana Wrongful Discharge from Employment Act*, was prompted by special circumstances. Between 1981 and 1986, an unusually large number of unjust dismissal suits, 182 in all, were filed in Billings, Montana. This flood of lawsuits was triggered by a downsizing of middle management in Montana's health and tourism industry. In a 1986 case, the Montana Supreme Court affirmed punitive damages of $1.3 million to an employee. The state court held that liability for wrongful discharge was not a 'covered occurrence' under a general liability policy. Legislative committees heard testimony that liability insurance to cover wrongful discharge could not be easily purchased by Montana employers. Some employers claimed they could face bankruptcy by reason of the expense of defending such litigation. When the state Supreme Court widened its interpretation of wrongful discharge to require that employers must investigate the claims on which dismissals are based, the legislature drafted and passed its *Wrongful Discharge Act*. See Jackson and Schantz (1990).
23. Influenced by the Montana policy, the National Conference of Commissioners on State Laws drafted and passed their own *Model Uniform Termination Act*. The Act was prompted by the belief that it was desirable to have uniformity regarding employees' substantive rights and remedies, as well as concerns with the high caseload resulting from the increase in wrongful discharge suits. Less generous than the Montana statute, the *Uniform Termination Act* was severely criticized by legal experts. Apparently, support for the Act came primarily from the National Association's employee representatives, who described the passage of the Act as a big victory for unorganized labour. Management representatives had voiced strong criticism throughout the three year drafting period, but agreed to participate in order to 'prevent worse'. The National Association of Labor Lawyers criticized the Act for its loopholes and potential ineffectiveness. Its spokesman, Dr Rosen, suggested that employers could void coverage by treating an employee as an independent contractor, by keeping an employee for less than 20 hours per week during some months, or by firing the employee before a year of employment passes. Plaintiff's attorney Golden of Southfield Michigan argued that the law was not intended to give rights to employees in states where they had none, but to neutralize employee claims in states where they did have some rights. He predicted that the Act would go nowhere in states where employees had already been given such rights. A discussion of these problems is provided in Mauk (1991).
24. The desire to preserve the undisputed managerial prerogative has been identified as a core theme of American managerial creed by several authors. See, for example Atleson (1983).
25. Myers (1994) describes the evolving insurance industry which provides coverage in case of wrongful discharge litigation and discusses insurance options available to management.
26. Hyman (1993).
27. See Lockton (1994). An economic evaluation of the Act can be found in Addison and Portugal (1993).
28. Birch (1995).
29. It has been observed that these compensation levels have fallen well below inflation. If statutory compensation limits had been increased in line with average earnings since the introduction of the Industrial Relations Act 1971, the maximum basic award would stand at £14,030, while the maximum compensatory award would amount to £48,000.

The cited figures pertain to terminations occurring on or after 27th September 1995. On the relevant legislation see the Employment Rights Act 1996 Part X (ss. 94–113) and preceding legislation.

30. See Dickens *et al.* (1984) at p. 529. An overview of the economics of UK dismissal litigation can be found in Frick, Brown and Sessions (1994).
31. Advisory Conciliation and Arbitration Service (1995).
32. Evans, Goodman and Hargreaves (1985).
33. Evans *et al.* (1985) and Flanagan (1987).
34. Picot and Wenger (1988) present a fierce critique of European dismissal law.
35. These issues are analysed in some detail in Hendy (1993) at p. 68. It must be remembered that a significant number of construction workers were excluded from dismissal protection as they were deemed to be independent contractors.
36. Hendy (1993) at p. 69.
37. Emerson (1988) provides an assessment of the level of dismissal regulation in the leading industrialized nations and highlights the *laissez faire* character of US labour market governance.
38. Flanagan (1987) at p. 23.
39. See Addison (1989), and also his 'Job Security in the United States: Law, Collective Bargaining, Policy, and Practice' (1986).
40. Picot (1988).
41. Grunfeld (1971) at p. 8.
42. Gunter, Minister of Labour, (1965) 26 April, 711 *Hansard* col 33.
43. Parker (1971).
44. See, for example, Streek (1992).
45. Turnbull and Wass (1995).
46. See note 29 above.
47. Turnbull (1995).
48. Editorial, 'The Unbearable Lightness of Business', (1995), *Management Today* 3.
49. Caulkin (1994).
50. Hendy (1993) at pp. 68–9 and pp. 78–80.
51. *Edwards v. Cardiff City Council* [1979] IRLR 303; *Marsden v. Fairey Steel Ltd.* [1979] IRLR 103. Both cases are discussed in Selwyn (1982), at pp. 245–6.
52. *Thompson v. Eaton Ltd* [1976] 3 all ER 384, [1976] ICR 336, [1976] IRLR 308.
53. *Power Packing Case Makers v. Faust* [1981] ICR 484, [1981] IRLR 120.
54. Hendy (1993) at pp. 78–80.
55. Mukherjee (1973).
56. Blackstone (1765–69).
57. Wood (1877) at para. 134.
58. Friedman (1985), at pp. 532–6.
59. Feinman (1976).
60. *Payne v. Western and Atlantic Railroad* (1884) 81 Tenn. 507.
61. *Comerford v. International Harvester Company*, 235 Ala 376 (Ala, 1932). In the politically relevant case of *Adair v. United States* (US SCt, 1908) 208 US 161, the US Supreme Court applied this doctrine in order to declare unconstitutional a statute prohibiting the discharge of railroad employees for union membership.
62. *National Labor Relations Act*, (49 Stat. 499) (Washington: USGPO, 1935). The NLRA was declared constitutional in *NLRB v. Jones & Laughlin Steel Corporation*, 301 US 1, 57 S.Ct. 615 (1937). *De facto* enforcement of the section 7 & 8 rules regarding dismissals started in 1934 with the formation of the first Labor Relations Board formed under *National Industrial Recovery Act* legislation.
63. *Fair Labor Standards Act* USCA 215 (a)(3) (1938/65).
64. Mendelsohn (1990) at p. 3 and Annexe A. Federal Acts providing some protection for employees from unjust discharge include: i) collective bargaining; *Railway Labor Act*, 45 USCA 152 (1976) ii) reporting of violations; *Energy Reorganization Act*, 42 USCA 5851; *Federal Water Pollution and Control Act*, 33 USCA 1367 (1978); *Air Pollution Prevention and Control Act*, 42 USCA 7622 (1983); *Occupational and Health*

and Safety Act, 29 USCA 660–61 (1975); *Coal Mine Safety Act*, 30, USCA 815 (1983); *Railroad Safety Act*, 45 USCA 441 (1983); *Fair Labor Standards Act*, USCA 215 (a)(3) (1965); *Employee Retirement Income Security Act*, 29 USCA 1140 (1975) iii) discrimination based on sex, race, colour, age, and national origin; 42 USCA 2000 (e)(2)(a) (1981); *Age Discrimination in Employment Act*, 29 USCA 623 623 (1975) (d) Veterans protection; 38 USCA 2021 (b)(1) (1979) iv) Garnishment: *Consumer Credit Protection Act*, 15 USCA 1674 (1982) v) Federal Employee Protection; *Civil Service Act* 5 USCA 4803 (a)(1983).

65. Grenig (1991); St Antoine (1984), estimates the unprotected workforce at 70 per cent.
66. *Peterman v. International Brotherhood of Teamsters Local*, 174 Cal. App. 2d 184 (1959).
67. *Frampton v. Central Indiana Gas Co.*, 297 N.E. 2d 425 (Ind. 1973).
68. *Trombetta v. Detroit, Toledo, & Ironton Railroad*, 265 N.W. 2d 385 (Mich. App. 1978).
69. *Fortune v. National Cash Register*, Co. 364 N.E. 2d 125 (Mass. 1977).
70. *Agis v. Howard Johnson Co.*, 335 N.E. 2d 315 (Mass. 1976).
71. *Pierce v. Orthopharmaceutical Co.*, 84 NJ 58, 417 A. 2d 505 (New Jersey 1980).
72. See *Tameny v. Atlantic Richfield* (1980) 27 Cal. 3d 167, for a case involving the refusal to violate a statute; *Clanton v. Cain-Sloan Co.* (Tenn 1984) 677 S.W. 2d 441, regarding the exercise of a legally protected right; *Hostettler v. Pioneer* (S.D. Ind. 1987) 2 I.E.R. Cases 1311, for a case where plaintiff's dismissal resulted from the expression of general societal concerns.
73. See *Toussaint v. Blue Cross and Blue Shields* (1980 Mich.) 292 N.W. 2d 880, where earlier oral promises and the personnel manual served as evidence for an implied contract.
74. *Fortune* (1977), *op. cit.*, in which the court found that the personnel manual contained an implied promise that the employer would act in good faith.
75. Krueger (1991).
76. See Mendelsohn (1990) at p. 2. The AMS survey is cited in Cregar (1987).
77. Dertouzos (1988) at p. 19.
78. Mendelsohn (1990) at pp. 3–4. On this theory of spillover effects see also Lieberman (1981). Lieberman suggests that the US legal system underwent a transformation from a contractual to a fiduciary legal system. The contractual model assigned rights and duties contractually, allowing a judge to adjudicate individual disputes on the basis of clear and unambiguous rules. Under the fiduciary model, by contrast, rights are based on trust and confidence among the parties. Because these rights are established by vague standards of care and potentially ill defined standards of trust, they must be inferred from the fiduciary relationship between litigants or between the state and its citizens. This encourages 'excessive' litigation and an entrepreneurial attitude, whereby judicial innovations spread quickly if they benefit a large enough group.
79. An AMS survey reported that between 1984 and 1986 more than 500 000 middle management jobs were cut in a group of 300 companies. See Bureau of National Affairs (1988).
80. Mendelsohn (1990) at p. 4; and Hoerr (1985).
81. Epstein (1984). Epstein gives a comprehensive overview of efficiency arguments in favour of employment-at-will. See also the earlier review by Harrison (1984).
82. Addison (1989). On the problems of reconciling incentives with job security see, for example, Lazear (1986) and Lazear and Moore (1984).
83. Becker (1989).
84. Gray (1993). Gray's analysis exemplifies an intellectual tradition which dominates much of the pro employment-at-will literature. This tradition typically attributes the success of economies solely to 'entrepreneurship'. Unfortunately this literature is largely void of any positive definition of entrepreneurship. Typically it lists factors which contribute to the rise of entrepreneurship as well as those which hamper it, while the sources of ideas and the pools from which 'entrepreneurs' are recruited are not spelled out. As a common denominator the 'entrepreneurship' argument against dismissal regulation stresses the need for the protection of managerial property rights, which are assumed to include the right to hire and fire at-will. References to

historical works are frequent and an 'empirical' correlation between entrepreneurial activity and institutional arrangements which protect individuals who hold property and allow them to act unconstrained is stressed.

85. Picot (1988).
86. Commons and Andrew (1936) at p. 505.
87. Commons and Andrew (1936) at p. 503.
88. Stieber (1980).
89. Epstein (1984).
90. See Note (1989) at pp. 510–11.
91. The notion that pay equals the marginal product applies only to conditions of competitive markets. For an introductory analysis of labour markets and remuneration models see Ehrenberg and Smith (1991) chapter 11; and Rees (1973) part 5.
92. See the extensive literature on dismissals as a disciplining device including Rebitzer (1989); Shapiro and Stiglitz (1984); and Gintis and Ishikawa (1987).
93. Becker and Stigler (1974).
94. Akerlof and Katz (1986), and Akerlof and Katz (1989).
95. See, for example, *HLR* Note (1989) and Parsons (1986).
96. See *HLR* Note (1989) at pp. 521–3.
97. On US studies of age-earnings profiles see, for example, Altonji and Shakotko (1987), Brown (1989), Hutchens (1989), Loewenstein and Sicherman (1991). UK studies include Brown and Sessions (1997).

    The cumulative evidence of these studies has led Harvard Law Professor Weiler to argue that, since deferral systems are a standard feature of pay systems in modern industry, there is an imperative for the legal protection of employees from employer opportunism. See Weiler (1990) at chapter 2.
98. Medoff and Abraham (1980a), and Medoff and Abraham (1980b).
99. Lazear (1979). See also Lazear (1981), and Lazear and Moore (1984).
100. See Epstein (1989).
101. See, for example, Mookherjee and Reichelstein (1990), Mookherjee (1993) and MacLeod and Malcomson (1989).
102. Malcomson (1984) and MacLeod and Malcolmson (1988).
103. See Fenn and Whelan (1984) at pp. 372–9.
104. *HLR* Note (1980) at p. 1831; and Note (1989) at p. 524.
105. *HLR* Note (1989) at p. 528.
106. See, for example, Hansmann (1996) and Barzel (1989).
107. See Williamson (1986) at pp. 265–8; and Keli, Crawford, and Alchian (1976).
108. Hansman (1988).
109. Hansman (1985).
110. Knight (1921). The pure Knightian entrepreneur meets her capital needs entirely by borrowing. All other factors of production are purchased on the market, while all products are sold on the market. The owner controls the firm and receives all its residual earnings.
111. See Ricketts (1987); chapters 4 and 5 describe the cost of contracting, including issues of asymmetric information, agency problems and issues of limited markets.
112. Williamson (1986) at chapter 2.
113. Heshizer (1985).
114. Peck (1979), and Drucker (1980).
115. *Glasbrook Bros v. Leyson* [1933] 2 KB 91, CA affirmed the earlier decision of *Managers of the Metropolitan Asylum District v. Hill* (1881) 6 App Cas 193, HL. In the latter case the appellants had been given statutory authority to provide asylums. The statute contained no provision for compensation. In this instance the appellants were restrained by an injunction from using the asylum in such a manner so as to cause a nuisance.
116. *Jones v. Leslie* (Wash SCt, 1918) 61 Wash 107.
117. *Perry v. Sinderman* (US SCt, 1972) 408 US 593.

118. Property interests and 14th amendment rights were acknowledged in the following Supreme Court cases: *Perry v. Sinderman* (US SCt 1972) 1 IER 33; *Cleveland Board of Education v. Loudermill* (US SCt 1985) 1 IER 424, *Brock v. Roadway Express Inc.* (US SCt 1987) 2 IER 1. The Supreme Court rejected such claims in: *State Colleges* (*Board of Regents*) *v. Roth* (US SCt 1972) 1 IER 23; *Paul v. Davis* (US SCt 1976) 1 IER 1827.
119. Peck (1979) at pp. 24–5.
120. Fryer (1974). It is perhaps not surprising that the UK academic literature on labour law has almost uniformly viewed British redundancy and dismissal protection provisions as insufficient and inadequate. See, for example, Forest (1980), Carty (1989), Collins (1992), Fitzpatrick (1994), Ford and Gibbons (1996).
121. Beck (1995) argues that the effectiveness of this litigation and legislation in the public sector has been limited, primarily because the current doctrine of exemptions is inapplicable to group dismissals, and hence allows employers to shift from the dismissal of single workers to the batch discharge of 'undesirable' employees.
122. Jacobsen, Lalonde and Sullivan (1994).
123. This computation is based on a working life of 40 years, and a non-linear wage profile that increases by 40 per cent over the working life. The initial wage starts at 20 per cent below the market value and increases to the market wage after 20 years.
124. Gould (1986) .
125. See, for example, Kay (1996). Professor Kay has been described as the principal intellectual influence on Tony Blair's economic thought. The title of his SES lecture is perhaps typical of the current narrow conception of stakeholding which seems to prevail among the current Labour party leadership. Whereas the rights of entrepreneurs and the need to provide certainty to businesses are consistently emphasized, the need to provide worker-stakeholders with a certain set of rights remains yet largely unacknowledged.
126. Kay and Silberston (1995) at p. 91.

ACKNOWLEDGEMENTS

The author would like to thank Miss Caroline Hunter, M.A. and Miss Helen Julia Paul, B.A. (Hons) for their valuable research assistance. Any errors are, of course, the author's sole responsibility.

REFERENCES

Addison, J. (1986), 'Job security in the United States: law, collective bargaining, policy, and practice', *British Journal of Industrial Relations*, **24**(3), pp. 381–418.

Addison, J. (1989), 'The absence of job protection legislation: a source of competitive advantage for the United States', in Libecap (ed), *Advances in the Study of Entrepreneurship, Innovation, and Economic Growth*, Washington: JAI Press.

Addison, J.T. and P. Portugal (1993), 'The UK labor market, institutions, law, and performance', in Hartog and Theuwes (eds), *Labor Market Contracts and Institutions*, Amsterdam: North Holland.

Advisory Conciliation and Arbitration Service (1995), *Annual Report*, Leicester: ACAS Publications.

Akerlof, G. and L.Katz (1986), 'Do Deferred Wages Dominate Involuntary Unemployment as a Worker Discipline Device?' Cambridge: National Bureau of Economic Research, Working Paper No 2025.

Akerlof, G. and L. Katz (1989), 'Workers' trust funds and the logic of wage profiles', *Quarterly Journal of Economics*, **104**(3), pp. 525–36.
Altonji, J. and R. Shakotko (1997), 'Do wages rise with job security', *Review of Economic Studies*, **54**(3), pp. 437–59.
Atleson, J.B. (1983), *Values and Assumptions of American Labor Law*, Amherst: University of Massachusetts Press.
Barzel, Y. (1989), *Economic Analysis of Property Rights*, Cambridge: Cambridge University Press.
Beck, M. (1995), 'Public policy exemptions, whistleblower statutes, and government worker layoffs: a case of adverse effects', *Journal of Collective Bargaining*, **24**(1), pp. 1–15.
Beck, M. and J. Allen (1994), 'Union agendas and the disintegration of job stability – an institutional perspective', *Journal of Interdisciplinary Economics*, **5**(2) pp. 79–105.
Becker, G. (1989), 'The courts shouldn't become pink slip police', *Business Week,* **14** (August).
Becker, G. and J. Stigler (1974), 'Law enforcement, malfeasance, and compensation of enforcers', *Journal of Legal Studies*, **3**(1), pp. 1–18.
Bellace, J.R. (1983), 'A right of fair dismissal', *University of Michigan Journal of Law* (16), p. 207.
Birch, T. (1995), *Croner's Guide to Managing Fair Dismissal*, Kingston: Croner Publications.
Blackstone, Sir W. (1769), *Commentaries on the Laws of England–IV*, London: T. Cadell.
Blair, M. (1995), *Ownership and Control: Rethinking Corporate Governance of the 21st Century*, Washington: Brookings Institution.
Brown, J. (1989), 'Why do wages increase with tenure?', *American Economic Review*, **79**(5), pp. 971–91.
Brown, S. and J. Sessions (1997), 'Age-earnings Profiles and the Cost of Agency', Loughborough: Loughborough University, Department of Economics, Economic Research Paper N. 97/16.
Bureau of National Affairs (1988), 'The American Management Survey', *Employment Relations Weekly*, 25 January, p. 99.
Bureau of National Affairs (1989), 'Collective bargaining, negotiation, and contracts', *Reports*, 9 March.
Carty, H. (1989), 'Dismissed employees: the search for a more effective remedy', *Modern Law Review*, **52**(4), pp. 449–68.
Caulkins, S. (1994), 'Editorial', The Observer, **29**.
Collins, H. (1992), 'The meaning of job security', *Industrial Law Journal*, **20**, 201–39.
Commons, J. and J. Andrews (1936), *Principles of Labor Legislation*, New York: Harper and Row.
Cregar, M. (1987) 'Terminate with care', *Management World*, **16**, pp. 12–13.
Dertouzos, J., E. Holland and P. Ebener (1988), *The Legal and Economic Consequences of Wrongful Termination*, Santa Monica: The Rand Corporation's Institute for Civil Justice, Report No R-3602-ICJ.
Dickens, W.T. *et al.* (1984), 'The British experience under a statute prohibiting unfair dismissal', *Industrial and Labor Relations Review*, **37**(4), pp. 497–514.
Drucker, P. (1980), 'The job as property right', *The Wall Street Journal*, 4 March.
Ehrenberg, R. and R. Smith (1991), *Modern Labour Economics*, New York: HarperCollins.

Emerson, M. (1988) 'Regulation or deregulation of the labour market: policy regimes for the recruitment and dismissal of employees of the industrialized countries', *European Economic Review*, **32**(4), pp. 775–817.

Epstein, R.A. (1984), 'In defense of the contract at-will', *University of Chicago Law Review*, (51), p. 947.

Estreicher, S. (1985), 'Unjust dismissal laws: some cautionary notes', *American Journal of Comparative Law*, **33**(2), pp. 310–23.

Evans, S., J. Goodman and L. Hargreaves (1985), *Unfair Dismissal Law and Employment Practice in the 1980s*, Manchester: University of Manchester, Department of Management Sciences, Research Paper No 53.

Feinman, J. (1976), 'The development of the employment-at-will rule', *American Journal of Legal History*, (20), p. 118.

Fenn, P. and C. Whelan (1984), 'Job security and the role of law: an economic analysis of employment-at-will', *Stanford Journal of International Law*, **20**(2), pp. 353–92.

Fitzpatrick, B. (1994), 'Unfair dismissal and industrial action, *Industrial Law Journal*, (23), p. 243.

Flanagan, R.J. (1987), 'Labour market behaviour and European economic growth', in Lawrence *et al.* (eds), *Barriers to European Growth*, Washington: Brookings.

Ford, M. and S. Gibbons (1996), 'Remedying unjust dismissal law', in McColgan (ed.), *The Future of Labour Law*, London: Mansell.

Forest, H. (1980), 'Political values in individual employment law', *Modern Law Review*, **43**(4), pp. 361–80.

Frick, B., S. Brown and J. Sessions (1994), *Unemployment, Vacancies and Unjust Dismissals: The Cyclical Demand for Individual Grievance Procedures*, Loughborough: University of Loughborough, Department of Economics, Research Paper No 94/7.

Friedman, L. (1985), *A History of American Law*, New York: Simon & Schuster.

Frierson, J. (1990), 'How to fire without getting burnt', *Personnel*, **67**(9), pp. 44–8.

Fryer, R. (1974), 'The myths of the Redundancy Payments Act', *Individual Law Journal*, **3**, pp. 1–16.

Grintis, H. and T. Ishikawa (1987), 'Wages, work intensity and unemployment in competitive labour markets', *Journal of Japanese and International Economics*, (1), p. 195.

Glendon, M. and E. Lev (1979), 'Changes in the bonding of the employment relationship', *Boston College Law Review*, (20), p. 457.

Gould, W. (1986), 'The rights of individual workers', *Center Magazine*, (17), p. 2.

Gould, W. (1988), 'Stemming the wrongful discharge tide: a case for arbitration', *Employee Relations Law Journal*, (13), p. 404.

Gould. W.B. (1986), 'The idea of the job as property in contemporary America', *Brigham Young Law Review*, p. 885.

Gray, J. (1993), *Beyond the New Right*, London: Routledge.

Grenig, J. (1991), 'The dismissal of employees in the United States', *International Labour Review*, pp. **130**(5–6), pp. 569–81.

Grunfield, C. (1971), *The Law of Redundancy*, London: Sweet and Maxwell.

Gunter, R., Minister of Labour (1965), House of Commons Debates, 26 April, 711 *Hansard* col 33.

Hansman, H. (1985), 'The organisation of insurance companies: mutual vs stock', *Journal of Law Economics and Organization*, (1), p. 125.

Hansman, H. (1988), *Toward a General Theory of Corporate Ownership*, New Haven: Yale University, Program in Law and Organisation, Yale Law School, Working Paper No 74.
Hansmann, H. (1996), *The Ownership of Enterprise*, Cambridge: The Belknap Press of Havard University Press.
Harrison, J.L. (1984), 'The "new" terminable-at-will employment contract: an interest and cost incidence analysis', *Iowa Law Review*, **69**(2), pp. 327–61.
Hendy, J. (1993), *A Law unto Themselves: Conservative Employment Laws – A National and International Assessment*, London: Institute of Employment Rights.
Heshizer, B. (1985), 'The new common law of employment: changes in the concept of employment-at-will', *Labor Law Journal*, **36**(2), pp. 95–107.
Hilgert, R. (1988), 'How at-will statements hurt employers', *Personnel Journal*, **67**(2), p. 75.
HLR Note (1980), 'Protecting at-will against wrongful discharge: the duty to terminate only in good faith', *Harvard Law Review*, (93), p. 1816
HLR Note (1989), 'Employer opportunism and the need for a just-cause standard', *Harvard Law Review*, (103), p. 510.
Hoerr, J. (1985), 'Beyond unions', *Business Week*, (July) p. 72.
Hutchens, R. (1989), 'Seniority, wages and productivity', *Journal of Economics Perspectives*, **3**(4), pp. 49–64.
Hyman, R. (1993), 'Labour law, labour market and the state: British industrial relations under the Conservatives', in Buechtemann (ed.), *Employment Security and Labour Market Behaviour*, Ithaca: Cornell University Press.
Jackson, J. and W. Schantz (1990), 'A new frontier in wrongful discharge', *Personnel Journal*, **70**(1), 101–104.
Jacobsen, L., R. Lalonde and D. Sullivan (1994), 'The cost of worker dislocation', *Challenge*, (37), p. 56.
Jenners, L. (1994), 'Employment-at-will liability: how protected are you?', *Human Resource Focus*, (71), p. 11.
Kay, J. (1996), 'A stakeholding society: what does it mean for business', third annual Royal Bank of Scotland/Scottish Economic Society lecture, 29 October.
Kay, J and A. Silberston (1995), 'Corporate governance', *National Institute Economic Review*, p. 84.
Keli, B., R. Crawford and A. Alchian (1976), 'Vertical integration, appropriable rents, and the competitive contracting process', *Journal of Law and Economics*, (21), p. 297.
Keppler, M. (1990), 'Halting traffic on the road to wrongful discharge – avoiding wrongful discharge suits', *Personnel*, **67**(3), pp. 48–53.
Knight, F. (1921), *Risk, Uncertainty, and Profit*, Boston: Houghton Mifflin.
Krueger, A. (1991), 'The evolution of unjust dismissal legislation in the United States', *Industrial and Labour Relations Review*, **64**(4), pp. 644–60.
Lazear, E. (1981), 'Agency, earnings profiles, productivity and hours restrictions', *American Economic Review*, **71**(4), pp. 606–20.
Lazear, E. (1979), 'Why is there mandatory retirement?', *Journal of Political Economy*, (87), p. 1261.
Lazear, E. (1986), 'Employment-at-will, job security and work incentives', Berlin: WZB, paper presented at the international conference on Employment, Unemployment, and Hours of Work in Berlin.
Lazear, E. and R. Moore (1984), 'Incentives, productivity and labor contracts', *Quarterly Journal of Economics*, **99**(2), pp. 275–96.

Lee, B. (1989), 'Something akin to a property right', *Business and Professional Ethics Journal*, (8), p. 63.

Lieberman, J. (1981), *The Litigious Society*, New York: Basic Books.

Lockton, D. (1994), *Employment Law*, London: Macmillan.

Loewenstein, G. and N. Sicherman (1991), 'Do workers prefer increasing wage profiles?', *Journal of Labour Economics*, **9**(1), pp. 67–84.

MacLeod, W. and J. Malcomson (1988), 'Reputation and hierarchy in dynamic models of employment', *Journal of Political Economy*, (96), p. 832.

MacLeod, W. and J. Malcomson (1989), 'Implicit contracts, incentive compatibility, and involuntary unemployment', *Econometrica*, **57**(2), pp. 447–80.

Malcomson, J. (1984), 'Work incentives, hierarchy, and internal labor markets', *Journal of Political Economy*, **92**(3), pp. 486–507.

Mauk, W. (1991), 'Model termination act is flawed', *Trial* (37), p. 28.

Medoff, J. and K. Abraham (1980a), 'Experience, performance, and earnings', *Quarterly Journal of Economics*, (95), 730.

Medoff, J. and K. Abraham (1980b), 'Are those paid more really more productive? The Case of Experience', *Journal of Human Resources*, (16), 186.

Mendelsohn, S. (1990), *Wrongful Termination Legislation in the United States and its Effects on the Employment Relationship*, Paris: OECD, OECD Labor Market and Social Policy Occasional Papers #3.

Mookherjee, D. (1995), 'Corruptible law enforces: how should they be compensated?', *Economic Journal*, **105**(428), pp. 145–159.

Mookherjee, D. and S. Reichelstein (1990), 'Implementation via augmented revelation mechanism', *Review of Economic Studies*, **57**(3), pp. 453–75.

Moon, R. (1990), 'Attack/counter attack: the continuing evolution of wrongful discharge claims', in *Labor Law Developments* 7–1, Institute on Labor Law, Washington: Bureau of National Affairs.

Mukherjee, S. (1973), *Through no Fault of their Own: Systems for Handling Redundancies in Britain, France, and Germany*, London: MacDonald.

Myers, R. (1994), 'Protecting against employment perils', *Nation's Business*, (82), p. 65.

Nye, D. (1995), 'When the fired fight back', *Across the Board*, (32), p. 31.

Parker S. (1971), *Effects of the Redundancy Payments Act*, London: HMSO.

Parsons, D. (1986), 'The employment relationship: job attachment, work effort and the nature of contracts', Ashenfelter and Layard (eds), *Handbook of Labour Economics* (2), New York: Wiley.

Peck, C. (1979), 'Unjust discharges from employment', *Ohio State Journal*, (40), p. 1.

Peritt, H. (1987), *Employee Dismissal: Law and Practice* (2nd edn), New York: Matthew Bender.

Picot, A. and E Wenger (1988), 'The employment relation from the transaction cost perspective', in Dorrow *et al.* (eds), *Management under Differing Labour Market and Employment Systems*, Berlin: de Gruyter.

Pilla, L. (1985), 'Unjust discharge arises', *Management World*, (14), 1 March.

Rauma, A. (1986), 'Fired workers are suing ex-bosses and winning', *Detroit News*, 25 November.

Rebitzer, J. (1989), 'Efficiency Wages and Implicit Contracts', in Drago and Perlman (eds), *Microeconomics Issues in Labour Economics*, New York: Harvester Wheatsheaf.

Rees, A. (1973), *The Economics of Work and Pay*, New York: Harper & Row.

Reich, C. (1964), 'The new property', *Yale Law Preview*, (73), p. 733.

Ricketts, M. (1987), *The Economics of Business Enterprise: New Approaches to the Firm*, New York: Harvester Wheatsheaf.
Schwoerer, C. and B. Rosen (1989), 'Effects of employment-at-will policies and compensation policies on corporate image and job pursuit intentions', *Journal of Applied Psychology*, **24**(4), pp. 653–6.
Selwyn, N. (1982), *Selwyn's Law of Employment*, London: Butterworths.
Shapiro, C. and J.E. Stiglitz (1984), 'Equilibrium unemployment as worker disciplining device, *American Economic Review*, **74**(3), pp. 433–44.
Simmons, G. (1984), 'Unjust dismissal of the unorganised workers in Canada', *Journal of International Law*, **20**(2), pp. 473–501.
Sombart, W. (1976, first published 1906), *Why is there no Socialism in the United States?*, Armonk, M.E. Sharpe.
St Antoine, T. (1984), 'Changing concepts of worker rights in the workplace', *Annals of the American Academy of the Political and Social Sciences*, **473**, pp. 108–15.
Stieber, J. (1980), 'The case for protection of unorganised employees against unjust discharge', Madison: Proceedings of the 32nd Annual Meeting of the Industrial Relations Association.
Streek, W. (1992), *Social Institutions and Economic Performance: Studies of Industrial Relations in Advanced Capitalist Economies*, London: Sage.
Summers, C. (1976), 'Individual protection against unjust dismissal', *Virginia Law Review*, (62), p. 481.
Thompson, A. (1981), 'A view from abroad', in Stieber *et al.* (eds), *US Industrial Relations 1950 to 1980*, Madison: Industrial Relations Research Association.
Turnbull, P. and V. Wass (1995), 'Anorexic organizations and labour market lemons', Durham: Paper for the British Universities Industrial Relations Association Annual Conference in Durham.
Weiler, P. (1990), *Governing the Workplace: The Future of Labour and Employment Law*, Cambridge: Harvard University Press.
Williams, K. and D. Lewis (1982), 'Legislating for job security: the British experience', *Employee Relations Law Journal*, (8), p. 482.
Williamson, O. (1985), *The Economic Institutions of Capitalism*, New York: Free Press.
Wood, H. (1887), *A Treatise on the Law of Master and Servant*, San Francisco: Bancroft.

5. Potential labour market repercussions of proposed reforms to the US Fair Labor Standards Act overtime hours law

Lonnie Golden

The United States House of Representatives in 1997 passed a bill (HR-1), by a narrow margin, that proposed significant amendments to the 1938 Fair Labor Standards Act (FLSA). A similar version of the bill (S-4) stalled in the US Senate. One aspect of the bill would allow private sector employers to substitute compensatory (comp) time for overtime pay if an employee signs on to such an agreement. Another provision would require overtime premium pay (or comp time) only if hours of work were to exceed 80 hours over a two-week period. Advocates tout the legislation as providing time-squeezed families with more choice and flexibility. Opponents, however, regard it as a 'wolf in sheep's clothing' designed to benefit employers at the expense of employees. An economic assessment of the repercussions of instituting the legislation would predict the impact on *efficiency, growth, equity* and *welfare*. This chapter is limited to the potential effect on the issue of worker welfare. The main question to be addressed is whether a proposed change in labour law will raise or reduce the economic welfare of the estimated 80 million non-exempt workers in the US?[1] The answer, as it is to most economic questions, is 'it depends'. In this case, it depends mainly on the response of employers, specific provisions included in the bill, and what ultimately happens to the average length of working time.

The first section of this chapter will briefly survey what various models of labour supply and demand in the economics literature imply are the causes and consequences of patterns in average work hours. A unique framework is developed which broadens the scope of the conventional notions of utility and cost. Worker utility from supplying labour can be influenced by dimensions of working time other than its weekly (or annual) duration. This includes its dynamic flexibility in response to changes in preferences or constraints, its volatility and its daily scheduling. A broadened firm labour cost function illustrates that employers may choose alternate 'low road' or 'high road' paths to the same destination of restraining unit labour costs. The low road consists of reducing current wage costs and a working time strategy of enhancing numerical and work-time flexibility. The latter means varying the number of workers and their hours in direct proportion to concurrent fluctuations in output demand. The high road involves improving organizational performance in the longer run via better matching of work hours and schedules with employee preferences and engaging in labour hoarding during downturn periods. The high road involves flexibility *for* workers rather than flexibility *of* workers. This chapter assumes actual hours are determined in workplaces and in the labour market through a bilateral monopoly-type process. Actual hours are a weighted average falling somewhere within the range between employer hours demanded and worker hours desired when the two diverge. The high and persistent incidence of both underemployment and overemployment (unaccompanied by fully compensating wage differentials) attests to the limitations of assuming a market-clearing process. The impact of FLSA reforms on worker welfare depends on the ultimate change to the level and timing of both hours demanded and desired. The impact on the actual level and path of average work hours depends on the effect of FLSA reforms on the institutional forces that mediate the determination of actual hours. Thus, a long run (market or bargaining) equilibrium is assumed indeterminate.

The second section will compare benefits and costs of hours regulation. The third section will project the effect of proposed FLSA regulations on worker utility by examining discrete, three-period intertemporal scenarios which may develop as a result of a worker selecting comp time over overtime pay. It will also integrate the predicted effect on average hours demanded per worker. Worker welfare under a new FLSA regime ultimately will depend on the extent to which employers pursue either the low-road or high-road strategy regarding working time. That is, worker welfare may increase only if employers, and the regulation, grant workers increased ability to control the number and timing of hours of overtime worked and comp time taken off, and if workers can turn comp time credits into cash on demand. If a new FLSA does not ensure this, worker utility will at best remain constant. Indeed, worker utility could well decline unless further amendments, legislation, regulations or labour market forces are forthcoming which shorten hours demanded, bid up wage rates and set an upper boundary to hours worked in a given week. The fourth section will present specific policy changes, including further FLSA reforms, more likely to enhance rather than diminish worker welfare and restrain rather than increase average weekly hours.

5.1 A MODEL TO ANALYSE REPERCUSSIONS OF CHANGING FLSA OVERTIME PAY PROVISIONS

Actual average weekly hours (H) worked are established by the interaction of three forces: (1) hours per week desired by the worker (H^*); (2) hours per week demanded by the employer (H^d); (3) the institutional environment in which hours decisions are mediated, such as labour law and regulations, collective bargaining and macro-economic climate. In a neoclassical labour supply allocation model, desired work hours of labour force participants stem from their preference for leisure, market wage rate, non-wage income and working conditions. The resulting income and number of leisure hours determines their level of utility. Some models incorporate a minimum workweek constraint established by employers. Employers set a bare minimum workweek for each job or shift because of fixed capital and start-up costs, particularly for continuous process production and fixed costs of labour such as training and insurance coverage.[2] The minimum hours constraint may leave a worker 'overemployed' – willing but unable to trade income for reduced work time at their current job – thus unable to optimize.[3] Hedonic labour market theory predicts workers facing mandatory overtime, inconvenient or inflexible work hours will receive a compensating wage differential. However, empirical evidence shows it is partial at most.[4] Thus, workers passing through a state of overemployment, facing a take-it-or-leave-it choice, will tend to absorb it and experience a suboptimal level of utility. In addition, overemployment (underemployment) can and does occur even in the absence of minimum (maximum) workweeks. Anytime workers are unable to make marginal adjustments downward (upward) in their work time voluntarily at their current job for a proportional adjustment in pay.

An expanded, multi-dimensional utility function for individuals illustrates that not only the level but the temporal aspects of worktime affects well-being as well. There are at least four separate dimensions of working time. This includes the mean duration of working time, which is the primary focus of research on working hours. It also includes the *volatility* (V) of hours over time for a given average duration of work hours.

$$\textit{Actual Mean Hours } (\bar{H}) = \frac{\sum_{t=0}^{n}(H_t)}{n};\ \textit{Desired Mean Hours } (\bar{H}^*) = \frac{\sum_{t=0}^{n} H_t^*}{n}$$

In addition, the degree to which actual hours (H) and schedules (I) respond to a change in the worker's desired length of hours (H^*) and daily interval (I^*) of work scheduled for a given H^* affects worker welfare.

Volatility (V) will reduce utility if desired hours H^* follows a different path than actual H varies, where:

$$\textit{Actual Mean Square Error } (v) = \sqrt{\frac{\sum_{t=0}^{n}(H_t - \bar{H}t)^2}{n}}$$

$$\textit{Desired Mean Square Error } (v^*) = \sqrt{\frac{\sum_{t=0}^{n}(H_t^* - \bar{H}t^*)^2}{n}}$$

Volatility (V) can be measured as the mean root discrepancy between actual and desired hours:

$$V = \sqrt{\frac{\sum_{t=0}^{n}(H_t - H_t^*)^2}{n}}$$

While actual H or desired H^* may vary over some time period, this can either reduce or increase V. This depends on whether a change in each decreases or increases the size of the gap this creates between H and H^*. Thus, V takes into account the possibility that a worker may desire variability in their weekly hours. It is *undesired* volatility in hours that diminishes the individual's utility.[5] It is reasonable to assume that since workers are also consumers, they may tend to prefer a smooth path over time in consumption spending and the income that finances it. Also, workers are part of a household and other groups and it is reasonable to presume they will find it easier to plan their leisure, household production and consumption-based activities when hours are predictable. Workers thus tend to prefer stable over unstable hours, *ceteris paribus*.

Squaring both sides of the preceding equation allows us to decompose variability into three separate elements:

$$V^2 = (\bar{H}^* - \bar{H}) + (v^* - v)^2 + 2\,(1 - \rho)vv^*$$

The first component represents the static or average deviation of actual from desired mean hours. The second term indicates the amount of undesired variation. If ρ is the correlation between H and H^*, the final expression reflects the lack of correlation between changes in actual and changes in desired hours of work, i.e., the degree to which the timing of such deviations is out of synchronization. The minimum possible value of V is zero. If the mean value of H and H^* are the same, V reduces to the standard deviation of hours over the time period. Suppose, however, n=2 and H^* over both periods is a constant 40 hours, while actual H is 50 in period 1 and H is 30 in period 2. The volatility factor will be equal to 10. V would double to 20 if H in the two periods were 60 and 20, respectively. The maximum possible V in 2 periods would be 40, where the worker is scheduled to work alternatively 80 hours the first week, and zero the next.

Flexibility to a worker means immediate and proportional adjustment of actual hours to anticipated as well as unanticipated deviations in H^*. Researchers have not sufficiently distinguished between the concepts of variability and flexibility in hours. Only the latter implies variation in hours on workers' terms. The degree of flexibility for workers can be portrayed as the term δ in the equation,

$$\Delta H_t = \delta(H_t^* - H_{t-1}) \quad 0 \leq \delta \leq 1$$

A δ of 1.0 means workers are able to customize their own average weekly hours, where actual hours of work adjust immediately and fully to a given change in the preferred workweek length.[6]

Workers are clearly not indifferent to the time slot or interval (I), the block of time in the course of a day over which work is scheduled. Even if their number of actual (H) and desired hours (H^*) are identical in each week over an entire time period, utility cannot be maximized unless their actual I is equal to their desired interval (I^*) each day. For example, a worker may prefer a regular, predictable, traditional 9am to 5pm (9:00 to 17:00) daily schedule of 8 hours each work day. Yet, the work is scheduled on an inconvient 8-hour evening or night shift. Alternatively, a worker may be on fixed daily schedule (I-bar) that deviates from their preferred schedule I^*. As an illustration, suppose $H = H^* = 8$ for all five days of the traditional workweek, but the worker's preferred daily schedule changes so that the desired timing of work deviates from their actual work schedule. For example, a worker enrolls in a college course that may conflict with her current, usual weekly work schedule in the late afternoon. Or, new child care (or eldercare) responsibilities lead a worker to prefer an earlier schedule.[7] Suppose, the worker now prefers to work a 7am to 3pm day, illustrated as,

```
                 I_0            I_n
|- - - - - ↓ - - |- - - - ↓ - - |- - - -|
Ø          I_0*           I_n*          T
          (7am)          (3pm)
```

The degree of inconvenience experienced by the worker each day is,

$$(I_0^* - I_0) + (I_n^* - I_n)$$

For a given level of average weekly hours (H), the degree of temporal flexibility in daily schedules can be represented by the expression,

$$\Delta I_t = \lambda(I_t^* - \overline{I_{t-1}}),\ \ 0 \leq \lambda \leq 1.$$

The term λ captures the degree of adjustment or responsiveness of the actual daily I, e.g., fixed at 9am to 5pm (17:00), toward the preferred daily schedule I^*.

The impact of working time dimensions on utility can be captured by the expression,[8]

$$U = U[Y, L; V, \delta, \lambda]$$

assuming: $dU/dY,\ dU/dL,\ dU/d\delta,\ dU/d\lambda > 0;\ dU/dV < 0$

Worker utility (U) increases not only in income (Y) and leisure time (L), but in the speed with which H and I adjust toward changes in desired hours (H^*) or schedules (I^*). Utility decreases in the volatility of hours (V), assuming optimal volatility (V^*) is zero. Suboptimal utility occurs if actual hours are slow to adjust toward either temporary or permanent changes in H^* or I^*. Utility may be suboptimal even in the event H and H^* are equal on average over the entire time period. Thus, the mere presence of constraints on hours and schedules, not just binding constraints, may diminish worker utility. Most workers comprehend that their H^* and I^* are likely to fluctuate as they progress through the lifecycle.

Suppose the actual schedule for a worker with an H of 40 is a fixed daily, nine-to-five schedule (I-bar) for five weekdays per week. Suppose the worker experiences a new, conflicting demand on their time which would require them to leave work at 3pm, two days per week. Utility in that week will depend on whether the worker is able to adjust their H down to 36, for a proportional (10 per cent) cut in compensation, or alternatively, to adjust their interval to begin work earlier, e.g., at 7am two days a week.

Assume for a given δ, as the absolute difference between H and H^* gets larger, utility diminishes at an increasing rate. The impact of V may be non-linear on utility, too, if large differences around the mean are disproportionally more important to welfare. The disutility due to a gap between H and H^* is assumed for simplicity to be symmetric, i.e., the same for overemployment as for underemployment. However, there is persuasive evidence that the estimated aversion to loss of goods (income) is greater than the aversion to the loss of time. This suggests that an underemployment gap erodes utility relatively more than an overemployment gap of identical size.[9] Nevertheless, the relative desirability of the 'goods' in the utility function, income, leisure and flexibility *vis-à-vis* each other (and the 'bad' of volatility) are unclear a *priori.*

5.1.1 Causes and Consequences of H^*

As a worker's desired hours (H^*) progresses on a path through time, workers are likely to experience periodic 'pressure points' in a few, but critical, junctures in the lifecycle. These may be either sustained or brief periods of overemployment or underemployment. This is better captured with a more comprehensive H^* function than those that focus solely on real wage rates and non-wage income.[10] It should include several personal characteristics, which in conventional neo-classical models are referred to as tastes and constraints, which alter either weekly, annual and lifetime H^* levels. Workers typically experience altered hours as an abrupt rather than the gradual adjustment implied by standard labour supply models. Such a model might better explain why overtime pay now comprises about 15 per cent of manufacturing production workers' total income, and the number of hourly workers receiving overtime pay in a given week rose from 10 to 13 per cent between 1985 and 1994.[11] A worker's desired labour supply also may vary (perhaps inversely) with the degree of hours and schedule flexibility they can access in the workplace.

While worker preferences may in part be exogenous – determined by personal choice factors such as marital status, number and age of children, schooling status – they are also influenced or moulded by the worker's cultural and workplace environment. Models that introduce the element of time and altering of worker preferences suggest an overemployed worker may eventually increase their preferred number of hours. Overemployed workers eventually shift their preferences from time-*using* toward more time-*saving* goods and services, raising their H^* to a level higher than if they possessed the option of adjusting their work hours downward through time [(Rothschild (1982)]. Schor (1991) goes further and argues that worker preferences regarding work hours eventually become endogenized – if workers do not get what they want from their employers they eventually want what they get. Schor argues that longer hours serve the interest of employers because the resulting higher unemployment in the labour market disciplines labour into greater work effort per hour. The root source of longer hours is culture more than employer strategy. Workers may begin with 'metapreferences' for shorter

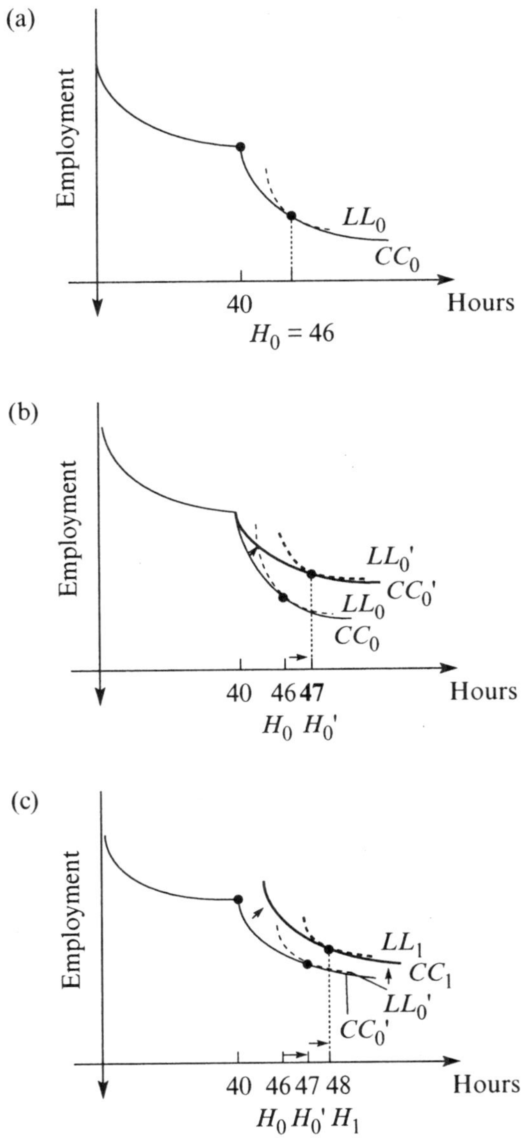

Figure 5.1 Optimal combination of workers and hours demanded (1)

working time, but the cumulative effects of intense product market promotional efforts eventually shifts worker preferences more toward income *vis-à-vis* leisure [(George (1997)].

5.1.2 Demand Side of Hours in the Labour Market

Neo-classical models of labour demand are designed to determine the optimal composition of labour input given the absolute and relative marginal costs of additional hours and employees. When adjusting labour input, employers consider the ratio (*FEC*/*w*). Fixed employment costs (*FEC*) are those labour costs that change less than proportionally when hours are altered. Variable wage (*w*) costs in the denominator include overtime premia in the event overtime hours are worked. This ratio increases when there is a decline in the wage rate; increase in private insurance premiums; increase in hiring and training costs (particularly with job–skill upgrading with more complex technology or teamwork systems); increase in discharge costs (severance pay, risk of litigation); more paid time off; and greater overhead expenses associated with administering and supervising an enlarged staff. A formal model of labour input demand determination shows the consequence will be a new optimal labour input mix composed of fewer workers with longer average hours. In the top frame of Figure 5.1, the input isocost function CC_0 contains a kink at *H*-bar, the standard workweek after which a premium wage must be paid. The assumed convexity of LL_0 implies that start-up costs and fatigue make hours and employees imperfect substitutes. The optimal combination of workers and hours demanded occurs at the point of tangency between *LL* and *CC* curves. This occurs at H_0^d and the second panel.

An expanded cost of labour is needed to better project changes in H^d. This includes not only the straight-time wage, overtime wage, non-wage labour costs, but the degree of numerical and worktime flexibility (*NWF*). *NWF* occurs with a proportionate response of worker-hours to fluctuations in the demand for output (Q^d), such as a surge or drop in orders or customers.[12] Without *NWF*, firms incur opportunity costs of lost economies of scale or a non-optimal level of inventories and *N*, i.e., undesired labour hoarding or unfilled vacancies. Organizations may also seek to gain 'efficiency hours' (*EH*). This involves establishing working time structures and procedures that lower labour costs in the longer run, such as boosting average labour productivity and minimizing personnel costs. Innovative working time arrangements such as flexitime tend to improve productivity and/or reduce costs associated with turnover, absenteeism, tardiness and perhaps sick leave, although they entail some additional, albeit small, costs of supervision (*S*).[13] Labour cost in period *t* is,

$$C_t = (WNH)_t\,(1-\alpha) + (1-\kappa)\,\alpha WN(H_t - \bar{H})\rho + bN_t + f(NH)_t$$
$$+\ \gamma(\Delta lnQ_t^{\,d} - \Delta lnNH_t^{\,d}) + \theta\,|\,H - H^{*}|\,^{\phi}_{t}(Q) + S$$

the sum of the wage bill – the product of the wage rate (W), hours per worker (H) and employment (N) with a premium wage rate (ρ) paid for the fraction of the workforce on overtime (α); non-wage labour costs (b) that are affixed only to N and those (f) that vary with total payroll NH, the extent of *NWF* or *EH*. The strategy of restraining unit labour cost [*ULC*–total cost (C) divided by total output (Q)] through *NWF* and a lower wage rate represents the 'low road'. *EH* constitutes the 'high road'. The *NWF* strategy is designed to curtail labour costs in the short run while the *EH* strategy aims to lower costs cumulatively over the longer run.[14] Short-run labour costs also can be reduced by raising the fraction κ, the share of the workforce working overtime and paid in comp time. Each strategy may imply divergent levels and paths over time in H^d. How firms allocate overtime hours and permit use of comp time off among workers depends on whether firms tend to choose the low road or high road working time strategy. More formally, firms' demand for hours relative to employees is,

$$H/N = [\underset{+}{b/w};\ \underset{-}{\rho};\ \underset{+}{\kappa}]$$

5.2 THE ECONOMIC EFFECT OF REGULATING HOURS OF WORK

The FLSA overtime premium was designed as a monetary (rather than statutory) deterrent against setting excessive weekly hours. It was intended to make employers bear more of the marginal social spillover cost, for example, on worker health and employment opportunities. Employers were allowed the latitude to use unlimited overtime hours, as long as they were willing to pay the premium.[15] Yet, current trends suggest the deterrence effect of the overtime pay premium is weakening. Overtime hours in manufacturing have recently climbed to a record peak of about five hours per week. In addition, the share of all workers working 49 or more hours per week has risen. Finally, compared to the two decades prior to 1979, labour input (in manufacturing industries) tends to adjust to shocks in output demand relatively more through variation in hours than via employment.[16] The FLSA overtime pay law takes on new relevance in the 1970s to the mid-1990s economic environment of a stagnant real hourly wage, growth in dual working couples and rise of involuntary underemployment. It counters structural bias toward longer hours caused by growth in FECs and prevents further erosion in real hourly earnings for workers.

The FLSA is certainly not costless. It may reduce profit for firms in competitive markets by requiring more employer record-keeping. It requires additional monitoring of job tasks under the often blurry rather than bright legal lines between exempt and non-exempt status for certain employees. Also, it may raise production costs or inhibit flexible setting of daily overtime hours. Finally, it denies income to workers with long-hour preferences and creates a deadweight loss for taxpayers to enforce the regulations.[17] A uniform standard workweek is arguably a 'second best', relatively less suboptimal policy solution to observed market failures–the imperfect sorting and matching in the labour market, chronic excess demand for flexible work schedules and absence of a fully compensating wage differential for inflexible work schedules.[18] The evidence of relatively inexpensive cost for regulatory enforcement and the high rate of recovery for reported violations may attest to the regulation's efficacy.[19]

The FLSA may also deliver a range of potential economic benefits. It improves *static efficiency* to the extent that it reduces incidence or duration of unemployment and underemployment. If it lowers the extent or duration of overemployment, it may reduce frictional unemployment due to the excessive turnover and job mobility stemming from hours-mismatches.[20] By constraining hours in the upward direction for hours per week and per day (as opposed to just annual hours), it limits the short-term volatility of hours and thus stabilizes fluctuations in workers' disposable income and consumption spending. Finally, it may lead managers to develop a more efficient production system over the work-day so as to avoid paying overtime. The FLSA may improve *dynamic efficiency* to the extent that it creates longer-term productivity gain by encouraging more leisure time used for recuperation (preventing fatigue, stress and accidents). To the extent that the demand-side outweighs the supply-side effect of the overtime pay premium on overtime hours, it provides more time for investing in social capital – civic and volunteering efforts that develop and strengthen communities building, and more time for parenting and caregiving activities that develop future human capital potentials of workers' offspring.[21] *Social Welfare* is enhanced on balance if the redistribution of hours triggers a utility gain to those receiving the hours that on balance exceeds the utility loss to those with long-hour preferences who must sacrifice income.

5.3 POTENTIAL EFFECTS OF AMENDMENTS TO THE FLSA ON HOURS AND WORKER WELFARE

Average hours are determined by the interaction of three forces, represented as,[22]

$$H = \beta H^* + (1 - \beta)H^d \ (\textit{where } 0 \leq \beta < 1)$$

weighted function of average hours desired by workers and demanded by employers where the weight (β) attached to H^* reflects the relative bargaining power of labour. The size of the β coefficient determines which party possesses the greater leverage to steer hours in the direction they desire. This depends on the FLSA, external economic factors, internal firm and union factors.[23] The β weight would be positive in union density, length of job tenure and opportunities for on-the-job leisure, and negative in costs of enduring a strike or quit (reflected by local unemployment rates). If the β weight were 0.5, both parties would be compromising equally on their desired hours and thus split the difference.[24] For example, actual weekly hours (H) of 44 may reflect a compromise between an employer's optimal hours demanded per worker of 46 and an employee's desired hours of 40, where β is equal to 0.33.[25]

$$|\rightarrow\rightarrow\rightarrow\rightarrow\rightarrow\rightarrow|\rightarrow\rightarrow\rightarrow\rightarrow|\leftarrow\leftarrow|\leftarrow\leftarrow\leftarrow\leftarrow\leftarrow\leftarrow|$$

0	H^*	H	H^d	T
	(40)	(44)	(46)	

However, if the β weight were zero, employees are working 46 hours per week – with 6 hours of overemployment. It may be the case that in some future period a worker may be willing to work even more overtime hours, e.g., 52 hours next week, as a temporary, stop-gap measure to earn more income. If the β weight were to remain zero, they would not be able to attain the four additional hours they desire, and become underemployed. The incidence of worker overemployment and underemployment hinges on the size of β for the typical hourly worker.

The eventual impact on worker welfare may be determined by two critical aspects of proposed FLSA legislation. One is that employers are allowed to retain the ability to offer the comp time option to only a subset of selected employees. The second is that employers have the right to refuse the use of comp time if they maintain it would cause an 'undue disruption of business'. Thus, workers who are able to select the comp time option may not be able to use the comp time during the times they need it the most.

The optimal hours-employees mix will change following the proposed overtime law reform, thus creating a new optimal hours demanded (H^d). Any market or policy change that heightens the ratio of fixed to variable labour costs (*FEC/w*) will rotate the *CC* curve from Figure 5.1(a) to a flatter isocost CC'_0 in Figure 5.1 (b) [see Hamermesh, Rees and Filer (1994)]. The term *w* in the denominator is reduced due to the lower effective average hourly wage being reduced without concurrent payment of an overtime premium. (Indeed, removing the premium pay requirement would eliminate entirely the kink in *CC* present at the standard workweek (*H*-bar), at least for the duration of this period and *CC* would become continuous.) In addition, an 80-hour standard would increase numerical flexibility and thus may reduce employers' short-run costs, too. The new tangent point shows the optimal workweek demanded will rise to H_0^{d1}. At the same time, the iso-labour function will shift upward to LL_1. And due to scale effects the isocost will shift upward to CC_1. Because total labour input has become relatively cheaper, firms will be left to substitute labour for capital input. And they will be able to produce a greater level of output. Scale effects would reinforce the within-labour input substitution effect. The new optimal point will be H_1^d, and unambiguously higher level of hours demanded. Figure 5.1 (c) illustrates a plausible case where the optimal workweek length demanded would rise from 46 to 48 hours. The H^d will rise by the degree to which the proportion of workers on overtime receive comp time rather than pay. The closer κ is to 1.0, the greater the increase in H^d.

The net impact on worker welfare depends crucially on whether employers pursue short-run or long-run strategies to restrain ULC. On the high road, the employer grants the comp time option to all those who request it, lets employees use it when they need it, applies no pressure regarding the selection or use of comp time and dutifully cashes out comp time credits upon request. On the 'low road', overtime hours are shifted more toward workers choosing the comp time option and pressure is applied to select the comp time option and to use it only when output demand slows.

The consequences on utility occur via worker income and leisure bundles across time periods. Suppose the worker is now scheduled to work 46 hours per week, but a new non-work demand on their time arises, changing their H^* to 40. Figure 5.2 illustrates a three-period, intertemporal model (with an hourly wage of \$10). Suppose the worker chooses to go on the comp time in lieu option, thus giving up income (\$90) in period 0. Working six overtime hours in period 0 to gain future comp time, s/he remains overemployed since average hours (*H*) of work will remain the same in the current period as with overtime pay only. In the case of the high-road employer, s/he is

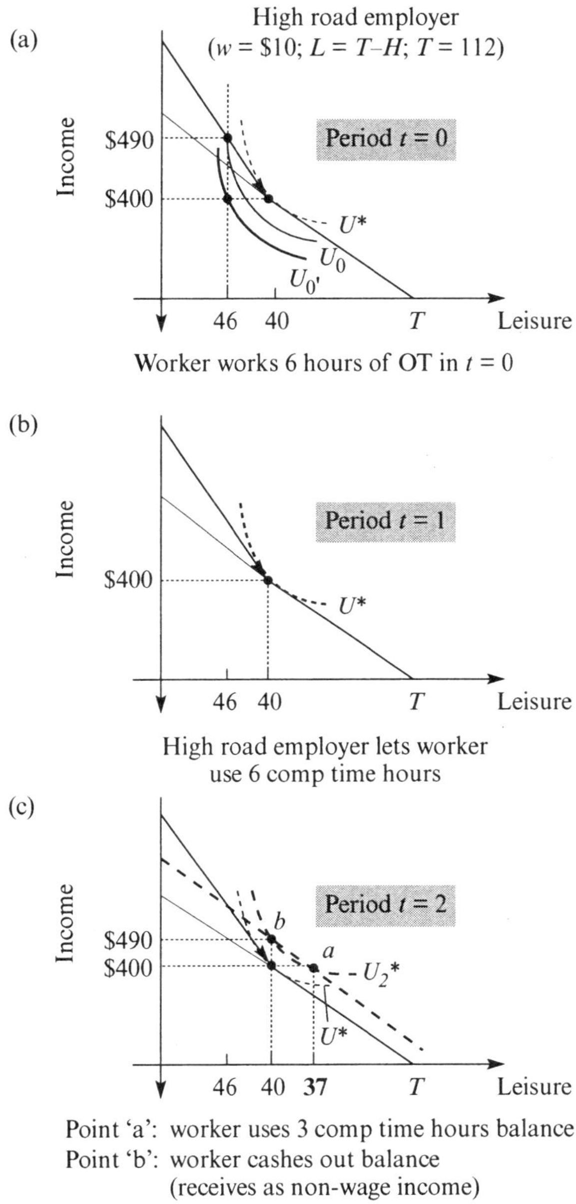

Figure 5.2 Optimal combination of workers and hours demanded (2)

able to use the six hours of comp time s/he desires in the next period, period 1, to get H^* of 40. At the end of period 2 s/he can cash out the balance of three remaining hours of comp time credits, which effectively provides an increase in non-wage income, thus shifting up the budget constraint. However, on the low road, the employer pressurizes workers into delaying the use of comp time until their H^d recedes, for example, not until period 2. Thus, the worker remains overemployed in both periods 0 and 1.

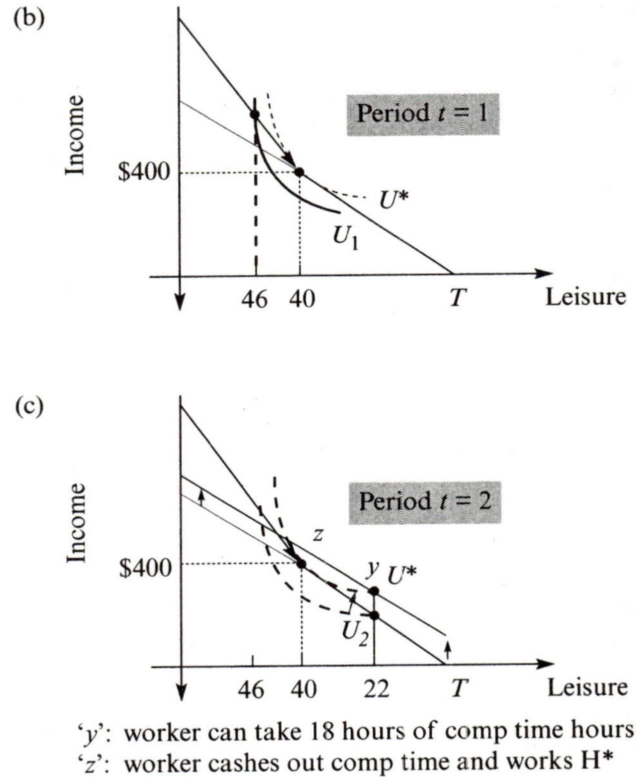

Note: Fig. 5.3(a) would be identical to Fig. 5.2(a).

Figure 5.3 Optimal combination of workers and hours demanded (3)

In period 2, the worker may either use or cash out the comp time credits. This scenario is shown in Figure 5.3. In addition, the worker experiences greater '*V*' since hours may vary from as much as 46 to 22 hours over the three periods – including up to twelve hours of overemployment.[26]

Moreover, a worker cashing out accumulated comp time credits at the end of the year is clearly not as well off as if they had received the cash in the week when overtime was worked. This is because people tend to discount future, deferred income and face some risk that the employer will either not exist by year's end or not comply with the regulation.[27] For example, suppose the rate of discount is 10 per cent between each time period. If a worker puts in 40 hours of overtime in the initial period and receives comp time, s/he forgoes $600 and gets 60 hours of comp time credits. If s/he simply receives all that $600 in cash in period 1, its net present value falls to $545.[28] If the income is not received until period 2, the net present value is only $496. Even if the discount rate were only 5 per cent, the present value declines to $571 and $544 respectively. Thus, the worker may not be as well off with just overtime pay even in the case of the high-road employer. In the case of the low-road employer, s/he may wind up with a substantial net loss in utility.

Thus, if an employer follows the low road, there will be even more intense pressure to schedule overtime in the initial period and to delay the workers' use of comp time credits until subsequent periods when demand recedes. For example, due to the unambiguous increase in H^d, hours demanded may rise from 46 up to, for example, 48, as will actual hours if the beta weight is near zero in the short run. Indeed, the cost savings for employers with a short time horizon are greatest if the overtime is worked by the subset of workers selecting the comp time option. Perversely, employers will have the incentive to assign the overtime hours demanded to already time-constrained workers who chose comp time, at least for the early part of the year. Indeed, with a low-road employer, an employee in need of time off might actually heighten their chances of securing shorter hours by expressing a preference for pay rather than comp time.[30] Hence, not only does the ability to substitute comp time for overtime erode the intended deterrent effect of the FLSA overtime requirement, but it may subvert it.

In sum, the predicted impact of the proposed comp time amendment to the FLSA is that it will increase average hours demanded per worker. The size of the increase in hours demanded will be a positive function of the proportion of the workforce for which overtime is compensated via future comp time (κ) and the proportion of firms choosing a strategy of flexibility *of* workers as opposed to flexibility *for* workers, which in turn depends positively on the length of the time horizon in firms' decision-making. The actual rise in average hours will depend on the existing and resulting β weight following the new labour law.

The threat of reduced worker welfare is heightened if it is accompanied by an increase in 'V', the degree of undesired volatility in weekly hours. This is particularly the case if the bill in the Congress is passed replacing the standard 40-hour workweek with an 80-hour two-week period. No overtime pay, nor comp time, would be owed for a week of, for example, 50 hours so long as the workweek is reduced to 30 hours the following week. While this would benefit employers by enhancing numerical and worktime flexibility, it may diminish workers' utility, in the event that their H^* does not follow the pattern of H^d through time. A further threat to worker welfare occurs if job opportunities are reduced as a result of an increase in average hours. If H^d dictates the trend in the reduced form in actual hours (H), fewer jobs will be created. Because empirical studies find that each 1 per cent reduction in standard hours, on the average, increases employment by slightly less than 0.5 per cent, the reverse implies a 2 per cent longer average hours will suppress employment by almost 1 per cent.[31] Some of the potential job losses may be offset if improved numerical and worktime flexibility (*NWF*) reduces production costs. However, the jobs saved or created may be qualitatively poorer, such as contingent jobs.

5.4 IMPLICATIONS FOR WORK HOURS LEGISLATION AND REGULATORY REFORM

This analysis suggests that additional measures are needed to prevent harm to worker utility and job opportunities. The revised versions of the bill in the House and Senate contained palliative amendments. The comp time option would not be available to workers with fewer than 1000 hours of employment, who may be relatively more vulnerable employees. Employees could accrue no more than 160 hours of comp time per year, after which overtime hours must be paid in cash. Employers who are found by the US Department of Labor to be in violation of the requirement not to coerce employees in their choice of comp time or premium pay nor in their use of comp time must pay the affected employee double damages based on their pay rate.

However, while such amendments may well reduce political resistance to the bill, they do not address the fundamental risk of lower utility for workers. Employers in European countries have been increasingly able in recent years to persuade workers to accept more variable hours. European governments have generally supported this to promote 'labour market flexibility'. For example, annualized hours, where weekly hours are established according to expected seasonal, and in some cases, unexpected cyclical fluctuations, have grown increasingly popular. However, the European case is vastly different from the comp time and 80-hour standard work period proposals in the US Congress. In Europe, workers tend to receive a host of compensating factors in return for yielding control over workweek variation – a reduction in standard weekly hours, an upper boundary to the range of variability, an effective gain in base pay, a reduced risk of layoff, input from worker representatives, etc.[32] Such measures mitigate the potential loss in utility.

To further cushion the potential blow to worker well-being, working time legislation in the US should be accompanied by several other policies, to address errors of both commission and omission in the existing proposals. This includes requiring compound interest on accumulated comp time credits;[33] the ability to 'borrow' up front as well as to 'lend' time or money to their employer; free movement (with some advance notice) between the comp time and overtime pay status; cashing out of comp time credits at any time (rather than after 30 days' notice); setting an extremely high standard for an 'undue business disruption' or eliminating the clause outright; preventing employers from offering the comp time option selectively among workers or through time; and banning mandatory overtime hours of work. Hours legislation should be accompanied by a statutory upper boundary on hours in any given week (as is the case in European agreements), and perhaps a shorter weekly standard for certain, targeted industries and occupations.[34] This would minimize V and increase leisure (L).

To make hours legislation truly 'family friendly', further policy is necessary. In terms of the model, tax incentives should be adopted which will increase the value of δ and λ – the flexibility in hours and schedules benefiting non-exempt workers – by closing the gap between H^d and H^* and between I and I^*. Preferential tax treatment or subsidies could help expand the offering of flexible work schedules desired by many workers, such as flexitime, job-sharing, 6 × 6 daily split shifts and voluntary paid leaves. In addition, extending the 1993 Family and Medical Leave Act to include, e.g., 24 hours per year of unpaid time off (with some advance notification) for time spent accompanying children or relatives to school or medical care would relieve some of the periodic time-pressures experienced by over-employed workers.[35] While this would be unpaid leave, it would be preferable to unpaid work, which is the case with the comp time proposal. Moreover, social and private insurance contribution systems must be redesigned to curb the extent to which labour costs have become fixed costs, to prevent the escalation in average hours employers will demand resulting from a cheaper average and marginal cost of overtime hours. Furthermore, laws that reverse the weakening position of labour (organized or not) in negotiations regarding working time would increase β and thus push actual hours in the direction of H^*. Finally, more resources for FLSA enforcement divisions to prevent an increase in non-compliance, coercion or abuse, would ensure that employers, go no lower than the low road.

Future research must develop a coherent macroeconomic schema that better integrates the causes and consequences of working time patterns. This would allow one more accurately to project the change in average aggregate work hours induced by the FLSA law change, and its potential macroeconomic consequences. Such change may reinforce the already existing upward structural trend in weekly hours for production and other FLSA-covered workers in the US. The direction and size of the policy induced change in aggregate hours will depend on its impact on the number of (weekly or annual) hours demanded by employers, hours desired by workers and the relative degree of bargaining leverage between employers and labour which mediates these when their work hours preferences diverge. The effect of the legislation on static efficiency depends on the secondary effects of FLSA reform on employment, productivity and consumption spending. A new FLSA that makes average work hours escalate and become more volatile would likely dampen the aggregate level of employment, labour productivity, leisure time and consumption spending, thus inadvertently exacerbating the already existing maldistribution of hours among workers in the US labour force.

NOTES

1. Hansen (1996). Previous legal analyses of the FLSA law include Martin, Aalberts and Clark (1993), DeChiara (1993), DiCesare (1995), Clark (1996) and Smith (1996). The 1997 bills were entitled, 'Family Friendly Workplace Act' and 'Working Families Flexibility Act', in the US Senate and House, respectively.
2. See, for example, Moffitt (1982), Dunn (1990).
3. Options such as absenteeism or tardiness, which risk discharge, are likely to be relatively less attractive than overemployment [Moss and Curtis (1985)]. Changing jobs is not viable because the compensation difference is such that overemployment is likely preferable to a part-time job with one's desired hours [Blank (1990), Rebitzer and Taylor (1994)].
4. For example, Ehrenberg and Schumann (1984), Duncan and Holmlund (1983), Altonji and Paxson (1988).
5. Hamermesh (1996) makes a useful distinction between hours per day and days per week components of weekly hours.
6. A more complex, distributed lag equation could be developed where actual hours adjust adaptively to such shocks in H^*. Shank (1986) found in a special CPS Supplement that 8 per cent of workers are overemployed, willing to trade income for work hours reduction but unable to do so at their current job, 27 per cent are underemployed and the remaining 65 per cent satisfied with their hours. Kahn and Lang (1995) found similar results in the PSID sample. Recent evidence points to growth in

both the extent of underemployment and overemployment and considerable excess demand for more flexible work hours and schedules (Galinsky, 1996; Schor, 1995).

7. A worker may prefer a later or entirely different shift, depending on how they arrange child care. Workers may also experience sudden, unanticipated shocks, such as having to care for a sick child or attend an unscheduled class, which can be accommodated by a flexible schedule.
8. Note that other possible dimensions of working time which can influence utility are left outside the scope of this chapter. This includes *intensity* of work per time period and '*congestion*' (otherwise referred to as 'multitasking' or 'polyphasing'). The latter is the extent to which work and leisure activities are performed simultaneously in the same block of time. Also note if the labour market were to create fully compensating wage differentials, the increase in income would offset the loss to utility generated by suboptimal and inflexible hours and schedules.
9. Dunn (1996). This asymmetry implies redistribution work hours from over-employed to under-employed individuals and would yield a considerable net gain to social welfare. This is because the under-employed would value the transferred hours (and income) more than the over-employed.
10. Desired hours can be represented as,

$$H^* = f[w, y; fc, \frac{A}{P}, \frac{C}{P}, \frac{w^*}{w}, OJL, P_L, U]$$

In addition to the usual determinants of labour supply – the wage rate (w), non-wage income (y) and fixed costs (fc) of working – a worker's desired hours per week (H^*) is influenced by their real net assets (A) (e.g., debt burden) and consumption (c) level, relative wage (w^*) *vis-à-vis* reference groups in positions ranked a step higher in the internal job hierarchy) [see Rima (1984), Bell and Freeman (1996), Axe and Golden (1991)], access to flexible working conditions and autonomy which makes possible on-the-job leisure (OJL) [Hamermesh (1995)], the direct price of leisure goods and services (P_L) and the unemployed (U) rate in the relevant labour market.

The sign on the unemployment term is ambiguous. Higher unemployment may decrease workers' desired worktime if they expect that work-sharing will prevent lay-offs and save jobs. But unemployment may increase H^* if workers believe they enhance their own job security by accepting more (voluntary or mandatory) overtime hours. For example, the growing supply of overtime hours may be due in part to rising consumer debt, wage inequality and job insecurity.

11. Carr (1986), EPI (1997) and author's calculations using Trejo (1993).
12. See, for example, Atkinson (1987), Rosenberg (1991), Fleischmann (1996).
13. For examples of the success of such flexible work practices, despite possible administrative or monitoring cost, see Clifton, Shephard and Kruse (1996), Rodgers (1992), Moss and Curtis (1985), Moen and Dempster-McClain (1987), Krausz and Freibach (1983), Ahmadi, Raiszedeh and Wells (1986). Despite the advantages, only about 15 per cent (10 per cent for blue-collar and clerical) of workers have access to formal flexible work schedule arrangements [Kush and Stroh (1994), US Department of Labor (1992)].
14. Employers using 'annualized hours' systems, varying weekly hours according to both cyclical and seasonal fluctuations in output, increase their NWF but entail longer run costs if they lack employee input and advance notification [e.g., Pickard (1991), Bosch (1995)].
15. See Ehrenberg (1986) and Rottenberg (1995) for contrasting views of hours regulation.
16. For evidence, see Glosser and Golden (1997), Hedges (1993), Rones (1996), Coleman and Pencavel (1993), and Leete and Schor (1994).
17. Rottenberg (1995). The courts have not provided consistent interpretations regarding exemption status, such as employee time spent 'on call', commuting in a company vehicle or in training programmes. The salary levels for salary basis test (established in 1975) are now archaic. Private and public sector employers face potentially large liabilities for, wilfully or not, treating or misclassifying exempt employees as non-exempt, e.g., docking pay for partial day absence.

18. The underlying cause of irrational inflexibility may be X-inefficiences within firms or the bounded rationality of managers. These stifle development of external or internal exchange mechanisms facilitating Pareto-improving trades of hours of work and income.
19. See Hansen (1996).
20. The pay premium also counters the creation of longer hours in jobs as part of an effort-regulation strategy adopted by employers to boost productivity. [Rebitzer and Taylor (1995)].
21. Moreover, shorter working time is likely to help *instrumental efficiency*, the full development of human capacities [Tool (1979)].
22. At the enterprise, industry and aggregate level, average weekly hours (H) can be represented by a simple equation which illustrates that H is influenced by standard hours per week (SH); average hours of part-time workers (PTH); and average overtime hours (OTH). Each component is weighted by the proportion of the workforce working exactly the standard workweek, part-time hours or overtime hours:

$$H = [\tau SH + \upsilon\, PTH + \omega\, OTH] \quad (\tau + \upsilon + \omega = 1)$$

For example, if 50 per cent of the workforce is working the standard 40 hours exactly, 20 per cent work a part-time schedule averaging 20 hours per week and 30 per cent work an average of 3⅓ overtime hours per week beyond the standard, the average H will be equal to 37 hours.
23. External pressures stemming from global competition and deregulation have led many employers to 'rationalize' work and production and more fully utilize expensive capital. In addition, the heightened incidence of underemployment (such as involuntary part-time and contingent employment), intensified job insecurity and weakened labour unions have eroded both the exit and voice mechanisms for labour to express dissatisfaction and enforce demands for improvement regarding work hours and schedules. Internally, within the labour movement, the traditional goal of shorter hours has been given lower priority than securing more regulated and predictable allocation of hours, and is overridden by the goal of preserving jobs and income.
24. The ratio $\beta/(1 - \beta)$ serves as an index that reflects the ability of employees to achieve the number of weekly hours they deem optimal. The index approaches zero as labour gets weaker.
25. Note that this model assumes a bilateral monopoly type of process in hours determination, where an indeterminate range of equilibrium average hours outcomes are possible. While price and price (wage) adjustments may influence both hours demanded and desired, the empirical evidence demonstrating binding constraints on many workers' hours without fully compensating wage differentials suggests this assumption is not unreasonable. The complexity of H^* function and indeterminacy of a unique equilibrium render a reduced form of hours unobservable here.
26. Thus, output remains the same until that future period when comp time is taken. In that future period, the firm may increase N to make up for lost hours, e.g., changing the composition of staffing toward part-time hours or temp workers, even with the risk of lower productivity, which raises the coefficient on PT in average H determination equation.
27. The risk of default is not negligible. The US Department of Labor Wage and Hour Division found $120 million in unpaid overtime violations, involving 180 000 private and public workers [Hansen (1996)]. Compliance with workplace labour regulations tends to be lower in the absence of labour unions [Weil (1996)].
28. The net present value computed using a rate of discount, r, is:

$$net\ PV = \Delta Y_0 + \frac{\Delta Y_1}{(1+r)} + \frac{\Delta Y_2}{(1+r)^2}$$

29. The net effect on employment is theoretically ambiguous. However, it will be negative if substitution effects are larger than scale effects.

30. This is reinforced in cases where employers use a request for comp time as a signal that the employee is less committed to their job, organization or workforce than if overtime for pay is requested. Thus, employees may perceive taking the comp time option and using all their earned comp time hours as detrimental to future promotion opportunities or pay increases. This would further discount the relative value workers attach to comp time *vis-à-vis* pay.
31. Bosch and Lehndorff (1997), International Labor Organization (1995), Mosely (1995), Booth and Schiantarelli (1993), author's calculations based on Ehrenberg and Schumann (1982).
32. Bosch (1995: 15).
33. Requiring comp time accounts to be interest-bearing, to enhance equity, however, may create a perverse incentive for workers to save rather than use comp time, which would be counter to the intention of alleviating over-employment, and in much the same way that the overtime premium has become a strong incentive for longer hours of labour supply rather than just a disincentive for hours of labour demanded.
34. Bosch and Stille (1991). Schor (1994) advocates FLSA reform legislation mandating that employers declare some 'standard' (possibly higher than forty) hours per week for each currently *exempt* job, understood at the time of the employment contracting. Employers would owe comp time for the 'overtime' worked in excess of this standard.
35. Follow-up studies of the FLMA find that few employers experience the increased costs that they feared, and that only 3 per cent of eligible workers actually take advantage of the FMLA entitlement of 6 weeks of unpaid leave. Thus, extending FMLA poses little threat to labour costs.

ACKNOWLEDGMENTS

The author gratefully acknowledges the helpful suggestions of Jacques Siegers, three anonymous referees, Edith Rasell and Eileen Appelbaum.

REFERENCES

Ahmadi, Raiszedeh and Wells (1986), 'Traditional vs. non-traditional work schedules: a case study of employee preference', *Industrial Management*, **28**(2), 20–23.

Altonji, J. and C. Paxson (1988), 'Labor supply preferences, hours constraints and wage-hour tradeoffs', *Journal of Labor Economics*, **6**(2), 254–76.

Atkinson, F. (1987), 'Flexibility or fragmentation? The U.K. labor market in the 1980s', *Labour and Society*, **12**, January, 87–105.

Axe, B. and L. Golden (1991), 'The augmented labor supply function: work time evidence from Japan', *Eastern Economics Journal*, **18**(3), July–September, 305–18.

Bell, L. and R. Freeman (1996), 'Earnings inequality and hours of work in Germany and the U.S.', National Bureau of Economic Research Working Paper #4808.

Blank, R. (1990), 'Are part-time jobs bad jobs?', in G. Burtless (ed.), *A Future of Lousy Jobs*?, Washington, DC: Brookings Institution.

Booth, A. and F. Schiantarelli (1993), 'Employment and length of the working week in a unionized economy in which hours of work influence productivity', *Economic Record*, **69**(207), December, 428–36.

Bosch, G. (1995), 'Annual working hours: an international comparison', Sixth International Symposium on Working Time, Blankenberg, Belgium, December.

Bosch, G. and B. Lehndorff (1997), 'The reduction of working time and employment', presented at the International Party on Labor Market Segmentation, 19th Conference, Porto, Portugal, July.

Bosch, G. and F. Stille (1991), 'Working time in Germany: trade and policy issues', *Economies et Societé, Serie du Travail*, **17**, 21–46.

Carr, D. (1986) 'Overtime work: an expanded view', *Monthly Labor Review*, November, 35–9.

Clark, N. (1996), 'FLSA reform – it's not broke, so don't fix it', *The Labor Lawyer*, **11**(3), Fall, 343–51.

Clifton, T. and E. Shephard (1994), 'Work and family programs and productivity: estimates applying a production function model', mimeo.

Clifton, T., E. Shephard and D. Kruse (1996), 'Flexible work hours and productivity: some evidence from the pharmaceutical industry', *Industrial Relations*, **35**(1), January, 123–39.

Coleman, M. and J. Pencavel (1993), 'Changes in work hours of male employees, 1940–1988', *Industrial and Labor Relations Review*, **46**(2), January, 262–83.

DeChiara, P. (1993), 'Rethinking the managerial-professional exemption of the FLSA', *American University Law Review*, **43**, 139–89.

DiCesare, C. B. (1995), 'Compensatory time', *Monthly Labor Review*, **118**(5), May, 62–3.

Duncan, G. and B. Holmlund (1983), 'Was Adam Smith right after all? Another test of the theory of compensating wage differentials', *Journal of Labor Economics*, **1**(4), 366–79.

Dunn, L.F. (1996), 'Loss aversion and adaptation in the labor market: empirical indifference functions and labor supply', *Review of Economics and Statistics*, **78**(3), August, 441–50.

Dunn, L.F. (1990), 'An empirical study of labor market disequilibrium under working hours constraints', *Review of Economics and Statistics*, **72**(2), May, 250–58.

Economic Policy Institute (1997), 'Family friend or foe? Working time, flexibility and the Fair Labor Standards Act', *Briefing Paper*, March.

Ehrenberg, R. (1986), 'Worker rights: rethinking protective labor legislation', in *Research in Labor Economics*, **8**, pt.B, 285–317.

Ehrenberg, R. and P. Schumann (1984), 'Compensating wage differentials for mandatory overtime?', *Economic Inquiry*, **22**(4), October, 460–78.

Ehrenberg, R. and P. Schumann (1982), *Longer Hours or More Jobs?*, Ithaca, NY: ILR Press.

Fleischmann, C. (1996), 'The endogeneity of employment adjustment costs: the tradeoff between efficiency and flexibility', Federal Reserve Board Finance and Economics Discussion Series, 1996–48.

Galinsky, E. (1996), 'Is the time famine real?', Families and Work Institute, March.

George, D. (1997), 'Working longer hours: pressure from the boss or from marketers?', *Review of Social Economy*, **55**(1), Spring, 33–65.

Glosser, S. and L. Golden (1997), 'Average work hours as a leading economic indicator in US manufacturing industries, 1958–1993', *International Journal of Forecasting*, June, 725–41.

Hamermesh, D. (1995), 'Labour demand and the source of adjustment costs', *Economic Journal*, **105**(430), May, 620–34.

Hamermesh, D. (1996), *Workdays, Work Hours and Work Schedules: Evidence for the United States and Germany*, W.E. Upjohn Institute for Employment Research.

Hamermesh, D., A. Rees and R.K. Filer (1994), *Economics of Work and Pay*, 6th edition, Harper-Collins.
Hansen, F. (1996), 'FLSA compliance and enforcement', *Compensation and Benefits Review*, **28**(4), 8–13.
Hedges, J.N. (1993), 'Worktime levels and trends: differences across demographic groups', *Industrial Relations Research Association 45th Proceedings*, pp.321–9.
International Labor Organization (1995), 'Working time and employment', *International Labor Review*, **135**, 259–72.
Kahn, S. and K. Lang (1995), 'The causes of hours constraints: evidence from Canada', *Canadian Journal of Economics*, **28**(4A), 914–28.
Krausz, M. and N. Freibach (1983), 'Effects of flexible working time for employed women upon satisfaction, training and absenteeism', *Journal of Occupational Psychology*, **2**, 155–9.
Kush, K. and L. Stroh (1994), 'Flextime: the imaginary innovation', *Business Horizons*, Fall.
Leete, L. and J., Schor (1994), 'Assessing the time-squeeze hypothesis: hours worked in the United States, 1969–89', *Industrial Relations*, **33**(1), January, 25–43.
Martin, C., M. Aalberts and L. Clark (1993), 'The Fair Labor Standards Act and the fluctuating workweek scheme: competitive compensation strategy or worker exploitation?', *Labor Law Journal*, February, 92–100.
Moen, P. and D. Dempster-McClain (1987), 'Employed parents: role strain, work time and preferences for working less', *Journal of Marriage and the Family*, **49**, August, 579–90.
Moffitt, R. (1982), 'The Tobit model, hours of work and institutional constraints', *Review of Economics and Statistics*, **64**, August, 510–14.
Mosely, H. (1995), 'Working time flexibility as an employment strategy: recent German experience', Sixth International Symposium on Working Time, Blankenberg, Belgium, December.
Moss, R.L. and T. D. Curtis (1985), 'The economics of flexitime', *Journal of Behavioral Economics*, Summer, 95–114.
Pickard, J. (1991), 'Annual hours: a year of living dangerously', *Personnel Management*, **23**(8), August, 38–43.
Rebitzer and Taylor (1995), 'Do labor markets provide enough short-hour jobs? An analysis of work hours and work incentives,' *Economic Inquiry*, **33**, April, 257–73.
Rima, I. (1984), 'Involuntary unemployment and the re-specified labor supply curve', *Journal of Post Keynesian Economics*, **6**(4), Summer, 540–50.
Rodgers, C. (1992), 'The flexible workplace: what have we learned?', in S. Lobel (ed.), *Human Resource Management*, Special Issue on Work and Family, **31**(3), Fall, 183–99.
Rones, P. (1996), 'Trends in work hours', *Changes in Working Time in the US and Canada Conference Proceedings*, Ottawa, Canada, June.
Rosenberg, S. (1991), 'From Segmentation to Flexibility: A Selective Survey', *Review of Radical Political Economy*, **23**(1/2), Spring–Summer, 71–9.
Rothschild, K. (1982), 'A note on some economic and welfare aspects of working time regulations', *Australian Economic Papers*, **21**, 214–18.
Rottenberg, S. (1995), 'The regulation of work hours and its externalities defenses', *Journal of Labor Research*, January, 98–109.
Schor, J. (1991), *The Overworked American*, Basic Books, NY.
Schor, J. (1994), 'Worktime in a contemporary context: amending the FLSA', *Chicago-Kent Law*, **70**(1), 157–72.

Schor, J. (1995), 'Why more people are dropping out of the rat race', *Working Woman*, August, 24.
Shank, S. (1986), 'Preferred hours of work and corresponding earnings', *Monthly Labor Review*, November, 40–44.
Smith, M. (1996), 'Mandatory overtime and quality of life in the 1990s', *Journal of Corporation Law*, **21**(3), 599–622.
Tool, M. (1979), *The Discretionary Economy: A Normative Theory of Political Economy*, Santa Monica, CA: Goodyear Co.
Trejo, S. (1993), 'Overtime pay, overtime hours and labor unions', *Journal of Labor Economics*, **11**(2), April, 253–78.
US Department of Labor, Bureau of Labor Statistics (1992), 'Workers on flexible and shift schedules', *BLS News*, August 14.
US Department of Labor, Bureau of Labor Statistics, *Employment and Earnings*, various issues.
US Department of Labor, Bureau of Labor Statistics, *Employee Benefits in Medium and Large Firms*, 1994.
Weil, D. (1996), 'Regulating the workplace: the vexing problem of implementation', *Advances in Industrial and Labor Relations*, **7** (21), 247–86.

6. Law and economics analysis of the European Works Council

Bernhard Nagel and Roman Jaich

6.1 INTRODUCTION

1996 saw the setting up of several hundred European Works Councils (EWC) in Europe's biggest companies. This was not an entirely voluntary development on the part of company management. The starting point was the EU directive of 22 September 1994 on the 'establishment of a European Works Council or a procedure in Community-scale undertakings and groups of undertakings for the purpose of informing and consulting employees'. In line with Article 14 Para. 1 of the directive, member states were obliged to have completed the transposition of the directive into national legislation by 22 September 1996 at the latest.

The core of the directive is a procedure for the establishment of a consultative body – a 'European Works Council'. As there is enormous variation in existing employment law regulations in the member states, the bulk of the text of the directive is taken up with the method of selection and the specific powers of a 'Special Negotiating Body', which has to negotiate the procedures and powers of the European Works Council with central management. In order to avoid central management spinning out or blocking the negotiations and so preventing the establishment of a European Works Council, Article 7 of the directive provides for 'subsidiary requirements' which automatically take effect three years after the negotiations have started. These subsidiary requirements, set out in an Annexe to the directive, lay down the powers of the European Works Council, which must be set up in these circumstances.

On the other hand the directive, in Article 13, 'rewards' those companies who reach a voluntary agreement to set up a European Works Council by 22 September 1996, at the latest. As long as the agreement covers the entire workforce and provides for the 'transnational information and consultation of employees' it remains in effect even after the transposition of the law in the member state in which the parent company has its headquarters.

If there is no voluntary agreement in line with Article 13, then, under Article 6, the Special Negotiating Body and central management must reach an agreement on the setting up, composition and powers of a European Works Council. The Article 6 procedure can be complicated and time consuming.

The legal sanctions which apply when central management fails to inform an established European Works Council correctly are weak, but they can be used as a suspending veto as the Renault case has recently indicated. There is no sanction at all if a member of the EWC cannot convince the majority of the EWC to ask for special information. The directive has no provisions protecting minorities.

Overall it is possible to describe the directive as operating through a combination of the carrot (the continued validity of voluntary agreements under Article 13) and the stick (the threat of the compulsory introduction of European Works Councils under Article 7).

Several hundred European companies have taken the carrot of Article 13 and set up European Works Councils on a 'compulsory/voluntary' basis. In other cases the management is waiting. The question arises as to whether these mutually agreed-upon voluntary EWCs make a positive contribution at all, or whether they are largely inconsequential, as Niedenhoff (1996) maintained. Niedenhoff argues that communication takes place at an overly high aggregate level and does not lead to any significant positive effect for management because of the diverse interests and cultures of the employees' representatives. In contrast, there is the view that the EWC at least make use of the right to information given them or even sometimes develop activities that go beyond what was legally expected and thus develop an unforeseen dynamism.

First, an evolutionary approach to this question can help toward a general clarification by showing the kind of development conceivable for a European Works Council. Then, the results of an empirical survey on the functioning of eight voluntary EWCs are to be weighed up against the theoretic approach.

6.2 THE EVOLUTIONARY APPROACH TO AN ANALYSIS OF THE EWC

The evolutionary approach in economics is a synthesis of the two traditional approaches in the social sciences, of methodological individualism and methodological collectivism (see Weise et al., 1993, p. 37ff.). In these two extreme positions on the analysis of social behaviour however, the dynamic element, i.e. institutional transformation or the evolutionary process, is neglected. The collectivistic approach describes the behaviour of individuals in their dependence on the state of the system.[1] According to this the system forces individuals into specific forms of behaviour. From the standpoint of this approach a society is regarded as a whole. Mostly very abstract, general characteristics are considered and specific societal phenomena are then examined as to their contribution to the realization of the stated characteristics. The system is accordingly not to be conceived as the sum of its single elements but as a self-sufficient whole capable of acting rather than one made up merely of elements possessing no choice. The coordination of social interdependency follows according to this approach via norms, whose development, however, cannot be satisfactorily explained and whose determination, according to Elias (1970, S.12), follows an arbitrary path, i.e. any change in behaviour in the system can only be explained by exogenous changes.

The individualistic approach, in contradistinction, chooses the individual as an object of investigation. In the process, the individual is equipped with certain qualities like rationality and complete information. If further assumptions are made, for example the absence of transaction costs, then institutional transformation can no longer be explained, since institutions no longer have any meaning. Thus according to this approach institutions only exist in an imperfect world. Institutions continue to be assumed as exogenous. Numerous modifications of the neoclassical approach such as the introduction of insecurity, information asymmetry, adjustment rigidity, institutional regulations and various forms of market failure have expanded the theoretical framework. With the New Institutional Economy various paths of action are being tried out in the interests of solving these problems. Transaction costs are being taken into consideration and are leading to the introduction of institutions,[2] the importance of property rights is being emphasized,[3] the consideration of opportunist behaviour is leading to a rent seeking theory[4] and to the principle-agent theory[5] and also to the theory of collective action.[6] These approaches share the idea of looking first and foremost at individuals seeking maximum profit and their own advantage in isolation from other individuals.

The only approach that explicitly takes institutional development into consideration is that of evolutionary economy. Here we are not talking of a homogeneous research body of knowledge, however, but rather of diverse standpoints which exist one beside the other. Thus evolutionary approaches are on the one hand understood as being a continuation of neoclassical theory and on the other as their dissolution.[7] Cited precursors of this are Schumpeter and von Hayek.[8] The approaches have the notion in common that time is irreversible and historical, that the rise and diffusion of new phenomena generate the evolution of hitherto unknown constellations of circumstances, and that the behaviour of the protagonists and their interaction demand more differentiated theoretic models than that of mere profit maximization. Various notions exist as to the correct approach procedures: Often model procedures are transferred from the natural sciences.

Here an approach is to be followed which was borrowed from the natural sciences. According to it, institutional changes can be described in terms of self-organization processes. It is a question of combining items examined by both individualistic and collectivist approaches. On the one hand the limitations to action on the part of the individual are examined at the macro-level, but these are, however, created by the individuals themselves by a collectivist self-organization process.[9] This is brought about by the individuals no longer acting in an isolated fashion but taking into account what other individuals do in their own behaviour.[10] Via their interrelatedness individuals thus create together an environment of action binding on all of them.

The forces which drive this process forward may be generally defined as follows:[11]

1. Conformity: The conformity force or the force of self-reinforcement can be defined as that force which effects an insistence on an existing institutional framework. When such a power is in force it is characteristic that there is little deviation from the behaviour of the majority since that is connected with costs. These are, for example:[12]

   Costs incurred through decision finding and information costs: If an individual orients himself in his decisions on the behaviour of others, decision finding costs and information costs decrease.[13]

   Coordination costs: If an individual orients himself on the behaviour of others, disadvantages may be avoided. That is the case in following the rules of traffic behaviour, for example.

   Sanction costs: If an individual orients himself on the behaviour of others, sanction costs otherwise effective in the case of deviation behaviour may be avoided. An example of this is the adherence to customs.[14]
2. Anticonformity: With an increasing force of conformity, anticonformity acts against it. In contrast to the force of conformity, which produces short-term reinforcement, anticonformity inhibits long-term.[15] This can be explained by the fact that the marginal advantage of conformist behaviour decreases with increasing conformity, i.e. the gains from anticonformist behaviour increase in the face of increasing

conformity on the part of other individuals.[16] The result is that for each individual, anticonformist behaviour creates more gains than conformist behaviour when already a large number of other individuals behave in a conformist way. The consequence of this is that in the face of increasing conformity pressure the pressure towards anticonformity also increases until both forces are equal, i.e. an equilibrium is reached.

3. Preference: Changes in relative prices – especially arising through changes in population density, technical progress or relative resource scarcities – lead to changes in the opportunity costs of existing institutions. If these climb beyond the level of second best alternative, a change in behaviour is stimulated. This explains why individuals show a preference for a certain institutional regulation. The force toward preference can continue to be largely influenced by ideology[17] and by the observation of other institutional arrangements and their effects.
4. Fluctuation: This makes it possible that a transformation can occur in institutions, i.e. if, given stable forces, a similarly balanced institutional framework is present, the fluctuation force ensures that the economic system does not remain in an equilibrium and drives it rather to a new equilibrium. Innovations are examples of this.

On the one hand an evolutionary approach contributes to an explanation as to why voluntary EWC agreements are made at all. The fact that it was possible to agree on the directive is to be explained by the already existing voluntary European Information Committees. Their existence attested to their functioning power and supported unions in their argumentation. On the other hand the implementation of the directive strengthened the institutionalization of EWC representatives, in the process of which the exponential growth of EWC facilities makes one draw the conclusion that each new agreement made it easier to introduce further EWC facilities.[18]

With regard to the EWC an evolutionary perspective means, furthermore, that the directive created by the EU Commission for the introduction of a European Works Council has as yet not created a new institution. For the agreement on the directive does not mean we can make any definite statements about the possible form of the future EWC. What we can say after a first acquaintance with the question is that two positions are conceivable. On the one hand the EWCs could be misused as an ineffective management committee for image purposes and so suffer a similar fate to global works councils in the 70s which more or less deteriorated to a form of union tourism. On the other hand it is just as conceivable that EWCs could develop into a committee to be reckoned with, which is capable of exerting influence on the decisions of management.

In the following the sphere of influence for EWC representatives will be described in order to show the possible use it can be put to by the protagonists.

6.3 ANALYSIS OF THE PRESENT ATMOSPHERE FOR THE DEVELOPMENT OF THE EWC

First it can be said that European groups still carry on the majority of their economic activities inside Europe. Thus the trading of commodities across borders on the part of European companies takes place largely inside Europe. European companies put more than two-thirds of their investment capital into Europe. It is, however, to be suspected that this European variant of globalization will be a temporary thing, that the momentary Eurocentric orientation of the big companies will decrease with increasing corporate growth, i.e. that in the long run the European market will prove to be too small. Thus most engagement of European companies across Europe is the adjustment to a bigger inland market. This intensifies the pressure of competition, however, and only allows those companies to survive which grow beyond the European market. A specific European globalization variant such as that envisaged by Dörre (1996), for example, is, at least as far as company activities are concerned, at best of a transitory nature. It is, however, not to be underestimated in this context that the single market has a considerable volume and so will secure the binding of large European companies to Europe, since market orientation still represents one of the most important location factors of companies. Thus 85 per cent of world production still orients itself on respective inland markets (Burchardt, 1997).

Beside the economic orientation of European businesses to Europe, a Europeanization of 'corporate culture' can be observed. Many companies are striving to establish common human resource strategies for the regions of the triad, i.e. independently of the global tendency to corporate strategy, common corporate strategies are being developed for the triad regions Europe, America and South East Asia, which are respectively connected with specific human resource conceptions. It is the aim of this strategy to reduce transaction costs. For management the EWC offers an advantage here, since it enhances the chances of a common European human resource strategy.

From an economic point of view the driving forces behind internationalization are the multinational companies,[19] which expand their economic activities beyond national borders and thus achieve additional profits. This gives those at the cutting edge cost advantages and drives other companies to similar behaviour in order to survive. The operative principle is competition, which forces companies to seek the most cost-effective alternatives. From the standpoint of neo-classical economy this development is regarded as positive and reference is made to the fact that free movement of commodities and finance are not to be regarded as a zero sum game. With the increase of international division of labour, respective national comparative cost advantages in production can be utilized. The consequence is competition leading to a more efficient utilization of resources. The subsequent consequence is an increase in commodities and services and thus a rise in income and assets.[20] According to neoclassical economic theory production factors are transferred in the ideal case to other countries so long as the marginal productivity of the factors of production inland and abroad are identical. This leads to production factors being diverted to uses that – in the individual economy and globally – offer the greatest advantage. What is usually not considered in this view, however, is difference in political power between the production factors. Thus as a result of the dismantling of trade barriers the production factor capital becomes increasingly more mobile than that of the production factor labour. This leads to relatively lower relocation costs, which effect a power shift in favour of the production factor capital. This enables capital owners to bring about productivity increases via changes in institutional conditions.[21]

With this backdrop the question becomes significant whether the EWC can develop at all in an environment characterized by production cuts and relocation. After the discussion was dominated even up to a few years ago by the attitude that internationalization for the developed West European nations was connected with national production dismantling in favour of cheap labour cost countries, recent publications more frequently come to the conclusion that internationalization is only to a limited degree the consequence of production relocation, location advantages, lower wages and deregulated labour markets.[22] Thus the study of Wortmann and Dörrenbächer (1997) shows that in the case of direct investments of German companies abroad only very few of them meant an export of workplaces. This can be translated to other European countries. The main motive for the introduction of production sites abroad is still the sales orientation of companies. What remains unconsidered in this argumentation, however, is that direct investment abroad, even if it is not connected with a relocation of production from inland to a country abroad, often represents missing investment at home. This can then lead via rationalization to job cuts. It also speaks in favour of the argument that labour costs in most business sectors are of limited significance in decisions on production relocation abroad, that the utilization of scale gains is an important motive in globalization. Because the fixed costs are of relevance for the realization of unit cost degression the production factor labour is still by and large a variable cost factor.[23]

Thus the idea of a nomadic company ready to change its location at a word's notice as soon as that will reduce production costs cannot be observed in reality. The majority of internationally active groups generates its profit now as in the past by and large in their own home countries or region. The reason for this is often strategic alliances in the subsystems politics and science, based on common cultural orientation and clearly lower opportunity costs.[24]

The decisive factor concerning the influence of global companies on works council representatives and/or national politics is, however, not so much how mobile companies actually behave, as the mobility potential they have at their disposal.[25] That is: the threat of production transfer or relocation already has the effect that works council representatives and political decision makers tend to acquiesce to the demands of management for extra workhours, a willingness to accept wage cuts and the dismantling of social standards. Management only needs to play the relocation 'card', it does not have to actually carry it out. Here there could be a job for the EWC in helping to assess the real threat of relocation through Europe-wide exchange of information.

Independently of the assessment of the effects that the internationalization of production has, changes in the strategic orientation of companies have a direct effect on labour relations. They are also not without effect on the EWC. A transformation in the reactions to globalization can be determined in the following behaviour changes of the management of transnationally active companies.

One of the new variants of globalization is the growing internationalization through takeovers of companies abroad since the beginning of the nineties. A reason for this is the ever more rapidly changing world of business. The consequence is that in the case of the opening-up of a new production site abroad, the opportunity costs in the form of the time required are considered as higher than the buying of an existing company. On the other hand globally active companies are striving for market leadership in their field. The acquisition of firms abroad therefore often serves to open up new markets and to get rid of competition through takeovers. The EWC is of interest for company management precisely for this reason, since the takeover of foreign companies has led to much bigger problems in the integration of these into the corporate group than the founding of a new company. For the takeover of a company often does not just mean a change of owner but of corporate culture. Existing structures are disrupted. The result is insecurity in the national management and in the employees. The EWC is of special interest to company management from this standpoint because it offers the possibility of integrating the acquired foreign locations better into a unified corporate strategy.

Whilst company expansions in the 70s and 80s were characterized by a broad spread of activities (horizontal integration), there has been a dominance of return to the core since the beginning of the 90s. Groups are retaining those areas of business in which they are market leaders, and other areas are disposed of. One cause of this development is the increased cost of R&D, which does not allow companies to cover the costs for R&D. Also the briefer lifespan of products makes companies concentrate on core production areas. There is a further motive in the reduction of insecurity. The result of the reduction to core areas is a rise in productivity, so that a potential for rationalization arises here. Beyond this the transformation of group structure has effects on the EWC. Because of restructuring, companies find themselves in a permanent process of change. Single elements of a group are sold or bought. The consequence for the EWC is that the employees' environment is in continual flux, and this effects the EWC, too. The manning of the EWC often varies and this renders communication difficult between the members and hinders the building-up of an effective committee.

The increasing importance of mixed groups and holding companies also has an effect on the EWC. The EWC's problem is that the directive only plan for it to be on one level. The question now is: on what level? If it is to be on the level of holdings, then the EWC will be in contact with management. Thus circumstances are created whereby employee representatives have access to strategic company information. On the other hand locating the EWC on the level of holdings has the consequence that, besides various nationalities, a variety of lobby interests represent a hindrance. If the EWC is to be located at division level, interest differences hardly pose any problems, but the contact to holding-management is no longer guaranteed. This is especially problematic when the seat of the group is in another country in which there are no contacts between employees and management as a result of the nature of national labour relations (e.g. Great Britain).

There are various perspectives for the EWC *vis-à-vis* the corporate strategy of a group. Medium-sized companies who are duty bound to have EWCs have by and large strong regional or national ties. Often they pursue an internationalization strategy which is still nationally oriented and concentrated on activities at home. They communicate via orders and directives from the group's headquarters to the affiliates. They translate organization and daily practices of the group's headquarters to the affiliates. This strategy is characterized by a low degree of differentiation and integration. Management concepts of the group headquarters are translated to the affiliates, for example by the sending of managers. The affiliates abroad generally do not have strong ties and are greatly dependent on the group headquarters. For the EWC this means that the strong position of the group headquarters and the ties to the homeland entail the problem of nationalization. In pursuing a national strategy, however, the employee representatives of affiliates abroad have a particularly strong interest in the EWC. But it is questionable whether they can assert themselves against disinterested employee representatives from the seat of the group who normally dominate the EWC.

Another example of this is the country-specific internationalization strategy. It is characterized by a low degree of integration and a high degree of differentiation. It takes into account that the unknown environment of other nationalities must find special consideration. The motive for a subsidiary abroad is usually to enter new markets and to build up a national image there in order to be accepted by companies of the country. To this end, use is made of the knowledge of regional managers. The group headquarters strives in each such case towards an optimization of individual national strategies, whereby the individual strategies are not integrated into an overall strategy. A decentral leadership and a low measure of connectedness of individual group companies is dominant here. For the EWC there are favourable conditions here. The foreign production sites are directed respectively to nationally or regionally defined markets, the individual markets are not connected to one another. In consequence there is hardly any location competition. The dominance of the parent company is not so strong that national overtones in the EWC are to be feared. This situation offers the chance of creating a climate of trust in the EWC, which enables it to achieve goals like Europe-wide job protection or unified social plans. It can further be expected that, in the face of increasing internationalization, multinational strategy will be replaced by a global strategy. The phase of multinational strategy then offers the EWC the chance of building up an atmosphere of trust among EWC members which in turn enhances effective EWC work in company restructuring.

We can indeed observe a transition from individual strategies of countries to an integration of subsidiaries into a global strategy of the total enterprise. This aims at unifying the national perspective of the parent company on the one hand and the multinational focus on local integration of subsidiaries on the other, and to realize the global efficiency of the total enterprise on the world market as desired by a global strategy. A global strategy must consider both the overall goals of the group and the local goals of the subsidiaries. This demands an informational strategy which not only runs from parent company to subsidiary, but also includes intensive communication between individual subsidiaries. The individual group companies are closely connected, partly via supply connections, partly via competition.

In recent publications some writers suspect that global strategy will move into network strategy (Flecker, 1996), in which no group headquarters will be discernible any longer. But it is to be observed that the integration of subsidiaries abroad into a global strategy is going hand in hand with an increase in central control. The dependence of subsidiaries is increasing. This development is promoted by technical progress in the communications sector, which makes central control possible even when group companies are far apart. With this backdrop the EWC acquires additional significance. The transition from decentral to central group control leads to an erosion of national information and codetermination rights. The national management is not informed about group strategy and cannot then hand on any information. In addition the national management can simply point to lack of decision powers on their part in cases of conflict. The EWC offers the possibility here to acquire important information about group strategy. But from the viewpoint of group management too the EWC can be of use. Pursuing a global strategy with central control demands a high level of control. The EWC can be used by group management in this situation as a second controlling level in order to acquire unfiltered information about the situation of individual locations.

All in all we can say that both employee representatives and management representatives have an interest in the EWC. These interests, however, are at best of a partial nature. The question arises then as to what character the EWC can develop.

6.4 DEVELOPMENT PERSPECTIVES FROM AN EVOLUTIONARY STANDPOINT

In the analysis of the development of the EWC four levels of action must be differentiated: the level of EWC members and group management, the level between EWC members, the level between national employee representatives and EWC members, and the level of EWC members and external protagonists – meaning mainly union representatives.

According to the directive and to the opinion of the protagonists concerned, the relations between EWC members and group management are in the foreground. It is on this basis that the EWC is defined and also how it defines itself. But it is important that the levels of action interact with one another. Especially between the levels of EWC members and group management on the one hand and that of the EWC members amongst themselves on the other, positive or negative feedback effects are to be expected. Thus the EWC can develop a strength *vis-à-vis* management if the EWC members manage to develop a unified position amongst themselves, that means if the EWC can establish itself as a homogeneous protagonist. On the other hand it is easier for the EWC to do that if it has a strong negotiation position *vis-à-vis* management. The level of EWC members and national employee representatives need not be examined at the present time. Most voluntarily introduced EWCs are either not at all or little connected to national interest groups. In the long term, however, a closer connection to national interest groups is necessary, for only this connection can give the EWC its legitimation. The relationship of EWC members to unions is in reality characterized by the fact that European or national unions supported the introduction of EWCs, but then retracted their engagement. In the following therefore, the influence of the unions will only be included as a positive or negative reinforcing effect.

What we have remaining is a model with two levels of action. On each of these the forces described in section two are in effect. These can be described as follows.[26]

At the level of EWC members amongst one another, the conformity force is in effect exerting pressure to homogeneous group behaviour, and the anticonformity force works counter to group pressure; this can be the influence of management, but also the presence of union representatives. The preference force can be expressed as the preference of EWC members for conflict-oriented relations or cooperation-oriented relations. The fluctuation force has the effect that an initially achieved balance does not stay. Thus it comes via elections or group restructuring to a new manning of the EWC, which can exert a pressure toward change on an existing balance.

At the level of the relations of EWC members to group management there is, beside the feedback to the level of the EWC members amongst themselves, also the anticonformity force in effect, which can be defined as the pressure of the EWC members on management, then the conformity force, which can be defined as the willingness of management to listen to the demands of the EWC, and the preference force, i.e. the preference of management for cooperative or conflict-oriented relations with the EWC.

The decisive factor is the assumption that in the end it is the level of EWC members which determines the success of the EWC. The protagonists themselves often define the EWC by its relations with management. But the driving force is in fact the EWC-internal level, since these act as regulators[27] *vis-à-vis* the level of management.

Various development tendencies for the EWC can be differentiated:

The EWC tends to dissolve itself. The EWC in this case does not develop into an independent protagonist. The causes for this can be many. There is no preference force at work, the employee representatives are not interested in the EWC or the anticonformity force dominates the conformity force, i.e. the interests of the employee representatives in the EWC are too diverse. The reason for this may be location competition – but in this case also the anticonformity force is too small. The group management does not succeed in motivating the EWC for its interests.

The EWC becomes an instrument of management. The only difference to the first case is that the anticonformity force in this case is clearly much stronger than the conformity force. Management in this case can use the EWC for its interests. The unions in this as in the preceding case have no interest in the EWC, or at least they cannot put it effectively into practice. This situation, however, tends to be unstable. If there is no force acting to help the EWC develop into an independent committee, the interests of management alone cannot stabilize it. If there is not enough interest on the part of the employee representatives, management cannot realize its interests. The consequence would be a slip back into the first situation. If then management wants to use the EWC for its own interests, it must promote the conformity force and try to develop the preference force towards the preference force.

The EWC develops into a European consultation committee. In this case the conformity force dominates the anticonformity force, and the preference force is more strongly oriented toward conflict.

The EWC develops into an independent protagonist. In this case, however, the EWC acquires its independence by carrying out projects such as job security and Europe-wide environmental standards together with the group management. The preference force which works in the direction of cooperation dominates conformity force and anticonformity force .These are more or less in equilibrium.

According to the directive the EWC is formed in such a way that it can go beyond the stipulated rights to information and consultation. This lies in the nature of the conformity force. It must be present so that an information committee can develop. When this has formed and stabilized itself, however, the demands on management will be more extensive.

Some recommendations can be concluded from these reflections:

It is necessary for the EWC to constitute itself internally. The level of the relations of EWC members to management should not be neglected, but the emphasis should be on the internal level. This can have a retroactive effect on the management level in the long run. It should be of primary importance to EWC representatives, then, to strengthen the conformity force.

This must be the starting point for unions, too. If they really want to strengthen the EWC and not be reduced to many voluntary EWCs, they should keep national differences (e.g. those that exist in competing unions in France) and intranational differences out of the EWC in order to strengthen the conformity force.

If management wants to use the EWC for its own interests, it should make some effort to promote the latter's inner constitutive process. In a case such as the second, there is a latent danger that the balance topples and a situation like the first one arises; however, then management can no longer use the EWC for its interests. In the worst case the EWC carries on a formal existence, is seen as a travel bureau and no information on group strategies can be transmitted.

6.5 CAN THE EWC BE EFFICIENT AND EFFECTIVE? AN ASSESSMENT *VIS-À-VIS* THE BACKDROP OF GERMAN CODETERMINATION

6.5.1 The Betriebsrat as a part of German industrial relations[28]

It would seem sensible in the analysis of European works council representatives to start from a reference model in order to investigate its possibilities. In this section the question is considered as to how far experience and insights from German codetermination can be applied to problems facing European works council representatives. Codetermination has to be analysed in connection with the German system of collective bargaining.[29] Codetermination is a democratic economic institution created by the German law in 1920. The employees of a firm elect their representatives. According to the present Betriebsverfassungsgesetz (works constitutional act) in force since 1972, there are also to be employee representatives at company level (Gesamtbetriebsräte) and at group level (Konzernbetriebsräte); the latter however are only optional. The powers of the Betriebsräte range from consultation rights and negotiation rights (Mitwirkungsrechten) to real codetermination rights. In the latter, where there is strong disagreement a committee in which both employer and employee are equally represented meet together with a neutral chairman whom both have to agree upon.

In Germany unions are not divided by professions or by the different political or religious affiliations of their members, they are unified (Einheitsgewerkschaften) which means that unions organize a whole branch like the metallurgic industry or the chemical industry (Industriegewerkschaften), not a profession like the electricians or chemical workers (Berufsgewerkschaften). Collective agreements normally cover one or several regions (Flächentarifverträge), not only one company (Firmentarifverträge). Nevertheless, 'Firmentarifverträge' are allowed under the German Act on Collective Agreement (Tarifvertragsgesetz). Less than one third of the collective agreements are single-company agreements, more than two thirds are regional agreements.

The employers' associations of important branches fit roughly, not exactly, to the organizational limits of the unions (Gesamtmetall – IG Metall, Bundesarbeitgeberverband Chemie – IG Chemie, now IG Bergbau, Chemie, Energie). There are personal connections between the systems of codetermination and collective bargaining on both sides. Union leaders have seats on the supervisory boards of important companies. The chairman of a works council usually has a seat on the supervisory board of his company, too. Most members of works councils are union members. In this capacity they are members of the collective bargaining commission of the union (Tarifkommission). Many members of the board of directors are also members of the collective bargaining committee of the employers' association. There they meet the same union leaders they have met before on the supervisory board of their company. Thus the two systems of collective bargaining and codetermination are linked.

The linkage between the two systems is a very special one. The system of codetermination is relatively peaceful. Works councils and management are bound by the legal duty of 'trustful cooperation' (vertrauensvolle Zusammenarbeit) under § 2 of the Works Constitution Act. The works council is not allowed to go on strike (§ 74 subs. 2). This is one of the rare cases in legislation where 'trust' is prescribed by law. What is prescribed is not only a form of behaviour (not to go on strike), but also an attitude (trust). The corresponding system of collective bargaining is more conflict-oriented. Here distrust and antagonizing behaviour is not illegal. The unions can threaten the employers' associations with a strike. But strikes are rare in Germany. As long as a collective agreement is valid the unions are not allowed to go on strike. After the expiry of a collective agreement the bargaining between employers' associations and unions can be very controversial, but in most cases the end of the game is a collective agreement without a strike, a more or less peaceful compromise. There is some evidence that there has been a 'spill-over-effect' of the system of codetermination to the system of collective bargaining and that an attitude of cooperation has developed in Germany.

The works council is responsible for the day-to-day work. It can bargain for agreements in its specific enterprise if there is no collective agreement covering the same subject, thus blocking the works council from acting in this field. Many collective agreements leave room for additional agreements with the works council on enterprise level, sometimes they even empower the works council to control whether the provisions of the collective agreement are observed by the employer or not. Under the concept of 'betriebsnahe Tarifpolitik' (collective bargaining close to the interests of the different enterprises) the unions try to bargain for collective agreements at company level in addition to the regional collective agreements. One of the goals of 'betriebsnahe Tarifpolitik' is to give the works councils more power so that they can bargain for specific solutions in their specific enterprises on the safe platform of a collective agreement. The employers' associations – for instance 'Gesamtmetall', the association of the employers in the metallurgic industry – try to replace collective agreements with the unions by direct agreements with the works councils. One of their reasons is that works councils are not allowed to go on strike, so they cannot exert as much pressure in the bargaining process as a union. Gesamtmetall also criticizes the 'Flächentarifvertrag' (a collective agreement for a region). This regional agreement is supposed to be too rigid because it treats weak firms and strong firms in a branch equally. The opposite position, taken by the unions, is that a mixture of collective agreements at regional and company level and direct agreements with the works councils at enterprise level is flexible enough to surmount the difficulties of diversity between the different firms of a branch.[30]

Critics arguing in favour of the decentralized Anglo-Saxon system of collective bargaining do not take into account the 'Betriebsegoismus' (enterprise-based egoism) of this system. Collective agreements on company level exploit the specific bargaining power of a union in this company. Collective bargaining at regional level as it exists in Germany exploits the bargaining power of a union in a region. It means less differentiation of wages because the collective agreement is mainly based on the average enterprise of the region. Some of the critics also forget that in Germany closed shops (jobs only for union members), union shops (employees must join a union) and agency shops (employees not joining the union must pay a substantial fee to this union representing them in the enterprise) are illegal. Every person has an individual right not to join a union (negative Koalitionsfreiheit). So unions must be flexible and attractive for their members, otherwise these members will leave.

Some employers' associations, among them 'Gesamtmetall', have been weakened by discontented members leaving the association. These firms try to escape the regional collective agreements and to bargain for collective agreements at company level or for agreements with works councils at enterprise level. The unions are less hostile to collective agreements at company level, even if they are worse than the regional agreement, than to agreements with works councils that cannot go on strike. Nevertheless, more and more works councils feel obliged to accept agreements at enterprise level worse than the conditions of the regional collective agreement. This is illegal. Under § 77 subs. 3 of the Works Constitution Act agreements at enterprise level bargained for by the works council shall not deal with wages and other conditions of employment that have been fixed or are normally fixed by collective agreement. The fact that this illegal behaviour is not rare gives an impression of the state of the systems of collective bargaining and codetermination in Germany. They are not as stable as they were in the seventies and in the eighties. Thus the specific achievements of industrial relations in Germany are considered to be at stake. These achievements are a high level of wages and a relatively small difference between the wages of the different groups of employees. The reasons for this decline of stability are discussed controversially in Germany. The most controversial subject of the discussion seems to be the economic analysis of the decline.

6.5.2 Game theory and codetermination

The Works Constitution Act (Betriebsverfassungsgesetz) states a duty of both the employer and the works council to cooperate in a trusting manner.[31] It further states that the employer has a duty to give full information to the works council in due time. If one uses a model with two actors (players), management and works council, both actors or players having the possibility to play cooperatively (sticking to the formal and informal rules) or defectively (acting opportunistically), the Works Constitution Act can be analysed by game theory.[32] If one adds a first assumption that sticking to the rules creates a positive climate in the enterprise with benefits for both sides and a second assumption that the game is played repeatedly, we are in a situation comparable to Robert Axelrod's famous computer game. In the 'shadow' of the Works Constitution Act, Rapoport, the winner of this computer game, could follow his strategy 'tit for tat' for repeated games. The strategy of Rapoport (first round playing cooperatively, then playing like the other player has played the round before) is friendly, Rapoport does not defect from cooperation first. The strategy is defensive, it reacts to defective playing immediately. The strategy is ready to pardon if the other player plays cooperatively again. The strategy is calculable, the other side knows exactly what the reaction will be. Axelrod[33] suggests that 'tit for tat' will work if the game is repeated often enough, if the future has a strong influence on the decisions of today, if every side remembers the former games, and if so-called cores of cooperation create a climate hostile to defective playing. The main danger for the success of 'tit for tat' are the so-called echo-effects; that means after one side has played defectively the defective playing goes on because both sides play defectively as an 'echo' to the earlier behaviour of the other side. There are at least three more dangers: First, too many players are in the game, so players lose track of what is going on; second, playing yieldingly can encourage defective playing on the other side; third, a high pay-off can be an incentive for defective playing.[34]

In Axelrod's computer game the players are free, there are no rules in the game preventing them from playing defectively. In the German 'codetermination game' there is a legal duty for both sides to play cooperatively. The German Works Constitution Act encourages cooperative playing by imposing the duty of truthful cooperation on both sides. This legal provision gives an incentive to start cooperatively and to overcome the deadlock of echo-effects. The duty of the employer to give full information in due time gives an incentive to play cooperatively and to overcome echo-effects, too. This incentive is intensified by other duties of codetermination and consultation stated in the Works Constitution Act, for instance in case of a substantial alteration in the enterprise. Since works councils are representative bodies, the number of actors in the game is not too high. Furthermore, there is a positive prerequisite for cooperative playing. Since rank and file workers exert some pressure on their representatives at the works councils as well as the shareholders do in relation to the managers, there is practically no incentive for playing yieldingly. Finally, empirical studies[35] have shown that in German enterprises 'cores of cooperation' have developed. These cores discourage defective playing even in times of an economic recession like in 1994. Nobody knows, however, whether these cores will hold out during a long period of unemployment and economic crisis.

Under certain circumstances management and works councils play sequential games. One example is an alteration in the enterprise under § 111 of the Works Constitution Act, for instance a reduction of operation or closure of the whole or important departments of the enterprise. A repeated game can only be played if the whole enterprise is not closed down. So, let us assume that management plans to close down an important department of an enterprise. A cooperative player gives full information to the works council in time. A defective player keeps the plan secret or gives incorrect information. The works council can answer cooperatively or defectively. A cooperative answer takes into account the situation of the company and the enterprise. A defective answer instigates employees against management with unjust accusations of incompetence. Under the condition that management must expect a defective answer if it plays cooperatively (by giving full information in time) it will play defectively. There will be a sequential game leading to the Nash-equilibrium. Management will play defectively because its expected pay-off resulting from the works council playing defectively will be smaller than its pay-off in the event of both sides playing defectively. If both sides played cooperatively the overall pay-off could be maximized. The model is shown in Figure 6.1.

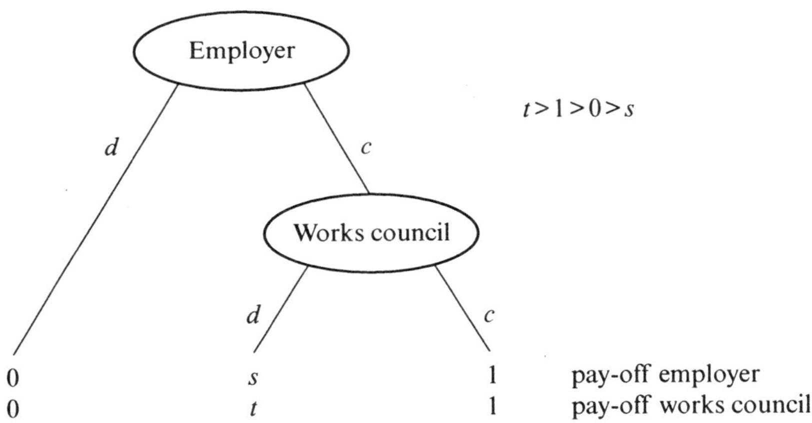

Notes: Works council will play defectively, because $t > 1$, therefore employer will play defectively, because $0 > s$. The result will be a Nash-equilibrium (0/0). If both sides played cooperatively the result would be 1/1, an overall optimum.

Figure 6.1 Model 1

In this situation the legislator acts again by imposing a duty of trustful cooperation upon both sides. In addition, the legislator imposes upon management a legal duty of giving full information to the works council in time. If as a result of this legislation both sides play cooperatively, the trade-off between working conditions (provided by the employer) and work quality (provided by the employee) can become more efficient provided that there are no negative externalities on unemployed persons and other third parties. 'In the shadow of the law' the game can change to the model in Figure 6.2.

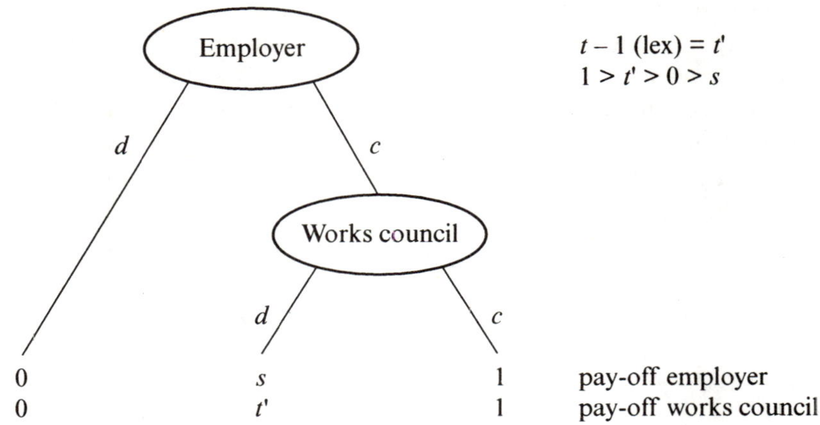

Notes: Works council will play cooperatively if $1 > t'$. Then employer will play cooperatively because 1 (expected pay-off in case of works council playing cooperatively) is greater than 0.[36]

Figure 6.2 Model 2

The legal rules of the Works Constitution Act exactly suggest such a game. The employer has a duty to give full information in time (§ 111). The works council can enforce this duty by its power to bargain for a reconciliation of interests and a social compensation plan (§ 112). If the bargaining for a reconciliation of interests does not result in an agreement, the works council can bargain for a social compensation plan. If no agreement is reached on the social compensation plan, the works council can move to a conciliation committee under §112 subs. 4. Its members are divided up equally between employer and works council with a neutral chairman chosen by both sides. The committee will decide the case. Where the employer gives defective information the works council can 'take revenge' by insisting on a very expensive social compensation plan. Where the works council plays defectively by launching false accusations against the managers the answer can be a very stubborn behaviour of the employer in the bargaining process, and the neutral chairman will be influenced by the fact that one side has played defectively. As a result it seems to be clear that the legislator of the Works Constitution Act has encouraged cooperative playing not only in the case of information in general (repeated one-shot-games) but also in the case of this sequential game. In the 'shadow' of these legal incentives the so-called cores of cooperation can develop. This is the result of a model with two players, management and works councils, playing repeatedly and acting independently from third parties, that means also independently from employers' associations, labour unions and collective bargaining. It is assumed that both sides profit from cooperation and that there are no externalities on third parties.

It could be argued that one cannot use game theory with its simple terms 'defective' and 'cooperative' for the explanation of codetermination. More adequate terms might be 'acting strategically' and 'acting communicatively'. Acting strategically means following a goal because it is profitable for a player himself. Acting communicatively in the terms of Jürgen Habermas[37] means reconciling the different interests because this reconciliation is profitable for both sides. Reconciliation is only possible if both sides have sufficient information. Habermas denies that game theory can explain even strategic human interactions sufficiently. He argues that a strategic interaction is not a mechanism for the production of an instrumental order. Strategic interactions take place in an already otherwise constituted 'Lebenswelt' (natural and cultural environment). The institutions of the 'Lebenswelt' are a social fact. They do not determine the reaching of agreement any more. But if the 'Lebenswelt' is strong enough to limit the actions of persons, these persons leave the egocentric view of the winner–loser orientation and enter into a rationality of communication, cooperation and reconciliation. Thus Habermas denies the applicability of the so-called REMM-hypothesis. In my opinion game theory serves as a tool to make a workable prognosis for human interaction. If it is a good tool, it can explain this interaction wholly or partially. The relationship between employers and employees in an enterprise is a very complicated field of interaction. Thus the most urgent need is empirical evidence on the nature and development of this relationship. If game theory is a helpful tool for this purpose, one should take advantage of it. We should not try to explain social development as a whole by the tool 'game theory'. Nor should we try to replace philosophy by game theory. But it is admissible to use game theory for this restricted purpose.

One could argue that there is no need for legislation because in a 'tit-for-tat' situation a cooperative game between employer and works council would develop by itself. But there is a historical and a logical argument against this assumption. There is some historic evidence that employers do not give away their dominant position in the relationship with employees if they are unsure of the benefits of cooperation.

In Imperial Germany works councils were introduced by law during World War I. This was in return for forcing workers into munitions factories under the 'Vaterländisches Hilfsdienstgesetz' (Law of The Service for the Fatherland). But if we look at the history of the development of works councils, the story becomes more complicated. At the end of the 19th century some employers introduced workers' committees on a voluntary basis. The members of the committees were appointed by the employers, not elected by the employees. But in 1905, after a bitter strike in the Prussian mining industry, Prussia introduced obligatory workers' committees in the mining industry. These committees were still considered by many employees as instruments of the employers. But in the long run this was one of the roots of the works councils introduced by the 'Betriebsrätegesetz' (Works Councils Act) in 1920. The historic development shows that voluntary and obligatory works are not mutually exclusive alternatives. Instead there was an evolution from pilot voluntary councils to obligatory works councils, starting with the demands of a minority in the National Assembly of 1848, picking up speed with the initiative of Emperor Wilhelm II in 1890 and coming to a preliminary end with the Works Councils Act of 1920.[38]

The logical argument is that an employer cannot play tit for tat with a works council or other committee that does not yet exist. Again, there has to be an evolution with the possible result of such a tit-for-tat situation. Then the cooperative game can be played in a non-cooperative situation.

6.5.3 Is the experience with German codetermination transferable to the EWC?

Concerning the EWC, there are a few differences to the preceding model. For example, we can no longer presuppose that the workers' representatives are a homogeneous group. If we cannot assume this for a member of a German Betriebsrat (works councillor), especially at the higher levels of the central works council for the company or the group works council, then, as you might expect, it is even less likely at a European level. The national interests of EWC members may lead to the formation of lobbies within the ranks of works councils. Thus it is to be suspected that in some cases the works council members already act out a prisoner-type dilemma game in which they do not pass on information they obtained from the national level and show little interest in the advantages that might come of cooperative behaviour. The EWC then becomes less effective, and individual groups can be played off against one another by management.

Likewise, the practice of substituting stand-ins for EWC members can also lead to the EWC not being able to develop as a homogeneous group. Because of their position, members of works councils and union representatives rarely pursue the same goals. Works council members mainly concentrate on representing the employees of the company, at best of the group, whereas the union representatives act on behalf of the whole inclusive workforce outside the group. The presence of union representatives in the EWC can consequently lead to negotiations between management and the works council not taking place because they run counter to the interests of the union. On the other hand, consultation between the EWC and unions is necessary, since the latter have greater experience, and they can ensure that works council members are not misled by false management information.

It is still the case that, depending on nationality, those designated as EWC works council members as a result of national codetermination have little or no experience in cooperative codetermination law. That means that the EWC is a body that by virtue of its structure is oriented towards cooperation. However, in some European states employees and employers have not developed a willingness to cooperate. In fact the development of cooperative structures depends on the emergence of informal institutions. So we can see, for example, that, if the German model of cooperative working functions, it is because it developed in a particular historical context and depended on specific starting conditions, which resulted from formal and informal rules.

6.6 CONSEQUENCES AND PERSPECTIVES

The fact that several hundred companies have reached 'voluntary/compulsory' agreements on EWCs in line with Article 13 of the directive does not mean this institution is now an effective player on the industrial relations stage. This will be possible if both management and works council representatives can see the advantage of it. The following scenarios are possible:

1. There is a nationalization – that means powerful employee representatives in the parent company use the EWC in their own national interest. In this scenario, cooperation between company management and the employee representatives in the parent company means that the EWC cannot develop as a united body. The employee representatives in the parent company try to obtain information from the EWC

representatives from other countries at EWC sessions, which they can then use as a bargaining counter with the central management. This scenario is particularly possible in EWCs with a German parent company, as in these cases there are often long-standing relationships between company management and employee representatives.

2. The EWC becomes a talking shop. If management has no interest in the EWC or possibly even sees it as a threat, there is a danger that the EWC degenerates into an ineffective body. One possibility for management is to 'sideline' the EWC by overwhelming it with a mass of unimportant information. Another possibility is to present the EWCs as a leisure pursuit – 'a jolly': with meetings held in an expensive hotel, possibly with spouses invited as well, leisure activities on offer.
3. The EWC is used by the unions for their own interests. One possible scenario here is that the EWC is used by the unions as a travel organizer.
4. Both management and works council representatives can see an advantage of the EWC. If management can see an advantage in having the EWC, whether in the form of the establishment of European corporate culture or of the prevention of unrest during a time of group restructuring, this advantage is a source of power for members of works councils. In this case the latter can assert their demands for comprehensive information and furtherance of EWC work. On the other hand, the EWC can only establish itself as a player if the members of works councils show an interest in it. If the majority of the EWC members are of the opinion that the committee cannot achieve much anyway, even an interested management cannot use the EWC for its own interests.

The existence of an effective EWC is only one possible scenario. The formation of functioning EWCs is supported by individual interests. Both the unions and employers' associations have incentives to promote the EWC in their own interests. Both have by and large organized themselves at European level. If companies now begin to grow beyond the European trade area, both the unions and the employers' association will be in danger of losing their legitimization basis. The EWC could represent an instrument capable of binding European groups more closely to their European basis.

Our reflections up to now have indicated that the EWC has several possible development paths. At present it is rather unlikely that the EWC will develop in the way that its creators originally intended. It is, of course, possible that this development will take place but it will be 'behind the backs' of the participants, to begin with without them knowing that it is happening. This evolutionary process can be best modelled using game theory where the actions of the works council are seen as a multidimensional game. This begins with a situation of non-cooperation, which the players, following their own interests, gradually abandon in favour of a cooperative game. This also systematically improves the chances of cooperation and defective games, in which, according to Rapoport's tit for tat rule, the most successful strategy is to cooperate in the first round and subsequently to do what other players have done in the immediately preceding round. This produces both cooperative and defective moves for the game. However, such a model has still to be developed.

NOTES

1. Luhmann (1968) is a representative of this approach. In later publications however, Luhmann includes institutional transformation explicitly by using the concept of autopoetic systems, as in Luhmann (1984). Also Becker (1976).
2. cf. on Williamson's (1985) notion of transaction costs.
3. On the theory of property rights cf. Alchian (1965).
4. See Buchanan *et al.* (1980).
5. See Jensen and Meckling (1976).
6. See Olson (1965).
7. cf. Erdmann (1993, S.5).
8. cf. Witt (1995).
9. cf. Weise (1990), for example.
10. This view is not new, thus in economic theory the Venblen effect has long been known, which arises because of interdependency among individuals.
11. cf. also Weise (1996).
12. cf. extensively Eger and Weise (1990, S.69ff.).
13. If an individual observes the consumer habits of others, for example, and if he orients himself on that, there are fewer decision making costs with respect to getting informed on the quality of goods.
14. The importance of the conformity force for institutions is also discussed as path dependency. See Kiwit and Voigt (1995) who argue that the cause of path dependency is specific investment in equipment and human capital, network effects and the cognitive anchoring of institutions. See also Leipold (1996).
15. On the subject of short-range reinforcement and long-range inhibition, see Gierer (1981).
16. Talking in game theory terminology, the more individuals play cooperatively, the greater is the attraction of playing 'defect' or anticonformist.
17. For the connection of ideology and institutional transformation, see North (1990) for example.
18. This view is demonstrable at least in Great Britain. Only fairly late were voluntary agreements reached here. That happened because companies who were willing to introduce EWCs did not initially do so since they did not want to betray the then Conservative government – which was against EWCs. After the first agreements were reached, the anti-attitude toward the EWCs dissolved, so-to-speak.
19. cf. the position of Dörre *et al.* (1997), who talk in this context of key companies.
20. cf. also Simons (1997). The positive effects of globalization are also emphasized by the Economic and Social Committee of the EU (1997).
21. cf. North (1990).
22. cf. Härtel *et al.* (1996), for example.
23. Thus following Kenichi Ohmae. Müller also (1997, S.34) describes fixed costs as a driving force in globalization, in order to put these on a broader market basis. But it is the fixed costs which generally lead to increasing scale income.

24. Barriers to the internationalization of companies are pointed out by Hirsch-Kreinsen (1997, S.489). These make it very doubtful whether nomadic companies can develop. The barriers he points to are the high management and organization costs, the organizatory limits to internationalization and the resistance (that should not be underestimated) against international activity on the part of national management and employee representatives.
25. See also Dörre (1996, S.22), who points out that employee representatives often cannot assess whether, when there is a threat of production relocation in the air, there is any real intention on the part of the company to relocate.
26. In principle this model can also be represented in mathematical form. For a similar model, see Eger and Weise (1991), for example.
27. For a closer inspection of the concept regulator in the view described here see Haken (1982), who means by it those parameters – in this case behaviour levels – which as a result of their slow adjustment enslave the fast parameters. In this view of things the EWC-internal level enslaves the EWC management level.
28. cf. also Nagel (1996a).
29. See Nagel (1996b).
30. For an economic assessment of the respective merits of centralized and decentralized collective bargaining see Revel (1994, p. 26 ff.).
31. Backhaus shows that binding social conventions can overcome the inherent instability of work organizations in a prisoner's dilemma situation. See Backhaus (1989, p. 241f.).
32. The structure of the game is very similar to the famous prisoner's dilemma.
33. See Axelrod (1984).
34. See Axelrod (1984) and Hengsbach (1995, pp. 56–60).
35. See Nagel *et al.* (1994); Kotthoff (1994); Nagel *et al.* (1996).
36. For another interpretation of this game see Baurmann and Kliemt (1995, pp. 13–44).
37. See Habermas (1987) and Habermas (1994 p. 43).
38. See Schneider and Kuda, (1969, pp. 53–86).

REFERENCES

Alchian, Armen A. (1965), 'Some economics of property rights', *Il Politico*, **30**, pp. 816–29.

Axelrod, Robert (1984), *The Evolution of Cooperation*, New York: Basic Books.

Backhaus, Jürgen (1989), 'Workers' participation stimulated by the economic failure of traditional organisation' in H.G. Nutzinger and J. Backhaus (eds), *Codetermination*, Berlin: Springer, pp. 229–67.

Baurmann, M. and H. Kliemt (1995), 'Zur Ökonomie der Tugend', in *Ökonomie und Gesellschaft, Jahrbuch 11: Markt, Norm und Moral*, Frankfurt am Main: Campus, pp. 13–44.

Becker, Gary S. (1976), *The Economic Approach to Human Behavior*, Chicago and London: University of Chicago Press.

Buchanan, James M., R.D. Tollison and Gordon Tullock (eds) (1980), *Toward a Theory of the Rent-Seeking Society*, Texas: A & M University Press.

Burchardt, Hans-Jürgen (1997), 'Die Globalisierungsdebatte: ahistorisches Ringelreihen und reduktionistische Prophezeihungen', in *Gewerkschaftliche Monatshefte*, July, pp. 397–409.

Dörre, Klaus (1996), 'Globalstrategien von Unternehmen – ein Desintegrationsphänomen. Zu den auswirkungen grenzüberschreitender Unternehmensaktivitäten auf die industriellen Beziehungen', in *SOFI-Mitteilungen*, 24/1996, pp. 15–27.

Dörre, Klaus, R. Elk-Anders and F. Speidel (1997), 'Globalisierung als Option: Internationalisierungspfade von Unternehmen, Standortpolitik und industrielle Beziehungen', in *SOFI-Mitteilungen* 25/1997, pp. 43–70.

Eger, Thomas and Peter Weise (1990), 'Normen als gesellschaftliche Ordner', in *Ökonomie und Gesellschaft*, Jahrbuch 8, Frankfurt am Main and New York, pp. 65–111.

Eger, Thomas and Peter Weise (1991), 'Latente Imitation und manifeste Transformation von Wirtschaftssystemen', in J. Backhaus (ed.), *Systemwandel und Reform in östlichen Wirtschaften*, Marburg, pp. 67–80.

Elias, Norbert (1970), *Was ist Soziologie?*, München: Juventa.

Erdmann, Georg (1993), *Elemente einer evolutorischen Innovationstheorie*, Tübingen: J.C.B. Mohr.

Flecker, Jörg (1996), 'Globalisierungsprozesse und industrielle Arbeitsbeziehungen', in Ulrich Steger (ed.), *Globalisierung der Wirtschaft: Konsequenzen für Arbeit, Technik und Umwelt*, Berlin, pp. 155–76

Gierer, A.(1981), 'Socioeconomic inequalties: effects of self-enhancement, depletion and redistribution', in *Jahrbücher für Nationalökonomie und Statistik*, (196), pp. 309–31.

Habermas, Jürgen (1987), *Theorie des kommunikativen Handelns*, 2 volumes, Frankfurt am main (4th edn): Suhrkamp.

Habermas, Jürgen (1994), *Faktizität und Geltung*, (4th edn), Frankfurt am Main: Suhrkamp.

Härtel, Hans-Hagen, R. Jungnickel, D. Keller, H. Feber, C. Borrmann, D. Winkler-Büttner and D. Lan (1996), *Grenzüberschreitende Produktion und Strukturwandel: Globalisierung der deutschen Wirtschaft*, Baden-Baden: Nomos.

Haken, Hermann (1982), *Synergetik: Eine Einführung*, Berlin, Heidelberg and New York: Springer.

Hengsbach, Friedhelm (1995), *Abschied von der Konkurrenzgesellschaft*, Munich: Kuaur.

Hirsch-Kreinsen, Hartmut (1997), 'Globalisierung der Industrie: ihre Grenzen und Folgen', *WSI-Mitteilungen*, 7/1997, 50, pp. 487–93.

Jensen, Michael C. and William H. Meckling (1976), 'Theory of firm: managerial behavior, agency costs and ownership structure', in *Journal of Financial Economics*, **3**, pp. 305–60.

Kiwit, D. and S. Voigt (1995), 'Überlegungen zum institutionellen Wandel unter Berücksichtigung des Verhältnisses interner und externer Institutionen', in *ORDO*, 46, pp. 117–47.

Kotthoff, Hermann (1994), *Betriebsräte und Bürgerstatus*, München: Hampp.

Leipold, H. (1996), 'Zur Pfadabhänigkeit der institutionellen Entwicklung', in D. Cassel (ed.), *Entstehung und Wettbewerb von Systemen*, Berlin: Duncker & Humblot, pp. 93–115.

Luhmann, Niklas (1968), 'Zweckbegriff und Systemrationalität', Tübingen: J.C.B. Mohr.

Luhmann, Niklas (1984), *Soziale Systeme: Grundriß einer allgemeinen Theorie*, Frankfurt am Main: Suhrkamp.

Müller, Hans-Erich (1997), 'Heimatlose Weltbürger?' in *Mitbestimmung*, (January), pp. 34–5.

Nagel, Bernhard (1996a), 'Entwicklungsperspektiven von Eurobetriebsräten und deutsche Mitbestimmung', in *WSI-Mitteilungen*, 8/1996, **49**, pp. 494–503.

Nagel, Bernhard (1996b), 'Wie effizient sind Tarifvertrag und Mitbestimmung?' in *Gewerkschaftliche Monatshefte*, February, pp. 97–111.

Nagel, Bernhard, Birgit Riess and Gisela Theis (1994): *Neue Konzernstrukturen und Mitbestimmung*, Baden-Baden: Nomos.

Nagel, Bernhard, Birgit Riess, Stefan Rüb and Andreas Beschorner (1996), *Information und Mitbestimmung im internationalen Konzern*, Baden-Baden: Nomos.

Niedenhoff, Horst-Udo (1996), 'Der Europäische Betriebsrat aus Arbeitgebersicht', in *WSI-Mitteilungen*, 8/1996, 49, pp. 489–93.

North, Douglass C. (1990), 'Institutions, Institutional Change and Economic Performance', Cambridge: Cambridge University Press.

Olson, Mancur (1965), *The Logic of Collective Action. Public Goods and the Theory of Groups*, Harvard: Harvard University Press.

Revel, Saul (1994), *Tarifverhandlungen in der Bundesrepublik Deutschland*, Baden-Baden: Nomos.

Schneider, Dieter/Kuda, Rudolf (1969), *Mitbestimmung, Weg zur industriellen Demokratie*?, Münich: Deutscher Taschenbuch Verlag.

Simons, Rolf (1997), 'Kein Nullsummenspiel', in *Die Mitbestimmung*, 1/97, pp. 12–17.

Weise, Peter (1990), 'Der synergetische Ansatz zur Analyse der gesellschaftlichen Selbstorganisation', in *Ökonomie und Gesellschaft*, Jahrbuch 8: Individuelles Verhalten und kollektive Phänomene, Frankfurt am Main and New York, pp. 12–64.

Weise, Peter (1996), 'Verhaltenskoordination durch soziale Kräfte und Normen', in Priddat, B.P. and G. Wegner (eds), *Zwischen Evolution und Institution. Neue Ansätze in der ökonomischen Theorie*, Marburg; Metropolis, pp. 187–209.

Weise, Peter, W. Brandes, T. Eger and M. Kraft (1993), *Neue Mikroökonomie*, 3rd edition, Heidelberg: Physica.

Williamson, Oliver E. (1985), *The Economic Institutions of Capitalism*, New York and London: Macmillan.

Wirtschafts- und Sozialausschuß der Europäischen Gemeinschaft (1997), *Stellungnahme zum Thema 'Beschäftigung, Wettbewerbsfähigkeit und Globalisierung der Wirtschaft'*, Brüssels: Amt für Veröffentlichungen der Europäische Gemeinschaft.

Witt, Ulrich (1995), 'Evolutorische Ökonomik – Umrisse eines neuen Forschungsprogramms', in Seifert, E.K. and B.P. Priddat (eds): *Neuorientierungen in der ökonomischen Theorie*, Marburg, pp. 153–79.

Wortmann, Michael and Christoph Dörrenbächer (1997), 'Multinationale Konzerne und der Standort Deutschland', in W. Fricke (ed.), *Jahrbuch für Arbeit du Technik: Globalisierung und institutionelle Reform*, Bonn: Dietz, pp. 28–42.

7. Severance pay in Germany: a contract perspective

Oliver Fabel, Steffen Welzmiller and Peter Chrubasik

7.1 THE GENERAL INSTITUTIONAL FRAMEWORK

Layoffs constitute a fundamental means of adjustment for firms facing significantly changing market facts and/or production technologies. While accepting this basic fact, all industrialized countries have also developed regulative rules governing the layoff process. In an early attempt to harmonize these quite varying national legislations[1] among its member states, the European Council[2] formulated a respective directive in 1975 which represents a short list of minimum standards. Massive layoffs thus necessitate consultations between firm and labour representatives on the possibilities of avoiding dismissals and the compensation of workers to be laid off. Yet, such consultations are not required to reach an agreement – the residual decision right always remaining with the firm. The EEC guideline was formally introduced to German labour law in 1978. The speed of this adaption most likely reflects the fact that the respective national legislation had already developed more detailed and binding rules.

Drawing upon the German tradition of codetermination rights, §§111–113 of the 'Industrial Relations Law' ('*Betriebsverfassungsgesetz*' – *BetrVG*[3]) of 1972 thus (i) defines a set of characteristic technological and/or organizational changes within a production site inducing a legal necessity to engage in firm–labour consultations, (ii) provides a list of possible adjustment instruments to be considered, (iii) ensures the involvement of labour representatives in the decision process, and (iv) determines procedures to reach an agreement to (v) compensate or ease the economic burden placed upon the inflicted workers while (vi) guaranteeing the continuation of the firm and its remaining labour contracts. The issue of compensating workers without endangering the economic survival of the firms has since become a focal point of legislative efforts. Examples are the introduction of guidelines for the calculation of severance payments and a requirement that the disadvantages for workers must actually be realized.[4] Judicial decisions have further led to firm-specific indices attempting to measure the financial burden placed upon firms.[5] This desire for further legal clarification must be attributed to the fact that the compensation costs are certainly significant in Germany. Hence, according to Hemmer (1988a, pp. 43–4) these costs exceeded gross profits or net investments for 20 per cent of the firms participating in a 1985/86 employer survey. A second study – roughly covering the same time-period – reports compensation costs between 5 and 10 per cent of the firms' revenue in 25 per cent of its sample cases.[6]

Among the list of compensation items – also including occupational pension claims, profit sharing agreements, subsidies for further education, and wage replacement payments for workers shifted to others jobs or unemployed, for instance – severance payments contribute by far the single most important cost factor.[7] Correspondingly, two controversial issues immediately arise. First, the employer's side frequently calls for a cap to be imposed on individual payments, or even an elimination of the respective rules of the BetrVG. Obviously, such proposals meet union criticism claiming that the severance pay allowances still do not compensate fully.[8] This chapter will thus attempt to introduce economic rationality into this apparently politically motivated dispute. Severance pay arrangements are viewed as an implicit contract designed to achieve efficient risk-shifting between retained and dismissed workers. Second, while the judicial majority opinion emphasizes that severance payments must compensate for future losses of dismissed workers,[9] the calculation of such payments is in practice based on employee characteristics such as age, tenure, and mean income attained under the labour contract to be terminated. Hence, section 7.3 will develop a benchmark economic model demonstrating that such computational rules may nevertheless reflect rational future expectations adequately.

7.2 SEVERANCE PAY AND EFFICIENT RISK-SHIFTING

7.2.1 The *ex ante* View Embodied in the Procedural Rules

On first sight, the available – though rather scarce – empirical evidence supports the importance of considering the individual severance pay as a determinant of total costs. Hence, Hemmer (1987, 1988a, p. 62) reports that 26 per cent of these benefits exceeded DM20 000, with an average payment of DM7400 in smaller firms and of DM8800 in larger firms. Over all firms the average worker received a payment amounting to 670 per cent of the monthly gross salary – usually averaged out over the preceding three to twelve months of employment. Hase, von Neumann-Cosel and Rupp (1992) calculate the severance pay–wage ratio for six representative worker types as ranging between 110 per cent (20 years of age, 2 tenure years) and 1210 per cent (55 years of age, 25 tenure years). Given these figures Hemmer (1988b) concludes that such payments often 'overcompensate'[10] and Dichmann (1988) therefore proposes to introduce upper limits. Currently, a legal cap only exists for firms in bankruptcy proceedings – limiting severance pay to 250 per cent of the final income attained.[11] Whether the limit of 1800 per cent derived from § 10 of the 'Dismissal Protection Law' ('*Kündigungsschutzgesetz*' – KSchG) generally also applies to massive layoff cases is still open for dispute.[12] Interestingly, the practice of negotiations shows that, even in cases in which both parties have at one point agreed on an upper limit, the actual payments made usually exceed this limit.[13] This can possibly be attributed to the fact that focusing solely on *ex-post* severance pay realizations in an attempt to decrease the respective labour costs may actually be rather misleading.

According to § 112 BetrVG, negotiations concerning the 'balance of interest' agreement ('*Interessenausgleich*') define whether layoffs must occur, the number of workers to be dismissed, and the layoff process. This must be accompanied by a separate 'social plan' agreement ('*Sozialplan*') which specifies the respective compensation package including severance pay claims. Nevertheless, the legally accepted practice holds that both agreements can be – and usually will be – negotiated simultaneously.[14] This is further stressed by the fact that the residual decision right concerning the 'balance of interest' always remains with the firm while the residual decision right concerning the 'social plan' is shifted towards a neutral third party – the 'conciliation board' ('*Einigungsstelle*') – upon failing to reach an agreement in bilateral negotiations. Thus, a need to reach agreement on both of these matters is maintained. Moreover, the calculation of 'social plan' benefits must always be carried out assuming ongoing 'balance of interest' negotiations – hence, before the layoffs are actually realized.[15] Thus, the legal framework necessarily prescribes an *ex ante* perspective, and severance pay arrangements should therefore be viewed as part of an implicit contract between a firm and all members of its original labour force.

7.2.2 A Very Basic Economic Model

Given the procedural rules, consider the following rather simple model of *ex ante* negotiations yielding a simultaneous determination of the wage income for workers to be retained and severance payments for those to be laid off. In order to concentrate entirely on the induced relative benefit level, assume it has already been agreed to lay off a fraction p of an initial workforce comprising M labourers.[16] The selection of workers to be retained is purely random. All M workers of the group under consideration exhibit identical socio-economic characteristics ruling out a preferential treatment of subgroups as otherwise possibly required by § 95 BetrVG and § 1 KSchG. Retained workers are expected to supply labour $l = 1$. To begin with, dismissed employees are assumed to remain unemployed. Their individual labour supply equals zero. The firm's objective is to choose a wage w and severance payment b such as to minimize total labour costs which can simply be calculated as $W = [(1-p)w + pb]M$.

Labourers share identical preferences over income c and labour supply which can be characterized by the utility function $u = U(c, l)$. The function $U(c, l)$ exhibits the usual properties – in particular, $U_c > 0$, $U_l < 0$, $U_{cc} < 0$, and $U_{ll} \leq 0$. In contracting, the labour representatives are assumed to ensure that the *ex ante* expected utility of a member of the initial workforce $V \equiv (1-p)U(w, 1) + pU(b + x, 0)$, where $x > 0$ denotes an exogenous public unemployment benefit does not fall short of a reservation utility level $\overline{V}$.

Given this participation constraint, solving the respective optimization problem[17] can easily be verified to imply the efficient risk-shifting condition

$$U_c(w^*, l) = U_c(b^* + x, 0), \tag{7.1}$$

with superscript * identifying the optimum. Unless the marginal utilities of income are equalized, redistributing income between employment states would bear the potential of further decreases in total labour costs while holding the workers' expected utility constant. As for the implied income differentials, the following relationship holds:

$$w^* - (b^* + x) = -\frac{U_{cl}(\tilde{c}, \tilde{l})}{U_{cc}(\tilde{c}, \tilde{l})}$$

$$\Rightarrow w^* - (b^* + x) \begin{Bmatrix} > \\ = \\ < \end{Bmatrix} 0, \textit{ if } U_{cl} \begin{Bmatrix} > \\ = \\ < \end{Bmatrix} 0 \tag{7.2}$$

with $(\tilde{c}, \tilde{l})$ defined by the mean value theorem. Obviously, if $U_{cl} < 0$ the efficient severance pay arrangement implies an 'overcompensation' in terms of income received by dismissed as compared to retained workers.

An alternative view may consider utility differentials.[18] Hence, define a reservation wage R^* for dismissed workers by $U(b^* + x, 0) \equiv U(b^* + x + R^*, 1)$.

As is well known

$$\frac{\partial R}{\partial c} = U_{cc}\frac{U_l}{U_c} - U_{cl}\begin{Bmatrix} > \\ = \\ < \end{Bmatrix} 0, \textit{ if labour is} \begin{cases} \textit{normal} \\ \textit{neutral} \\ \textit{inferior} \end{cases} \tag{7.3}$$

Inserting into the efficient risk-shifting condition implies

$$U_c(w^*, 1) = U_c(b^* + x, 0) \equiv U_c(b^* + x + R^*, 1)\,(1 + \frac{\partial R^*}{\partial c})$$

$$\Rightarrow w^* \begin{Bmatrix} > \\ = \\ < \end{Bmatrix} b^* + x + R^*, \textit{ if labour is} \begin{cases} \textit{normal} \\ \textit{neutral} \\ \textit{inferior} \end{cases} \tag{7.4}$$

Concluding dismissed workers will always enjoy a higher utility under efficient risk-shifting, if labour is assumed to be normal. However, the normality of labour is usually taken to constitute a plausible economic assumption.[19]

7.2.3 Second-best Risk-shifting with Uncertain Job Alternatives

According to Witte and Servatin (1983) 53 per cent of the workers questioned upon being dismissed by a southern German firm in 1983 reported experiencing no financial problems at all and 75 per cent did not face a financial crisis. While this may be due to the severance payments received, it also reflects the fact that 35.3 per cent of these workers found alternative employment immediately and another 37.6 per cent after an average search period of eight months. To some extent, these findings are supported by Hemmer (1988a, pp. 74–7) who notes that 46 per cent of the dismissed workers are younger than 40, 25 per cent even younger than 30 years. Hence, the representative dismissed worker should not encounter age-specific labour market problems.[20] Consequently, Vogel (1989) concludes that severance payments are typically seen as a financial 'extra' with little or no relevance for social policy. In particular, these arrangements are seen to conflict with the legal requirement of adequately accounting for the individually realized economic disadvantages of the dismissed.

While an intensive analysis of whether such arrangements may still be viewed as adequate in this sense must be deferred to the next section, it should be recalled that the legal procedural rules actually force the negotiating parties to calculate benefits on an *ex ante* basis prior to the actual layoff decisions. As a first approach towards analysing the effect of alternative income opportunities, suppose that the certain income x introduced above is replaced by uncertain income opportunities $\tilde{x}$ fluctuating over the non-negative interval $X = [x_L, x_U]$ subject to a distribution function $F(\tilde{x})$. The value x_L may clearly be interpreted as a certain unemployment benefit now. Also, assume that the workers' utility function is specified as $U(c, l) = v(c) - g(l)$, with $v' > 0$, $v'' < 0$, $g(1) = G > 0$, and $g(0) = 0$. Hence, the utility function implies normal labour and, if severance payments could be made contingent on the realization of $\tilde{x}$, first-best efficient risk-shifting would imply the equality of income comparing retained and dismissed workers. However, as this cannot be achieved, given the discussion above, the firm must solve

$$Min_{(w,\, b)}[1 - p)w + pb]M$$
$$\textit{subject to: } (1 - p)[v(w) - G] + p \int_X v(b + \tilde{x})dF(\tilde{x})d\tilde{x} \geq \bar{V} \tag{7.5}$$

Investigating the first-order conditions, it is easily seen that second-best risk-shifting now implies

$$v'(w^{**}) = \int_X v'(b^{**} + \tilde{x})dF(\tilde{x}) \tag{7.6}$$

with superscript ** identifying the respective optimal values.[21] Defining $B^{**} = b^{**} + \int \tilde{x} dF(\tilde{x})$ as the expected income of a dismissed worker, a second-order Taylor-approximation reveals

$$\int_X v'(b^{**} + \tilde{x})dF(\tilde{x}) - v'(B^{**}) = v'''(B^{**}) \int_X [(b^{**} + \tilde{x}) - B^{**}]^2 dF(\tilde{x}) \tag{7.7}$$

Again, plausibility considerations concerning the sign of v''' can be derived from standard economic theory. Thus, the well-known Arrow-Pratt measure of absolute risk-aversion $A(c) \equiv -v''(c)/v'(c)$ is generally assumed to decrease with income.[22] However,

$$A'(c) = -\frac{v'''(c)v'(c) - [v''(c)]^2}{[v'(c)]^2} \tag{7.8}$$

Consequently, $v''' > 0$ is necessary for decreasing absolute risk-aversion. The second-best risk-shifting condition can then easily be verified to imply that the expected income of dismissed workers will exceed the certain income of retained labourers in this case.

7.3 COMMON SEVERANCE PAY RULES

7.3.1 Legal Requirements and Business Practice

Although admittedly simple, the previous analysis has made very clear that efficient risk-shifting rules will induce an 'overcompensation' of dismissed workers whenever severance pay arrangements constitute part of an implicit *ex ante* contract. This holds both in terms of income and utility differentials given the economically plausible assumptions of normal labour and decreasing risk-aversion. While the *ex ante* perspective constitutes a legal necessity, the question of whether to base the actual calculations on worker characteristics associated with her/his work history within the firm is still under dispute. Both § 112 of the BetrVG, requiring firms to account for future labour market opportunities, and the judicial majority opinion, generally support a future orientation – the latter only additionally allowing for attributes derived from the workers' past to enter the calculations.[23] Yet the law contains only a few hints concerning the concrete characteristics to be considered. Indirectly, § 3, no. 9 of the 'Income Tax Law' ('*Einkommensteuergesetz*' – EStG) provides a benchmark by specifying tax exemptions for severance payments which increase with age and tenure attained under the terminated labour contract. Court, decisions also regularly emphasize age and tenure as the most important attributes to be included.[24]

In business practice the most commonly used calculation method is the so-called 'multiplicative formula'. Individual severance allowances result as the sum of a fixed payment and a past-period average income – the latter most commonly multiplied with the product of age and tenure divided by a figure which then again decreases with age. As this income multiplier, the fixed payment usually also increases with both age and tenure. Furthermore, in the majority of cases utilizing the so-called 'table method' for benefit calculations the procedure is virtually identical. A difference only arises due to the fact that there exists a table of age and tenure specific income multipliers. Only a minority of 'social plans' – either using a 'table method' or the so-called 'additive formula'[25] – does not include income-based calculations – solely specifying age and tenure specific fixed payments. According to Hemmer (1988a, pp. 81–2) and Hase *et al.* (1992, p. 248), 72.5 and 68.6 per cent respectively of the individual severance payments were contingent on income. Further, 98.5 and 99.2 per cent differentiated accounting for tenure and 77.9 and 87.0 per cent for age.

There appears to exist a general understanding that the benefits should increase with age reflecting diminished labour market opportunities.[26] On the other hand, Neumann (1988) and Schellhaaß (1989) agree that the tenure effect must be interpreted as a compensation for bygone firm-specific capital human investments of the workers. Yet this contrasts with a purely future-oriented calculation.[27] Finally, Hase *et al.* (1992, pp. 248–9) criticize the 'discriminatory nature' of the income-contingency of the benefits. Since higher incomes should be associated with superior human capital endowments, they rather indicate improved labour market opportunities. Interestingly the following attempt to economically motivate the existing calculation rule based solely on productivity expectations shows that the tenure and income effects can be derived straightforwardly. At the same time, however, the impact of age should generally be regarded as ambiguous.

7.3.2 A Model based on Productivity Expectations

Within a firm's initial labour-force worker-types are distinguished by referring to their biological age i, $i = (I^E + 1), \ldots, (I^L - 1)$ where I^E, I^L refer to common ages of entering and leaving the economy's workforce respectively, and tenure years completed j, $j = 1, \ldots, [I^L - (I^E + 1)]$, as of date $t = 0$ of the layoff decision. The length of a production period also equals one year. Retained workers will be assumed to be contracted for the entire length of their remaining work-life. The same applies whenever a dismissed worker allocates an alternative employment contract. Hence, the analysis abstracts from explicitly considering future temporary layoff spells. Such future employment risks should affect all employed workers of the economy alike.

Per period revenue from employing a single worker equals

$$y_t^e = K^e[l_t^e + \eta^e + \varepsilon_t^e] \tag{7.9}$$

with superscript $e = \{o, n, a\}$ identifying respectively the old (0), the new (n), or an alternative (a) production environment. Technical production uncertainty is reflected by the disturbance $\varepsilon_t^e \sim N(0, \zeta^2)$, $\forall t$ and $\forall e$, taken to be uncorrelated serially and across production environments. The parameter η^e is associated with a worker's individual productivity. It is *ex ante* random, realized at the beginning of each labour contract and remaining constant over the full length of the contract. The realizations thus reflect labour market matching of individual abilities and firm-specific requirements. For each representative group of workers the unconditional distribution of productivity parameters is given by $N(0, \sigma^2)$. Further, human capital cannot be transferred as workers change firms. Hence, $Cov(\eta^a, \eta^o) = 0$ and $Cov(\eta^a, \eta^n) = 0$. Moreover, $Cov(\varepsilon_t^e, \eta^e) = 0$, $\forall e$ and $\forall t$. However, for continued contracts within the firm the correlation coefficient $\bar{\rho} \equiv \rho(\eta^o, \eta^n) \geq 0$ indicates that previous job experiences are relevant for future productivities. This reflects improved matching within the more narrow borders of the internal labour market, in comparison with the external labour market rather than indicating a transfer of human capital.

The firm has not utilized a particular selection method when hiring workers. Hence, all worker groups are representative in the above sense as of date $t = 0$. However, both firms and workers can use their observances of past individual revenues to calculate a series of signals $\{z_t\}$, with $z_t \equiv [K^o]^{-1} y_t^o - 1 = \eta^o + \varepsilon_t^o$, for $t = 1, \ldots, j$, given that the worker has actually supplied labour $l_t^o = 1$. In the following let $\bar{z} \equiv [j]^{-1} \Sigma_{t=1}^{j} z_t$ and note that

$$\bar{z} = \bar{z}(j) \sim N(0, \sigma^2 + \frac{1}{j}\zeta^2) \tag{7.10}$$

The conditional expectation concerning a retained worker's productivity under the renewed contract can then be obtained as

$$E\{\eta^n | \bar{z}\} = E(\eta^n) \frac{Cov\{\eta^n, \bar{z}\}}{\text{Var}\,\{\bar{z}\}} [E\{\eta^a\} - \bar{z}] \tag{7.11}$$

$$= \bar{\rho} \frac{\sigma^2}{\sigma^2 + \frac{1}{j}\zeta^2} \bar{z} \tag{7.12}$$

following de Groot (1970, p. 167) and Judge *et al.* (1982, pp. 252–5). Note that the respective conditional variance

$$Var\,\{\eta^n | \bar{z}\} = \sigma^2 \left(1 - \rho^{-2} \frac{\sigma^2}{\sigma^2 + \frac{1}{j}\zeta^2}\right) \tag{7.13}$$

only depends on age and tenure without accounting for the realization of the signal $\bar{z}$.

7.3.3 Expected Lifetime Utilities

For simplicity, let the workers' instantaneous utility function be defined by $U(c, l) = -exp\{-r[c - \bar{g}\, l]\}$ with $r, \bar{g} > 0$. All firms in the economy provide linear incentive wages $w_t^e = \alpha_t^e + \beta_t^e y_t^e$. Let

$$\Omega_t \equiv s_t + \alpha_t^e + \beta_t^e y_t^e - \bar{g} l_t^e \tag{7.14}$$

denote per-period consumption net of the disutility of labour, with s_t as (dis-) savings. Obviously, choosing the contracts' effort intensities, such that $\beta_t^e = [K^e]^{-1}\bar{g}$ implies that the workers are indifferent with respect to their individual choice of labour supply in which case they are assumed to agree with the firms' intended level $l_t^e = 1$. The risk-neutral firms will claim a fraction γ^e, with $0 \leq \gamma^e < 1$ of each worker's revenue in order to satisfy their shareholders. Hence, an employed worker's per-period expected income is given by $(1 - \gamma^e)E\{y_t^e\}$ and the income variance by $(\bar{g}[K^e]^{-1})^2 Var(y_t^e)$.

Now, consider a retained worker and assume that the subjective discount rate δ matches the market discount rate of a perfect capital market. If wealth as of the decision date 0 equals zero, and no wealth is shifted towards retirement, the optimal per-period saving s_t clearly equals zero as well.[28] Hence, accounting for the properties of the exponential utility function and the normal distribution derive the per-period certainty equivalent income – with expectations taken as of date 0 – as

$$C_R^c(\bar{z}(j)) \equiv (1 - \gamma^n)K^n \left(1 + \frac{\bar{\rho}\sigma^2\bar{z}(j)}{\sigma^2 + \frac{1}{j}\zeta^2}\right)$$

$$- \frac{r_g^{-2}}{2}\left(\zeta^2 + \sigma^2\left(1 - \frac{p^{-2}\sigma^2}{\sigma^2 + \frac{1}{j}\zeta^2}\right)\right) \tag{7.15}$$

and note that the respective expected discounted lifetime utility equals

$$\tilde{V}_R^i(\bar{z})(j)) \equiv -\sum_{t=1}^{IL-i} \delta^{(t-1)} \exp\{-r[c_R^c(\bar{z}(j)) - \bar{g}]\} \tag{7.16}$$

Turning to dismissed workers let ϕ denote the replacement ratio in the public unemployment benefit scheme. In Germany such benefits only replace regularly received labour income. In particular, yearly bonus payments are not replaced. Let this rule imply that the benefits are calculated as a fraction of the workers' historic fixed labour income $\alpha^o = (1 - \gamma^o - \beta^o)K^o$. If there further exists an actuarially fair private unemployment insurance possibility, savings s_t refer to the respective premium and benefit payments. Receiving severance payments $A^i(\bar{z}(j))$ when being dismissed, intertemporal optimization then yields an expected discounted lifetime utility.[29]

$$\widetilde{V}_D^i(A^i(\overline{z}(j))) \equiv -\sum_{t=1}^{IL-i} \delta^{(t-1)} exp\Big\{-r\Big(\sum_{t=1}^{IL-i} \delta^{(t-1)}\Big)^{-1}\Big[A^i(\overline{z}(j))$$

$$+\sum_{t=1}^{IL-i} \delta^{(t-1)} Q_t(i)\Big((1-\gamma^a)K^a - \overline{g} - \frac{r\overline{g}^2}{2}(\sigma^2+\zeta^2)\Big)$$

$$+\sum_{t=1}^{IL-i} \delta^{(t-1)}(1-Q_t(i)\,\phi\,(1-\gamma^o-\beta^o)K^o\Big]\Big\} \quad (7.17)$$

Note that, the per-period income expression in this case constitutes a weighted sum of the certainty equivalent income if being re-employed and the certain public unemployment benefit. The weight $Q_t(i)$ denotes the age-specific re-employment probability as of date 0 which – assuming no labour market discrimination – can be calculated from the respective unemployment rates in the economy. Finally, it appears plausible to assume that the change of the production environment which takes place in the firm equalizes the expected wage income of an average retained worker and the expected wage income which can be attained in alternative employments. Hence, $(1-\gamma^n)K^n = (1-\gamma^a)K^a$.

7.3.4 The Induced Severance Pay Calculations

As seen before, the neutrality of labour, constant absolute risk-aversion and efficient risk-shifting assuming a random retention choice among workers with identical personal characteristics implies an equalization of the marginal expected discounted lifetime utilities. In this case, imposing voluntary participation/separation constraints – hence, requiring an equality of the respective utility levels – yields the same calculation rule for severance pay. However, the true reason for developing such a highly stylized model must be seen in the fact that the induced rule for calculating severance pay claims actually exactly matches the 'multiplicative' method noted to constitute common practice in Germany. Hence, the model exposed should be viewed as an adequate benchmark. In particular, let

$$\Delta C \equiv (1-\gamma^a)K^a - \phi(1-\gamma^o)K^o - \frac{r\overline{g}^2}{2}(\sigma^2+\zeta^2) - (1-\phi)\overline{g} \quad (7.18)$$

define the pure certainty equivalent income disadvantage incurred by a dismissed worker in every future period being unemployed rather than newly hired by an alternative firm. Then the calculation rule for severance pay can easily be derived as

$$A^i(\overline{z}(j)) = \hat{A}^{ij} + B^{ij}\overline{z} \quad (7.19)$$

with fixed payment

$$\hat{A}^{ij} \equiv \sum_{t=1}^{IL-i} \delta^{(t-1)} \left\{ (1 - Q_t(i))\, \Delta C + \frac{r\bar{g}^2\bar{\rho}^2\sigma^4}{2\,(\sigma^2 + \frac{1}{j}\zeta^2)} \right\} \tag{7.20}$$

and multiplier

$$B^{ij} \equiv \sum_{t=1}^{IL-i} \delta^{(t-1)}\, K^n(1 - \gamma^n)\, \frac{\bar{\rho}\sigma^2}{(\sigma^2 + \frac{1}{j}\zeta^2} \tag{7.21}$$

Observe that, due to the linear incentive wage assumption, the worker's average past wage income $w \equiv [j]^{-1}\, \Sigma_{t=1}^{j} w_t$ actually constitutes a linear function of $\bar{z}$ with $\delta\bar{w}/\delta\bar{z} = (1 - \gamma^o)K^o > 0$. Hence, with only slight modification the multiplier derived above can be interpreted as an income multiplier.

Thus, whenever tenure within the firm improves job matching under the new production environment, $\bar{\rho} > 0$, severance pay claims must increase with tenure and the historic level of wage income attained. If, due to very drastic changes in the technology, this does not apply, the claims will be only age-contingent and both tenure and wage effects cannot be motivated. This must be attributed to the fact that the present model solely considers learning-through-tenure about future productivities and perfectly ignores a necessity to compensate for bygone human capital investments. More specifically, the tenure effect on the fixed payment part can be verified to capture the generally decreased future wage-risk of workers with higher tenure. In contrast, the tenure and wage effect on the income multiplier – derived from assuming a positive correlation coefficient – reflects the fact that higher historic incomes more accurately signal superior productivities under the new production environment.

While these results are obvious, the total age effect on severance pay is generally ambiguous. Quite in contrast to empirical findings the income multiplier must decrease with age, however. Clearly, older workers can economize the advantage of being able to signal future productivities upon being retained only over a shorter length of remaining work-life. The same effect also yields a tendency towards lower fixed payments which may, however, be overcompensated by the additional effect of unemployment rates which increase with age. Hence, note that, if unemployment, rates were constant, the fixed payment would also unambiguously decrease with age. On the other hand, setting the discount rate δ equal to zero – such that only the first period after dismissal matters in comparing benefits – increasing age-specific unemployment rates will always imply higher fixed payments for older workers. More generally, lower discount rates, strongly increasing age-specific unemployment rates, and a rather significant labour market income disadvantage ΔC contribute a tendency to increase the fixed payment with age. However, this trades off against the income risk reduction effect of retainment. For actual calculations these qualifications must therefore be carefully assessed given the labour market facts when determining whether total benefits should increase as well.

7.4 CONCLUDING COMMENTS

In addition to introducing the basic principles of institutionalized severance pay negotiations as laid out in the German 'Industrial Relations Law', the current paper has discussed two controversial issues which arise when this legal framework is applied. First, since the available evidence suggests the existence of rather significant labour force adjustment costs with severance pay claims constituting the single most important cost item, the proposition to impose legal caps on individual payments frequently reoccurs in the political sphere. However, the procedural rules implied by the law require that severance pay must be determined *ex ante* – prior to the actual layoffs – and generally support simultaneous negotiations of the adjustments within the firm and the benefits extended to those to be dismissed. However, under economically plausible assumptions – for example, the normality of labour in the workers' utility function and decreasing absolute risk-aversion – 'overcompensating' severance pay has been shown to result from efficient risk-shifting between retained and dismissed members of an initial workforce. Hence, despite apparently generous severance pay awards, law-makers will be ill advised to introduce upper limits on such payments. If binding, the caps will only generate deviations from the efficient risk-shifting rule, necessarily implying higher total adjustment costs.

When bilateral negotiations do not reach agreement or firms have not complied with legal procedural rules,[30] third parties have to decide on the compensation for dismissed workers. The judicial majority opinion holds that severance pay calculations must generally be carried out prospectively – accounting only for future losses of the individual worker, while the business practice usually associates higher ages, tenure, and wage income with increased benefits. There appears to exist an understanding that the age effect compensates for diminished labour market opportunities. The impact of tenure is usually rationalized by pointing at firm-specific human capital investments of workers which, however, have been acquired over past employment periods. Moreover, this argument, would rather imply a negative tenure effect, since more returns on initial investments would already have been collected over post production periods. Finally, the income effect is critically seen as ' discriminatory'. In contrast, the analysis of section 7.3 – intentionally ignoring human capital investments by workers – has shown that both positive tenure and income effects can still be motivated economically, if tenure improves the quality of job matching in the firm's internal labour market. Yet the impact of age is generally ambiguous, since diminished labour market opportunities must always be balanced against the fact that older workers are characterized by a shorter length of remaining work-life. Hence, whatever the disadvantage associated with unemployment, the maximum length of time over which this burden must possibly be incurred is certainly shorter. Although the model from which these results have been derived is rather specific – yielding the 'multiplicative' calculation rule most commonly applied, however – these arguments should be judged qualitatively robust.

NOTES

1. For an international overview see Emerson (1988).
2. Directive 75/129/EEC.
3. German laws will generally be referred to by their official abbreviation in the following.
4. Both changes enacted in 1985 – the latter in the 'Law for the Promotion of Employment' ('*Arbeitsförderungsgesetz*').
5. Targan (1993) provides an account of such figures in use by courts.
6. Hase *et al.* (1989).
7. Compare Vogel (1989), Von Hoyningen-Huene (1990, p. 314), Zöllner and Loritz (1992, p. 535), and Fitting and Kaiser (1996, p. 1738) for instance.
8. Hase *et al.* (1989).
9. Zöllner and Loritz (1992, p. 535), Popp (1993), Fitting and Kaiser (1996, pp. 1734–5).
10. Accounting for the existing social security standards in Germany, Vogel (1989) even suggests that severance pay arrangements are regularly superfluous.
11. § 2 of the 'Law on Social Plans in Bankruptcy and Composition Proceedings' (*Gesetz über den Sozialplan in Konkurs- und Vergleichsverfahren*').
12. Von Hoyningen-Huene (1990, p. 316),
13. Schellhaaß (1989) notes that the same applies to the legal limit for firms filing for bankruptcy.
14. Von Hoyningen-Huene (1990, pp. 311–12), Fitting and Kaiser (1996, p. 1723).
15. Fitting and Kaiser (1996, p. 1737).
16. Since the problem of determining an optimal employment level is not addressed, it should be noted that the current analysis is compatible with Fabel (1990b) deriving efficient production rules given uncertain product demand, for instance.
17. Wolfstetter *et al.* (1984) show that the respective dual problem of maximizing the workers' expected utility subject to a labour cost constraint yields qualitatively identical results.
18. Also see Wolfstetter (1985) and Fabel (1990a, pp. 68–71).
19. Stiglitz (1984) also notes the existing 'overcompensation problem' which arises in this case.

20. This must be qualified, however, as the German 'Federal Labour Office' ('*Bundesanstalt für Arbeit*') notes significant age and industry-specific differences in the layoff infliction rates. See Hemmer (1988a, pp. 105–109).
21. Similar conditions are investigated by Kahn (1985) and Moore (1985).
22. See Arrow (1964) himself, for instance.
23. Von Hoyningen-Huene (1990, p. 313), Zöllner and Loritz (1992, p. 535), Popp (1993), and Fitting and Kaiser (1996, pp. 1734–5).
24. Popp (1993) and Fitting and Kaiser (1996, pp. 1735–8).
25. The widely used distinction of 'multiplicative', 'additive', and 'table' methods stems from Gessner and Plett (1982).
26. Hase *et al.* (1989, 1992 – p. 250).
27. Further, note that recent empirical findings do not support the existence of significant human capital investments by workers. See Knoll and Koss (1995).
28. This assumption only serves to simplify the argument. In order to maintain the qualitative results it would actually only be necessary to let optimal savings equalize the per-period expected utilities of consumption.
29. Again, no wealth is shifted towards retirement. Explicit derivations are omitted due to space limitations. The authors will be pleased to supply a treatment of the intertemporal optimization problem upon request, however.
30. By § 113 BetrVG the labour side then acquires the right to demand a 'Compensation of Disadvantage' ('*Nachteilsausgleich*').

REFERENCES

Arrow, K.J. (1964), 'The role of securities in the optimal allocation of risk-bearing', *Review of Economic Studies*, **31**, 91–6.

De Groot, M.H. (1970), *Optimal Statistical Decisions*, New York: McGraw-Hill.

Dichmann, W. (1988), 'Die Problematik des Sozialplans', *Wirtschaftsdienst*, **88** (11), 98–104.

Emerson, M. (1988), 'Regulation or deregulation of the labour market – policy regimes for the recruitment and dismissal of employees in the industrialized countries', *European Economic Review*, **32**, 775–817.

Fabel, O. (1990a), *Insurance and Incentives in Labour Contracts*, Frankfurt-am-Main: Hain.

Fabel, O. (1990b), 'Implicit contracts with effort incentives', *Journal of Economics – Zeitschrift für Nationalökonomie*, **52**, 25–42.

Fitting, K. and H. Kaiser (1996), *Betriebsverfasstungsgesetz: Handkommentar*, Munich: Vahlen, (18th edn).

Gessner, V. and K. Plett (1982), *Der Sozialplan im Konkursunternehmen*, Cologne: Bundesanzeiger.

Hase, D., R. von Neumann-Cosel and R. Rupp (1989), '"Weit oberhalb der Belastungsgrenze" oder "welt unterhalb eines angemessenen Nachteilsausgleichs" – Zwei Untersuchungen zur Sozialplanpraxis', *Die Mitbestimmung*, (1), Beilage.

Hase, D., R. von Neumann-Cosel and R. Rupp (1992), *Handbuch Interessenausgleich und Sozialplan*, Cologne: Bund-Verlag.

Hemmer, E. (1987), 'Welt oberhalb der Belastungsgrenze – Zwischenresultate einer IW-Studie über Sozialpläne und ihre Auswirkungen', *Gewerkschaftsreport*, **87** (3), 13–17.

Hemmer, E. (1988a), *Sozialplanpraxis in der Bundesrepublik Deutschland – Eine empirische Untersuchung*, Cologne: Deutscher Institutsverlag.

Hemmer, E. (1988b), 'Sozialpläne (I) – Theorie der Sozialpläne', *Der Arbeitgeber*, **40** (21), 790–94.

Judge, G.G., R.C. Hill, W. Griffiths, H. Lütkepohl and T.-C. Lee (1982), *An Introduction to the Theory and Practise of Econometrics*, New York: Wiley.

Kahn, C. M. (1985), 'Optimal severance pay with incomplete information', *Journal of Political Economy*, **93**, 435–51.

Knoll, L. and B. Koss (1995), 'Spezifisches Humankapital: ökonomische Theorie und betriebliche Praxis', *Zeitschrift für Personalforschung*, (4), 401–15.

Moore, J. (1985), 'Optimal labour contracts when workers have a variety of privately observed reservation wages', *Review of Economic Studies*, **52**, 37–67.

Neumann, H. (1988), 'Effiziente Entlassungen durch Sozialpläne?', *Jahrbücher für Nationalökonomie und Statistik*, **205**, 506–18.

Popp, G.J. (1993), 'Abfindungen aus dem Arbeitsverhältnis – Rechtsnatur und Bemessungsgrundlagen', *Der Betrieb*, **46**, 734–6.

Schellhaaß, H.-M. (1989), 'Sozialpläne aus ökonomischer Sicht', *Zeitschrift für Arbeitsrecht*, **20**, 167–207.

Stiglitz, J.E. (1984), 'Theories of wage rigidity', *NBER Working Paper*, (1442).

Targan, N. (1993), 'Wirtschaftliche Vertretbarkeit von Sozialplänen', *Arbeit und Arbeitsrecht*, **93** (2), 42–4.

Vogel, O. (1989), 'Rahmenbedingungen für personelle Umstrukturierungen', *Zeitschrift für betriebswirtschaftliche Forschung*, **41**, 883–95.

Von Hoyningen-Huene, G. (1990), *Betriebsverfassungsrecht*, Munich: Beck, 2nd edn.

Witte, E. and K. Servatin (1983), *Berufliche, soziale und persönliche Auswirkungen der Entlassung von Arbeitnehmern – Eine Fallstudie*, Düsseldorf: Deutsche Gesellschaft für Personalfürhrung, (53).

Wolfstetter, E. (1985), 'Contract theory and involuntary unemployment: a review', *Discussion Papers on Political Economy*, Freie Universität Berlin, (3).

Wolfstetter, E., M. Brown and G. Meran (1984), 'Optimal employment and risk sharing in Illyria: the labour managed firm reconsidered', *Zeitschrift für die gesamte Staatswissenschaft – Journal of Institutional and Theoretical Economics*, **140**, 655–68.

Zöllner, W. and K.-G Loritz (1992), *Arbeitsrecht*, Munich: Beck, 4th edn.

8. The codetermined corporation as a player in the labour market

Jürgen G. Backhaus

8.1 INTRODUCTION

On October 22, the *Wall Street Journal Europe* ran the following story on Daimler Benz:

> Frankfurt – Top officials of Daimler-Benz AG will attempt to smooth out differences over the German company's future management structure today, but a final decision might well be delayed until next year, company officials said.
>
> The routine meeting of Daimler's four man steering committee comes amid growing impatience among the company's management with the discord within their ranks.
>
> Daimler Chairman Juergen Schrempp is championing a merger of the holding company with automobile maker Mercedes-Benz AG, its biggest unit, in order to streamline management and expedite decision-making within the group. Mercedes Chairman Helmut Werner and worker representatives reportedly oppose Mr. Schrempp's plans, arguing that they would slam workers' morale amid a critical drive to diversify its products and markets.
>
> Neither Mr. Schrempp nor Mr. Werner would comment on the restructuring proposals, but Karl Feuerstein, chairman of Daimler's in-house works council and deputy chairman of its supervisory board, told the Reuters news service that Mercedes must under no circumstances be split up along business lines in any restructuring. 'We will measure all proposals according to this demand,' Mr. Feuerstein said. 'We must discuss this comprehensively in the supervisory board. Maybe the decision won't be taken this year,' he added.
>
> Mr. Feuerstein is one of two employee representatives on the steering committee, which also includes Hilmar Kopper, the chairman of Deutsche Bank AG – Daimler's biggest shareholder with a 24.3% stake – and a lawyer who represents other financial backers of the group.

> Both sides are said to be keen on keeping Mr. Werner behind the wheel at Mercedes, which provides 80% of the sales and most of the profits for Daimler, a transportation group with interests in aerospace engineering, telecommunications and financial services. German media have reported that Mr. Werner threatened to resign if Mercedes were to be swallowed by Daimler.

With a few broad brushes, the story shows how different is decision making in German corporate board rooms from similar processes elsewhere, for instance in the United States. To begin with, boards are split into two, the managing and the supervisory board. Works councils elect the powerful chairmen, who can end up on supervisory boards and more importantly, the steering committees. In addition, investment bankers may join forces with employee representatives in controlling management appointments. How did this system come about, which events shaped it, and why is it being continued by globally operating companies? In other respects, this same company has been a leader in introducing deep changes in the world of German corporations, leading the way to being listed on the New York stock exchange and therefore obliging with the requisite SEC as well as EC rules on corporate accountability. In fact, the company now uses two competing accounting systems for the consumption of German and US stockholders respectively.

For a law and economics contribution this chapter has a peculiar structure. Not only does the argument jump back and forth between factual and theoretical themes; the design of the chapter is to arrive at a particular model (bonding) by demonstrating, not simply assuming, that the codetermination system makes sense. This is done in great detail with respect to the different institutional turning points and the historical starting point. This 'making sense' can scarcely be translated into the suggestion that codetermination is a single solution, the optimal solution or in fact the only efficient solution that could be arrived at given the specific circumstances which have to be held responsible for the ultimate outcome. However, the main point of the argument is that codetermination is clearly a viable outcome that has many efficient characteristics. Some critics have suggested that the chapter is overly optimistic with respect to codetermination as a model of firm governance. However, that is nowhere stated here. The chapter only suggests that codetermination is a viable system that reflects highly peculiar circumstances under which bonding became sensible as a solution. Nowhere is a suggestion ventured that codetermination as a system can be exported into different legal, economic and cultural environments. It may even be impossible to do so, if an effort were tried.

On the other hand, codetermination as a highly peculiar system of governance does reveal certain strengths which no other system of firm governance knows. In particular, it is extremely well fitted for an environment that knows a strong and taxing state which is also expected to provide a substantial piece of infrastructure on which the codetermined firm in fact relies. It is also a system of firm governance which takes into account that labour mobility is low. Finally, it is a system that enables all its participants to take a very long view of investment decisions, not only in productive capital in the firm, but also in the environment, the infrastructure and last, but by no means least, the human capital investment.

8.2 ANTECEDENTS OF CODETERMINATION

With the exception of the economic theory of the labour managed firm, little consideration has been given to understanding how a codetermined corporation behaves as a player in the labour market. Codetermination does not imply labour management, which is why the economic theory of labour managed firms is not applicable to codetermined corporations.

Codetermination has a long intellectual and legislative history in Germany. The issue was already discussed by the very first democratic German parliament which gathered in the Frankfurt Church of Saint Paul in 1848. Still during the First World War, the first legislative measures were taken. The Weimar constitution of post-World War I republican Germany, in article 165, introduced codetermination both at the plant level as well as beyond, as regional, industry-wide and central councils were to be formed. The specific feature of adding labour representatives to the supervisory board was first established in an act passed on February 15, 1922. The notion of establishing councils carried through the ideas of the German November revolution of 1918 which led to the collapse of the German empire and the demise of German monarchies.

After the second World War, the situation was completely different. Not only had the organizations of German statehood collapsed, the country itself lay in ruins and her productive capacity had been largely destroyed with plants being damaged, the workforce dispersed and slowly returning often disabled, and an allied de-industrialization policy being added on top which found its most obvious form in the large scale demountation of German industrial infrastructure including plants, machinery and equipment and railroad equipment. In the population there reigned a widespread belief that not only were political forces to blame for the catastrophe, but that, in addition, the economic constitution of pre-war Germany had enabled the political leadership to conduct its disastrous policies. As gradually a German statehood was re-establishing itself, the newly established states that would later form the Federal

Republic adopted constitutions which typically established forms of worker participation if not outright socialization of industry, such as was provided in the constitution of the State of Hesse (article 41). This article transferred into forms of social property the entire mining industries, companies being involved in the production of iron and steel, the entire energy sector and all forms of public transportation requiring either rail or suspended power lines, such as an electrified railroad, a tram or a trolley bus. It is interesting to note that, since energy and public transportation were already in the public domain, the article supported by 71.9 per cent of the voting population in a separate referendum, has not only a socialist but also an antistatist slant. The mining, iron and steel industries, on the other hand, had previously been predominantly private sector activities. From the point of view of codetermination, it is interesting to look at the corporate governance structures finally suggested in the organization act required by the constitution. The act foresaw two levels of corporate governance. At the plant level, control would be shared by representatives of the workers, representatives of the municipality where the plant was located and representatives of a state holding entity, to which all the socialized corporations belonged. This tripartite representation was to be on equal terms. The holding entity, on the other hand, was to have a tripartite governance structure again, with the first third of governors being elected by the Trade Union Federation of the State of Hesse, the second third being proportionately elected by the Federations of the State of Hesse of the Cities, the Counties and the Municipalities (a city being part of a county), and the remaining third being elected by the State Parliament on the one hand and appointed by the Ministries of Economic Affairs, Labour Relations and Finance on the other.

Two ideas clearly underlie this scheme of a corporate governance structure of the socialized key industries of the State of Hesse. The first idea is the notion of involving all kinds of stakeholders in the corporation; the workers, the local municipalities, the counties and cities; that is, all those who had to provide for the proper infrastructure in which the corporation was to thrive. The second idea is the notion that decisions be taken as much at the plant level as possible, with the entire set of socialized industries being subject to a very loose state guidance, which can only indicate but never direct (never more than one third of the vote). An idea prominently absent from this proposed set of governance structures is the notion that corporate governance could rely on markets, such as capital markets, markets for managers or other markets for corporate control.[1]

8.3 THE SITUATION IN 1949

On August 14, 1949, the first parliament in West Germany was elected. It had a large spectrum of parties: the Communists and the Social-Democrats, still pushing for a centrally planned economy; the Bavarian Party and Centre Party representing segments of the Catholic population; the Christian Social Union from Bavaria; the Christian Democratic Party and the Free Democratic Party standing for market values; the mildly conservative German Party from Lower Saxony continuing the long tradition of the 'Welfen' [Ghibellines] in Hanover; the Federation of Refugees and the Dispossessed (BHE), the National Conservative All German Party and the Socialist All German Party, covering the spectrum from left to right. Later, the constitutional court would forbid the Communist Party and the Socialist All German Party as not operating within the premise of the Basic Law (Grundgesetz) of 1949. With a hair thin majority of one vote, the first Chancellor Konrad Adenauer was elected on September 15, and could be appointed by the new President who had just been elected on September 12. Thus, a broad centre–right coalition government was formed which included as yet no Minister of Foreign Affairs. Even prior to electing a chancellor, thereby forming a government, the Parliament had initiated its work by passing the following resolution introduced by the faction of the Social Democratic Party:

> Petition of the faction of the Social Democratic Party.
>
> Reference: Demountations.
>
> The Bundestag is requested to decide: The German Bundestag states that the continuing demountations prevent the reconstitution of the German economy and amount to an insupportable burden on the new democratic state. …
>
> The Bundestag hopes that the governments of France, Great Britain and the United States of America will expedite a re-examination of the demountation lists and, as long as a full review has not been completed, will stop the current demountations.[2]

The grim climate in the industrial heartlands of Germany in the Autumn of 1949 is well expressed by the communist MP Paul, who even speaks of an acceleration of demountation efforts and conflicts between the demountation teams and the workers at these sites so fierce that in the case of the Gelsenberg mine both state and local police had to get involved. But the issue remained beyond the jurisdiction of the parliament, which is why in this instance the matter was referred to the parliament's committee on occupation and foreign affairs.[3]

This forms part of the backdrop for the unusual petition on the part of the joint faction of the Christian Democratic and Christian Social Union asking the government, of which these parties were the two leading partners, to introduce legislation covering the legal relationships between workers and employers in accordance with the coalition programme introduced in the parliament on 20 September 1949. The new legislation was to replace the works council legislation of the Allied Control Council as well as state legislation and introduce 'according to an order that befits our times, the codetermination right of workers once and for all'.[4]

What might have driven this unusual petition – the leading faction petitioning its own administration to introduce a piece of legislation that only weeks ago it had formally announced as a priority? At first blush this is by no means obvious. In presenting the petition, the speaker for the joint faction of the Christian Democratic and Christian Social Union first offered a historical review of German codetermination starting in 1920. He then put forward a reason that is suggested to have triggered the initiative. The Allied Control Council had passed with act number 22 a framework legislation which, in the different zones, had been implemented differently. These implementation rules were, however, suspended by the allied powers as having become the prerogative of the newly established German parliament. Thus, a kind of legislative vacuum had been created, which the Christian Democrats saw a need to fill. He concluded by arguing strongly for the continuation of those institutions in which the labour representatives in recent times had shown their ability to take responsibility for economic decisions.[5]

The ensuing debate involved speakers of the Social Democrats, the Communists and the (promarket) Free Democrats. All three speakers supported the initiative. On the left side, the Communists preferred, however, building on the provisions of the state constitutions, of which we have already noted the Hessean example. The Social Democrats squarely supported the initiative, and also the speaker of the Free Democrats did so. In the margin, he noted that even without this initiative the government would shortly have introduced the relevant legislation, and that, although he broadly supported the idea of codetermination, there was room for disagreement about details. Yet, specifically, he mentions both the institutions of works councils and the general notion of codetermination ('Mitbestimmung') as being what his party intended to support. Petition number 117 then passed with an 'overwhelming' majority.

The details proved to be thorny indeed. It took more than a year until, on February 9 1951, the Chancellor introduced an act about the codetermination ('Mitbestimmung') of workers in companies in mining and iron and steel production, on the same day that the Bundesrat, the representation of the states that constitute the Federal Republic, had passed the government's draft act. The Bundesrat then acted under the chairmanship of the Prime Minister of the State of Northrhine Westfalia, the location of the West German industrial heartlands. The chairmanship of the Federal Council (Bundesrat) changes on a biannual basis between the Prime Ministers of the Federal German States. Accordingly, the chairman acted within weeks of assuming his position.

The animated debate on February 14 1951 extends over some 30 pages of the official register.[6] The entire event shows a sense of great haste. The Chancellor himself introduced the act, being interrupted several times, mostly by the Communists but also from the right. He variously received applause from the Social Democrats, his own faction and, according to the minutes, a not clearly specified 'right'. The official motivation for the legislation was still lacking, it had not yet been printed and distributed. The members of parliament worked on the basis of the printed draft act, the changes requested by the Federal Council and the oral presentations. After the Chancellor had spoken, the Minister of Labour Relations (responsible for this legislation) read the official motivation but dared not depart from the written text which provoked sarcastic criticism from the Social Democrats (Dr. Schumacher).

The Chancellor's speech consisted of essentially three points. He first explained the circumstances under which the legislation had been introduced. The Minister of Economic Affairs, he said, when asked in a committee about the future representation of workers in the mining and iron and steel industry, once Allied legislation would have to be substituted by German legislation, had given an answer that had led worker representatives, but in particular the trade unions, to the conclusion that he wanted to take away from them the rights they now possessed. However, the Chancellor said, the Minister of Economic Affairs strongly denied that what he intended to say could have been interpreted this way, 'this restlessness has spread and led to those notices (of labour agreements of trade unions and companies) being served that first occurred in the iron and steel industry, later in mining' (p. 4431). Under German law, before a strike can occur, these notices have to be served. The Chancellor continued by saying that from the very start he had pointed out that as this was not a dispute in the realm of collective bargaining, a strike 'against the constitutional body of legislation' could not be allowed to take place. Yet, the Chancellor said, he had also pointed out how in his experience the policies of the German Trade Union Congress had always been moderate.

Secondly, the Chancellor reviewed the recent history of worker representation in the mining and iron and steel industry, notably in the Rhineland and Westfalia. He emphasized the rights granted to the worker representatives there, and by the occupation powers, by act of 1947, stressing that it was a specific, and not a general, arrangement. Finally, and in conclusion, the Chancellor emphasized the important role that workers and the representatives had played in fighting the demountations. On numerous occasions, the Chancellor pointed out, he was impressed by the deep affection the workers had displayed towards their plants.

A central feature of German post-World War II codetermination is its strict reliance on the two tier system as far as the aspect of corporate governance is concerned, next to the system of works councils that, of course, emphasizes issues of plant organization. Obviously, most corporations in this range comprise many different plants with many different work-related arrangements and challenges. The mountain and steel related codetermination act of 1951 is different in that, next to the supervisory board of the corporation, the managing board also has an element of worker representation, in that one of the three or more managing directors, the one with personnel and labour relations in his portfolio, was to be appointed with a majority of the votes of the worker representatives on the supervisory board, and he was to work on equal terms with his colleagues in the governing board. The most interesting portion of the speech by the Labour Minister, who was in charge of this legislation, concerns this very point, and he was actually pressed by the chairman of the Social Democratic Party to emphasize and clarify the position of the so-called Labour Director (Arbeitsdirektor), which he did.

The parliamentary debate of the act (in the first reading) lasted for only three hours. Yet, all the relevant arguments necessary to explain codetermination as a result of the specific conditions in Germany were made. In what seems to be a generous use of arithmetic, the speaker had assigned 36 minutes to each of the major factions and 15 to each of the smaller factions, there being only two major factions, the Social Democrats and the joint faction of the Christian Democratic and Christian Social Unions. The speaker for the Social Democratic Party, Mr. Imig, started the debate with an interesting review of the recent history of codetermination. He revealed that on January 19, 1947, Dr. Jarres, the chairman of the supervisory board of the steelmaker Klöckner, suggested to the trade union (here the metal union) the following: 'We here at Klöckner think that a new arrangement must be found for the iron industry that fits the changed times: and that there should be a practical parity, i.e. an equal representation, but also equal responsibility of capital and labour.' Specifically, he wanted to realize this parity in the supervisory board of the Klöckner works.[7] On the same day, a similar suggestion was made by Dr. Reusch and Dr. Hilbert, both members of the board of the Gute Hoffnung mine. And thirdly, on January 21, 1947, Dr. Hillman of the steel company Otto Wolff followed suit.

Secondly, the speaker pointed out that codetermination is also about political control, as the workers had not yet forgotten that the product of their work had been used against themselves, suggesting that at least the last war could have been prevented had codetermination already been introduced.

Thirdly, he pointed out that the workers, on the basis of the Allied acts number 75 and number 27, had gathered the requisite experience that they would now need.

Different Christian Democrat speakers added no substantively new information. The first speaker emphasized a broad consensus on which the act had been based, the issue of parity, again, and the solution to realize this parity in the supervisory board. Later, a second Christian Democrat speaker, himself the member of a supervisory board of a mine in Haspe, confirmed the account of the origin of the codetermination idea and added that the Allied policies of decomposing large conglomerates (Entflechtung) had also played a role in this decision (p. 4446). The first Christian Democrat speaker, by the way, had this interesting sentence in his remarks: 'A sensible application of codetermination can, as we know from experience, increase both productivity and the creditworthiness of the corporations concerned' (p. 4441).

The speakers of the Free Democrats, a coalition partner, were the most critical of the codetermination initiative. Points of interest are: the idea that there may be a certain tension with article 14 of the German Basic Law which guarantees private property, that the strike threat by the unions puts the parliament under duress and that article 105 of the penal code would therefore be relevant. Also, and importantly, one of the speakers (Dr. Becker) outlined the following essentials of the Free Democrats with respect to codetermination:

1. Complete codetermination in all social matters;
2. Participation in hiring and firing;
3. Consultation in all economic affairs in commissions of which thirty per cent are labour representatives;
4. Thirty per cent of labour representation on the supervisory boards;
5. All labour representatives must be employed in the firm itself (i.e. no external trade union representatives).

We see then, that even the most pro-market political party supported codetermination to a very great extent.

A Christian Social Union speaker (Dr. Semler) quoted the constitution of his home state of Bavaria which required codetermination, in support of codetermination. A speaker for the mildly conservative Ghibelline German Party supported codetermination above all with a view to social peace. A speaker for the Bavarian Party was not critical of the act itself, but of the trade union tactics that had brought it about and he was anxious to avoid a repetition of this scenario. The speaker for the Catholic Centre Party found that codetermination was the basic requirement for a new social and economic order. The speaker for the Federation of Refugees and the Dispossessed emphasized the 'divine right to private property' and was therefore critical of the role of the trade unions, rather wishing more co-entrepreneurship. The Socialist All German Party speaker linked the notion of codetermination and participation in the company profit: in a crafty mélange of different facets, he was trying to emphasize discord in the governing coalition. Similarly, the member of the Communists (Agatz) placed the act already in the context of the Cold War and a possible German rearmament, but he also quite accurately depicted the way in which the workers and their representatives took an active part in the post-war reconstruction of not only plants but also corporations. He felt that codetermination was a way to engage workers in the firms so that they could find their codetermined companies worth defending (p. 4458), implying that this might be a military defence.

Finally, the arch-conservative speaker for the All German Party also emphasized codetermination through co-entrepreneurship and was likewise critical of the role ascribed to the trade unions in the draft act.

After the debate was over, apparently reasonably on time, there was a certain amount of procedural manoeuvring. It is, however, noteworthy that a speaker for the Free Democrats, 'in the interest of expediting the procedure' (p. 4460) suggested that the draft act should only be sent to two committees, the Committee for Finance and Tax Matters (in the United States the Ways and Means Committee) and, in a subordinated way, to the Committee of Justice. This proposal was then accepted without any dissent. The final act passed with an overwhelming majority, (only fifty votes not being cast in its favour).

8.4 SHIFTING CONSTRAINTS 1946–1947–1948–1951

The sequence of events in post-World War II Western Germany is then characterized by the following legal events. In 1946 most of the reconstituting states passed constitutional documents, and most of these documents contain some provision of codetermination. In 1947, various academically trained industry leaders, and we know of at least four, for their respective industries in coal, iron and steel suggested that there be a parity representation of labour and capital in the supervisory boards of the respective companies. This was still under the conditions of an administered economy with no workable currency in place and no access to international capital markets; actually no prospect for any type of capital investment in sight. In 1948 there was the currency reform and, gradually, markets developed which meant that companies could sell their products and have a claim on resources in return, not a claim on resources as a consequence of a plan document. At this point, the consensus on codetermination began to fragment. At least the Free Democrats, still in principle supporting codetermination, thought of market-based forms of participation. Various groups in society were wary of the strong power of the trade unions, this being strong political power but also economic power through the institutions of codetermination. In 1949, however, the government immediately announced its intention to introduce codetermination by act of parliament, and it was encouraged to do so by its own leading coalition partner, the joint faction of the Christian Democratic and Christian Social Union.

In 1950 at the end of the year, and apparently in early 1951 in the middle of the winter, the metal workers' and coal miners' unions threatened to strike if codetermination were not finally passed, at least for their industries. The parliament obliged, and the act was passed with an overwhelming majority.

In this way, the law and economics interpretation of codetermination can take two completely different directions. On the one hand, we could think of the German parliament, still a very young democratic institution, as being forced by the trade unions who were politically strong into a situation whereby they had to decide under duress. A strike threat in the middle of the winter, and memories of the bitter winter of 1946 still being fresh, was no light matter. On the other hand, however, the parliament obliged swiftly: the relevant debate took only three hours, all parties agreed that time was of the essence, and little criticism of the compromised draft act was actually voiced. More significantly, there was no alternative to the legislation proposed. No alternative organization model was seriously being discussed that would satisfy the conditions reasonably unanimously detailed by all the relevant parties. The parliament was not exactly rubberstamping the proposed legislation, but the speakers did not argue from different legislative designs in order to criticize the draft. This insight begets the notion that the act may, under the circumstances, have essentially been without a conceivable alternative. The remainder of this chapter is devoted to exploring this possibility.

In order to do so, let us return to the parliament, still in 1951. There was an episode to follow which was to mar the entire carefully erected edifice.

An interesting afterplay occurred when, in an interpellation with respect to the performance of the Federal Minister of Justice, the social democratic faction asked the Federal Government to state whether the Minister of Justice, 'in either the towns of Goslar or Uslar' had described the freshly passed codetermination legislation as an expression of injustice and suggested that the trade union leaders should be put in jail. The Social Democratic faction asked the government to answer whether, 1. the Minister of Justice had said such things and, 2. whether the government subscribed to his views.[8]

As the reader recalls, the Free Democratic Party, along with other parties, had all along complained that they were being put under duress by the threat of strike in the coal industry; particularly as this had happened before in the winter time (1946) and the consequences of yet another winter without coal were still very fresh in people's memories. Bear in mind that at the time both heating and transportation were dependent on a regular supply of coal, and lack of heat and food during the winter surely meant death for many citizens. The Chancellor himself, in introducing the legislation, had pointed out that he had rejected the threat of a strike already in December, but according to the record it had been repeated sometime in January. During state election campaigns in Lower Saxony, the Minister of Justice campaigning for the Free Democratic Party referred to this recent experience. Under the penal code as cited above, a jail sentence was required for whoever put a legislature under duress. In introducing the interpellation, the speaker for the Social Democratic Party, after reviewing the history of codetermination under Allied control, said this:

> What did the workers in the coal and steel industry actually do? In 1945, they were willing to take full responsibility, they were ready to re-construct our heavily damaged key industries. When their responsible positions in these industries were all of a sudden becoming uncertain, they served notice of their labour agreements to their social partners (the employers) if these social partners would withhold their codetermination right in the future. Is a worker violating the law, if he wants to continue his work only under the condition that he, through his trade union, can be a partner through codetermination in the enterprise? Is the Minister of Justice for forced labour under feudal conditions?[9]

Indeed, nothing new was revealed during the debate except for the fact that the Minister of Justice stood by his words. He, and many others who had campaigned in Northern Germany at that time, felt that the minister was within his rights, as a campaigner, to say what he had said. The fine line between what the minister bound by the Coalition Agreement and the party campaigner can say was clearly brought out in parliament.

Little new emerged from this discourse. After the final speaker, the arch-conservative von Thadden (then the youngest Member of Parliament) had spoken, the speaker declared the agenda 'exhausted', prompting calls from the centre 'for heaven's sake, we too!' (p. 5595). Without further ado, the matter was closed.

8.5 BÖHM'S CRITIQUE

All these debates did not occur in an intellectual vacuum. There was a lively political and literary culture.

There were, in particular, no want of critics of codetermination. Only the most intelligent critiques should be dealt with carefully. After all, codetermination has served one of the less likely leaders of the industrial world, after two crushing defeats on the battlefield, well in regaining its own.

On the face of it, the scheme is an unlikely one. In order to explore the background of its inception, its story can also be told against the background of one of its most fervent critics: Franz Böhm. Böhm's influential study, however, is the often cited complete misunderstanding of what codetermination is about from an economic point of view.

Franz Böhm was not only a scholar, he was also a politician. He left his chair at the University of Freiburg for a chair at the University of Frankfurt, because he felt that Frankfurt would provide him with better chances for political influence. His massive contribution to codetermination, which was published in the scholarly yearbook ORDO, dominated that year's edition, running over 229 printed pages, and can be variously regarded as a scholarly or as a political contribution. I tend to see it more as a political contribution in scholarly disguise. It is not illegitimate for a lawyer to present political arguments as scholarly arguments. Böhm could be a skilful, shrewd and unusually determined politician who would resort to any means available to him in order to further his cause. His finally successful negotiations intended to lead to a reconciliation between the German and the Jewish people give ample evidence of Böhm's character in this respect. Even where we do not agree with him, we should respect the sincerity of his convictions and look for the merits of his arguments.

Böhm is unusually critical of the institution of codetermination, associating all kinds of ills with it, but almost completely neglecting the positive effects that codetermination was expected to have by those who brought about the institution.

For this reason it is sensible to look again at the origin of codetermination as a legislative proposal, since this is the background against which Böhm wrote his article in 1950.

The free German parliament in the three western zones of Germany that were constituted as the Federal Republic of Germany had barely met, when – this is the second printed matter of the entire parliamentary proceedings – on September 7, 1949, the faction of the Social Democratic Party introduced a petition to the governments of France, Great Britain and the United States to re-examine the demountation register, not to consider further demountations and to stop the currently ongoing demountations. The demountations of industrial sites, according to the parliamentary record, had been intensified during recent months and there had been violent clashes between the workers who were seeking to defend *their* machines against the demountation teams that were, by taking down and shipping away the machinery, destroying their working places. Luddites in reverse gear!

It is important to know that this practice was still going on in the industrial heartland of the German Federal Republic, the Rhine–Ruhr region, in the Autumn of 1949 after the new state had already been constituted.

Against this background, we have to see the motion being introduced seemingly superfluously by the faction of the Christian Democratic Union, to which the first chancellor belonged, to ask the government to prepare a codetermination act pursuant to the government programme that had just been presented by the chancellor and defended in parliament. This motion, printed matter number 117, is dated October 1949. The purpose of such legislation was to override state legislation which had been halted by Allied decrees (issued by the Allied Control Council) which had precedence over German law, even over German constitutional (state) law. The motion received a large majority, being in fact supported by all parties from the very left (the Communists) to – located on the right wing – the liberals (the Free Democrats). The Free Democrats emphasized substantial differences in opinion about which codetermination rights would finally be established, but they supported the government move. The Communists, while supporting the government in its move, preferred immediate implementation of the state legislation which had been halted by Allied decree. At that time, Böhm, who was a member of the Christian Democratic Union, was not yet a member of the Bundestag. He became a member of parliament in 1953 in the second legislative period.

If we read Böhm's article from today's point of view without taking this historical background information into account, we cannot really understand why codetermination was ever introduced in Germany. As a matter of fact, Böhm himself postulates (page 143) that the vast majority of the people in their capacity as consumers, subjects under the private law and citizens were opposed to codetermination if only they understood what it was. On the other hand, he saw the unions and the entrepeneurs (I believe he means the managers) as supporters of codetermination, while the workers, to the extent that they were not directly involved in codetermination, were seen by Böhm as indifferent. Interestingly enough, he talks about codetermination of workers in the firm, when indeed codetermination was always supposed to take place at the corporate, not the plant, level.

The heated debate in the first German parliament, which preceded the introduction of codetermination, is somewhat at variance with the unanimous support of the measure as such. In fact, the debate never touched on any of the important issues of how to craft a proper governance structure for those companies that where supposed to be the parts in the engine of growth that should pull Germany out of distress and into democracy and prosperity. Today, if we look at the minutes of the parliamentary sessions, we cannot even see where the conflict could conceivably have been located. The heated rhetoric has a thoroughly empty taste. In fact, no alternatives were ever presented in the parliamentary debate except for the summary reference by the Communists to the state constitutional legislations and here notably to the legislations of the state of Hesse and its socialization article of 1946 and its failed socialization act of 1948. Despite the richness in the German literature on different organizational models for corporate governance, no such alternative landscape had been provided for discussion in the German parliament when codetermination was passed. The stilted conflict over supposed remarks by the Minister of Justice, when the opposition could not even decide where these remarks had actually been made, shows clearly that bones were to be picked that had their origin in a different barnyard.

Having reviewed this parliamentary record in considerable detail, the question that arises is this: Why, if there was such widespread agreement about a particular piece of legislation, was there such hefty debate in parliament at all? Clearly, the speakers were not posturing; they were speaking about clearly identifiable matters that mattered.

Part of the parliamentary record can be explained by the large diversity of factions. The spectrum of political views, after the shattering defeat of Germany and the splintered structure of its statehood, was still very large. How, otherwise, could the Ghibelline Party have its own representation in parliament? Similarly, the Centre Party or the Bavarian Party? Secondly, the appeal of those who had suffered under National Socialism, next to those who had suffered in their health, often visibly by missing limbs, was strong. The leader of the Social Democratic Party had to be supported by an aide as he moved to the podium. Sound minds in badly wounded bodies were in fact discussing the future of German economic order. Yet the interesting thing is that, while they were in large agreement about the future of the German economic order, there was a substantial extent of agreement between the far right and the far left comprising the entire middle including the Free Democrats. The heavy-handed tactics of the metal trade union, then calling the shots in the trade union congress on the one hand, against the background of the heavy-handed tactics of the demountation commissions on the other, gave the entire debate dimensions which otherwise it would never have had. The underlying issue, noticeable only upon reflection, was the emergence of markets in the recently established western part of Germany. Interestingly, in introducing the legislation, the Chancellor blamed his own Minister of Economic Affairs for having caused the 'restlessness' (i.e. the threat to strike in the core industry), and then immediately started to defend his own minister, without this minister ever being heard in this debate. The Minister of Justice, who also had qualms about the legislation, vented his views likewise not in parliament (only after the interpellation) but rather during campaign speeches in Lower Saxony. If there was so much consensus, and since the demountations indeed soon stopped in the western part of Germany, what was the disagreement about? The answer is patently obvious, and it is also the answer that explains why the Minister of Economic Affairs did not even have to raise his voice. Under Allied Control, there was in fact no monetary economy. The allied forces had imposed a strict system of a planned economy, stringent regulation and a system of allocations and allotments. Upon this system could thrive a class of people, called 'functionaries', who were dealing odds that sometimes could be decisive of life or death. This system, coupled with the de-nazification attempt, bred widespread discontent and a support of market principles even in quarters that never had thought of markets very fondly, let alone deeply. In 1948, Ludwig Erhard, the silenced Minister of Economic Affairs, at a stroke introduced with the new German currency access to world markets (albeit at this time still rather limited), but with this introduction came the possibility of attracting investment. Indeed, the attractiveness for investment turned up in the legislative debate about the first codetermination act, although the speaker didn't quite know how to handle it. Clearly, the Labour Union Movement was surprised by the advent of capital markets. The threat of a strike by the ailing leader of the Trade Union Movement, Hans Böckler, who died shortly thereafter, did not change the course of the legislation any; it only changed the tone of the debate and it gave some fringe parties arguments which they used astutely, to the embarrassment of the Minister of Justice who happened to have to campaign against these very arch conservatives in Lower Saxony.

Yet the deeper point was that with markets emerging, responsibilities had to be defined more clearly. No longer could you model management as some kind of ruling group in the corporation. Responsibilities between the Supervisory Board, the Managing Board and the Works Councils had to be clearly circumscribed. Dealing with coal shipments to preferred constituencies had to end, since coal now had a price, a market price that would bear on the bottom line and thereby on the ability of unions to extract wage concessions.

The upshot of these shifting constraints is aptly demonstrated in the parliamentary orchestra. The Chancellor in acting on his guideline competence gives a general and very informative speech. The Minister of Labour Relations, clearly unhappy about his role, does not dare deviate one inch from his prepared speech. Upon criticism by the chairman of the Social Democratic Party, he even insists that the legal matters are so involved that he wants to stick to his text. Yet the Minister of Justice is not even heard in the debate until after the fact. And the Minister of Economic Affairs, who set all this in motion according to the Chancellor's account, is nowhere to be seen. Yet, by setting it in motion, he could furthermore remain silent, because he understood the order of the market economy and how the cards would ultimately be dealt. In this context, the special position of the mountain industries also needs particular attention.

Böhm saw codetermination essentially as an enabling institution to form cartels of producers against consumers. Whereas in the bulk of economic literature on firms with labour participation the emphasis is on the conflict between labour and capital, Böhm emphasized the conflict between producers and consumers. Böhm's analysis is essentially static and does not capture any of the reasons which genetically were responsible for codetermination to take shape. Clearly, codetermination was seen by its originators as an enabling institution, to rebuild corporations in specific locations, where they had previously been and where their workers had their homes and families. Hence, the emphasis was, historically speaking, on the attempt to arrive at parallelizing the interest of consumers and producers instead of pitting them one against the other. As far as the labour market is concerned, codetermination can hardly lead to any form of cartelization, since there always remains a large segment of the labour market which is unaffected by codetermination.

8.6 CODETERMINATION AS AN INTERLOCKING SYSTEM

Codetermination is an interrelated set of institutions consisting of five major elements (see Table 8.1). Codetermination at the plant level involves the representation of workers in works councils. Works councils need to be heard in many matters referring to the daily practice of work, they need to be involved in discussions with respect to such issues as hours, time and form of payment, hiring and firing of individual workers. They need to agree in economic matters that essentially concern them, in particular if a plant is to be closed. In that case, a social plan needs to be implemented. Obviously, the works councils have no say in what is being produced, what the prices are, what kinds of investments are being taken and so on. But the crucial fact is that they determine the exit costs and thereby the entry costs of a potential investor.

Next to the works councils, codetermination provides for the representation of labour representatives on the supervisory boards of corporations. The supervisory boards appoint management and supervise management activities. Under different codetermination acts, workers have either one third or one half of the seats on the supervisory board. In the supervisory boards, the long-term investment plans of companies are determined. Thirdly, codetermination may involve the appointment of one member of the managing board of the company, who is in charge of personnel affairs and has the special trust of the labour representatives on the board. In this, and only in this sense, labour can participate in the managing of some corporations, but the personnel director will always be in the minority. Under German corporate law, the board acts jointly.

Table 8.1 Codetermination as an Interlocking System

	Works Council	Collective bargaining	Two tier board	Bonding of investment	Competition between locations
Works Council	x	1	2	3	4
Collective bargaining	5	x	6	7	8
Two tier board	9	10	x	11	12
Bonding of investment	13	14	15	x	16
Competition between locations/Gewerbesteuer	17	18	19	20	x

The acts establishing codetermination in Germany were passed by the German federal parliament in 1951, 1952, 1965 and 1976. The 1976 act, for instance, which generalized the codetermination model, and which had in its original form been confined to the so-called 'mountain' industries (mining and steel), carried a majority in the parliament of more than 90 per cent. In the context of European Union harmonization attempts of corporate law, Germany is trying to introduce codetermination as an element into European corporate law; this is being resisted by some other European Union Members. The reason for Germany's stance in this matter is the fact that codetermination is part of the German consensus and departing from it is not supported by any one of the stronger political movements in the country.

From a law and economics point of view, the question remains as to why Germany opted for this peculiar form of company organization, which is at substantial variance with the classical model of the business firm. The answer to this question has to be given in two parts. Part one of the answer needs to address the issue of why codetermination was introduced in the first place. Part two of the answer needs to address the issue of why codetermination is being clung to as a generally desired form of corporate organization.

In 1949, Germany still lay in ruins. The reconstruction effort had not really taken off, because the institutional prerequisites (stable money, stable legislative framework, labour peace, a supporting tax system and consistent economic policy) were not yet quite in place. Codetermination was one aspect of this package of implementing the institutional prerequisites for the reconstruction of post-World War II Germany. Since the physical plants had been largely destroyed or were still subject to demountation, productive capital was actually embodied in human capital. The human capital, of course, needed to be won over in any investment decision. It is for this reason that human capital was systematically introduced into the organized forms of capital representation in the corporation. Only in this way did it seem possible to re-invest unpaid wages and dividends into the company. In 1951 and in 1952 pursuant to the government programme, West Germany introduced the system of codetermination as we now know it. It was chosen over a number of different organizational alternatives which would all have been much less compatible with the functioning of a market economy. In 1965, with the reform of the act on joint stock companies, codetermination was again expanded into sectors not hitherto covered. It was further expanded in 1976. The legislative record is completely at odds with Böhm's predictions. It is difficult to conceive of an interest group driven scenario of parliamentary legislative decision making that could explain the consistency of the record and the large supporting majorities. The system has clearly proven workable, but it has interesting implications with respect to which industries can expand in Germany and which are driven abroad typically with the active co-operation of the labour representatives on the supervisory board – Volkswagen do Brasil probably having been the first highly visible example of the approach. In a nutshell the system is geared towards company structures with a near parity of human and physical capital. Only some lines of production lend themselves to this model, and herein lies a clear strategic choice of the codetermination legislation, although it may not have been made consciously.

Codetermination as a model cannot be superimposed on any country. Legislators keen on copying Germany's legislation should carefully consider Böhm's argument in order to find out whether the conditions that prevailed in Germany and that made codetermination a worthwhile legislative experiment would prevail in the candidate country as well. Otherwise, they might do well to heed Böhm's warning.

In reviewing the parliamentary debate in 1951, one is surprised to note how little time was spent in hammering out the details of the legislation. Indeed, much of the relevant knowledge was probably shared by the members of parliament, but it was going to take almost thirty years until, in 1979, the German Constitutional Court emphasized the extent to which the different institutions making up the German codetermination system are interdependent, even interlocking.[10] The system makes sense only because its five different pillars support each other; taking one element away can result in serious shortcomings. The five elements have been listed in Table 8.1, and their interdependence will be discussed in turn in the sequence of the numbers indicated.

The works councils are the oldest element; they were introduced during the First World War originally in the ammunition industry in order to allow workers who threatened to strike to participate in decisions about the organization of their working environment, schedules and the like. Today, the works councils are an omnipresent part of the management structure of the German company. They are also present in the public service with slightly different functions, since civil servants in Germany do not have the right to strike.

1. The works councils relate to the institutions of collective bargaining in terms of the division of tasks. Works councils deal with aspects that are not, in principle, subject to collective bargaining. For instance, collective bargaining will set the base wage. Works councils will discuss with management when and how the wage is paid. This division of the task is extremely important since works councils, in

order to be effective, have to be able to reach their goals by convincing management of the superiority of their proposed solution in the interest of the entire company. Works councils participate in decision making in the sense that they cannot be ignored: rarely can they take decisions on their own. Only in one case (when the firm is to be liquidated) can works councils impose a serious damage on the firm's owner by withholding their agreement to the social plan. The institution of collective bargaining, on the other hand, by definition uses powerful sanctions on either side. The workers can strike, the companies can lock them out. In both cases, serious losses can be imposed. Unions may not be able to strike because they may not be able to pay the striking workers their compensation which typically they are understood to do. This division of tasks is extremely important in particular as we compare the German situation to the American one. In the United States, collective bargaining will also cover work rules, a practice which can result in very formalistic agreements about which disputes are likely to arise. On the other hand, union leaders used to collective bargaining may find it difficult to cooperate in company boards when given the chance, such as in the case of Eastern Airlines (under the chairmanship of Frank Bormann).

2. The works councils are often the recruiting ground for the labour member in the supervisory board of German cooperations. It is here that we realize that the two-tier system is a precondition for co-determination to be possible. If the works councils were to send representatives on to the managing board, they would end up negotiating with themselves. Incidentally, the labour directors mentioned above were always recruited from the outside in order to avoid such a conflict. By being able to rely on the works councils, the supervisory boards have a second channel of information at their disposal, the first one being management which, as they also have to control it, may be withholding information that could be damaging. It is for this reason that the system of codetermination can strengthen owners' rights in the firm, at the expense of managers. In this sense, codetermination is one conceivable answer to the problem posed by Berle and Means.
3. Bonding is a device to protect sensitive investments in specific assets. When highly specific human capital is deployed in the production process, the owners may be interested in seeking protection against the loss that can occur if inappropriate management decisions are being taken. The works councils can provide such protection on the one hand through the day-to-day consultation with management, on the other hand through their links with the supervisory board.

Here, both labour and capital can seek to protect the value of the investment by monitoring management that, through its operation, determines the marginal productivity of both capital and labour.

4. In Germany (as in the United States) local communities depend for their tax revenue on the profitability and presence of corporations within their jurisdiction. There exists a symmetry in the interest of the local communities and the employees of corporations, who are typically tied to these communities by virtue of their home ownership, family and other ties and generally their roots. German workers tend to be much less mobile than their American counterparts. Thus, the works councils also act in the interest of the local communities from where they stem in guarding the presence of the corporation at its current location. This, by the way, does not prevent codetermined firms from sometimes making large investments overseas, if these investments are perceived by labour representatives as implicitly enhancing the stability of their own jobs.
5. By virtue of the division of tasks between the system of collective bargaining on the one hand, where employers' associations and the trade unions negotiate the base wage, and the system of works councils on the other, where the day-to-day operation of the working routines is being discussed, the works councils are relieved of those issues which necessarily would result in acrimonious disputes. Thus, the two systems mutually support each other.
6. Since labour representatives sit on the boards of corporations, the unions possess much more detailed information about specific companies than their American counterparts. They are therefore unlikely to overshoot in their bargaining, more inclined to take a long-term view and maximize lifetime earnings rather than per annum wages.
7. The first German post-World War II parliament has given the hair thin majority of the governing coalition 'an overwhelming majority'; this result strikes me as a very important show of a consensus living in the post-World War II West German democracy. The families of the workers are typically tied to the location likewise, hence they also count among these stakeholders of the corporation. Unions make these investments, because the investment they make in wage concessions can be guarded through the codetermination structures.
8. Very often, trade unions also guard the interests of the corporation in the towns where they operate. They thereby help in creating a business environment that is hospitable to the corporate activities.
9. The two-tier board can function effectively because through the works councils information can be gathered in a systematic manner.

The board is able to collect information which sometimes is not even available to management.

10. Since the supervisory board and the managing board are separate, the managing board is free to bargain with the unions, who are not represented there. A single-tier system would not allow for this separation of interests.
11. The two-tier system, again, helps in safeguarding investments against excessive demands from either side. This is true both for labour and capital.
12. Although through the corporate city tax (Gewerbesteuer) the German city is in fact a stakeholder in its corporations, and although the city is expected to furnish services from basics to schools and sometimes even theatres and symphony orchestras, no attempt has been made to my knowledge to repeat the features of the Hesse organization act and grant the city seats on the supervisory board. The instrument that is used is typically a plain contract. This contract is a public contract, but many communities preferred to contract privately through development boards (Entwicklungsgesellschaften).
13. Since bonding of investments is one of the key strategies used under codetermination, the works councils chairmen have a specific role that is far beyond that of a shop steward, for instance, in the British system. They are selected not for their aggressive negotiation skills, impressive confrontational methods or rhetoric, but rather for guaranteeing smooth working relationships and an avenue for resolving the many conflicts that necessarily develop when people have to work together, certainly if highly committed and highly skilled people are involved.
14. Collective bargaining is also conducted differently when bonding of investments is a part of the set of strategies. Tactics need to be more subtle not only in view of strike funds but also in view of human capital investments at stake.
15. Bonding is an attractive alternative strategy because the supervisory board allows for keeping an eye on the specific investments made.
16. Since bonding strategies are available, cities, in turn, are able to make long-term commitments, which, after all, they have to finance out of tax revenues. These investments can go far beyond what is usually practised in the United States by, for instance, a county development board. For instance, establishing schools, theatres, public pools and the like requires not only the initial investment, but also the continued commitment to cover the sometimes substantial operating costs.
17. Cities, through the works councils, often have a venue to press their wishes into firm decision making as well. At least some logical

politicians will serve simultaneously on city and company boards. This is important when issues of city planning and work organization overlap (for instance bus schedules). Short communication lines can substantially cut transactions costs.

18. When a strike is being called, the mayor holds his breath. The city can lose twice, not only because of the reduced income and therefore likely increased level of entitlements that need to be paid out – in Germany the entitlements have to paid by the cities, not the state or the federal government – but also because depressed corporate revenues mean depressed corporate tax revenues, putting the city budget into a squeeze. It is obvious that through various channels a moderating influence is present.
19. Most cities in Germany operate a bank, the so-called Sparkasse. This is a leftover from traditional cameralist policies. These banking institutions also get involved, as they can in Germany, with locally operating companies, since commercial and investment banking can be done through one and the same institution in the German banking systems. In this way, the city can exert an influence through the supervisory board if, as is customary, the major local banks and firms take seats on this board. The city mayor, in turn, typically appoints the bank manager. Often times, the city also relies to a not insignificant extent on the bank revenues for its own budgetary requirements.
20. Since the interest of the city and the workers (its citizens) coincide to a large extent or are even parallel, the city where the company is operating is also interested in keeping the strategy of bonding investments viable. It tries to create an environment that makes the strategy attractive.

In this way (as well as in others not detailed), the five pillars of codetermination interlock to support the entire structure. Removing any one of them will lead to multifarious consequences, and these consequences are very difficult to predict.

Codetermination creates a specific player in the labour market that is strongly committed to human capital formation and to the location where the works are sited. This is a different position than that of the typical American or multinational corporation, which tends not to maintain close ties to any specific location. The consequence is that codetermination tends to open a different arena where, next to labour market exchange, decisions can be taken. These decisions refer to shaping the production function, not to the formation of wages. The latter distinction also points to the reason why codetermination has to be the result of legislative decision making and cannot conceivably be the outcome of collective bargaining. It is not a bargain, it is rather a constitution in which production functions can be shaped.

8.7 LEGISLATION OF BACKGROUND LAW AND DEAL LAW

The guiding hypothesis of this study had originally been the suspicion that ideological or specific political factors were decisive for codetermination to emerge in Germany and nowhere else. The parliamentary record, however, does not show such specific ideological or political considerations to have been important. Rather, despite some oddities of the political process, notably the trade unions' strike threat, codetermination appears to have been largely uncontroversial. The previous section tried to show how the different elements of which codetermination is made up as an interlocking system fit together. This raises the different question of whether, under specific conditions, public choice processes can also lead to efficient legislation. To this issue we now turn.

8.7.1 The Efficiency of the Common Law Debate

A steady flow of papers over the past two decades in the economic analysis of law suggests that the common law evolves toward efficiency,[11] the implication being that statute law does not. Despite the different formulations, the suggestion turns on the proposition that inefficient law creates large transactions costs: hence, parties gain from having inefficient legal arrangements removed. It follows that inefficient legal rules will be litigated again and again, until they approach efficiency. Michelman (1980) showed that this tendency should hold for judicial behaviour under either type of law, common or enacted. We should therefore observe a tendency toward efficiency in judicial rule making, independent of the particular legal culture in which a judge opines.

Whereas Michelman's amendment to the Posnerian argument considerably weakens the case for the superiority and singular efficiency of the common law, it refocuses attention on the body of law to which judicial decision making gives rise. That judicial decision making tends toward 'efficient' (defined as wealth maximizing)[12] legal rules is quite consistent with another contention, dating back to Bentham,[13] that the common law, as a system of rules, lacks coherence and rationality and hence is less efficient than a code (one might add 'can conceivably be'). The successive judicial decisions groping towards efficiency may reach a local optimum, an optimum that can be inferior to an inefficient solution reached otherwise.

Further doubt is cast on the notion that the common law converges towards efficiency, since the supposition that inefficient rules will be relitigated rests on the assumption that the judiciary is a monopolistic provider of legal decisions. Inefficient legal arrangements need not be re-litigated. Parties will engage in litigation only if each expects the benefits from litigation to exceed the costs. When inefficient verdicts are expected, parties will be reluctant to litigate and prefer rather to settle out of court. The tendency toward efficiency is not a dependable one. As Priest and Klein (1984) have shown, litigation depends largely on how close parties estimate the dispute to remain to the court's established decision standard. 'Close' cases are most likely to be re-litigated, as are those in which one party has a relatively larger stake than the other. It follows that both efficient and inefficient decision rules can be perpetuated.[14] Disregarding for the moment private avenues of adjudication, it appears that whether the law is efficient will depend more on the performance of legislatures than the prevailing literature suggests.

In this section I propose three variations of a simple model to show under which conditions we can expect a legislature to enact efficient law.

8.7.2 Three Simple Models

In keeping with Michelman's (1980) distinction, we assume that there are two types of law in any society: law that every incremental enactment or judicial opinion builds on,[15] and law that was a 'deal' to redistribute income away from one group and toward another. In this transfer, the legislator is seen as a broker who acts for a fee.[16] 'Deal law' may then be efficient in maximizing the wealth of the society in the long run, but it need not be. Conventionally, 'background law' should tend toward efficiency, although my preceding remarks leave this supposition in doubt. 'Background law' may be either common law or codified case law, consisting of pure codifications or a combination of these elements. Hence, we can assume, in each jurisdiction, that there will be a certain amount of competition between the legislature and the judiciary in providing 'background law'. While Michelman's distinction between 'background law' and 'deal law' is a straightforward one, identifying a particular piece of legislation as either being 'background law' or 'deal law' may be less so. It is perfectly possible that an act of parliament contains both. As Posner has pointed out, the distinction may require some deeper analysis in each individual case. He notes that 'courts cannot readily identify purely redistributive legislation, in part because such redistributive legislation may be defensible on efficiency grounds by reference to problems of social peace, free rider problems and so forth'.[17]

In this terminology, the question then can be put as follows: do we have to consider the codetermination legislation as background law, or rather as deal law? And if it is deal law, does it constitute an efficient deal or is it mainly of a redistributive nature?

8.7.2.1 Political entrepreneurs

Assume a legislature made up of representatives who broker their legislative services for a fee. They are individual wealth maximizers.[18]

The demand for legislative income transfers is fairly straightforward. It requires a group so small that the benefit bestowed upon it is clearly perceptible for each member; a group that is well organized so as to prevent dissipation of the benefit, and that is able to provide the brokerage fee in terms of either votes or pecuniary (and lawful) benefits.

The suppliers of wealth transfers, in turn, must be difficult to organize, and inelastic in their response to legislation. A threat of facing a one dollar loss as a consequence of legislation will not result in a one dollar increase in expenditure to fight such legislation; the individual expected costs of mounting a political defence exceed the expected individual gains (from not being coerced into a wealth transfer) and being able to suffer the income loss. The opportunity costs of resisting the wealth transfer must exceed the amounts (per person) transferred. The more durable the enactment and the larger the transfer it provides, the more the receiving interest group is willing to pay. Yet, for the providing group, the more durable the enactment and the larger the transfer, the higher will be the benefit from resisting the transfer, whereas opportunity costs remain unaffected. Hence, wealth transfers are subject to a scale restriction that is determined by the (transactions) costs of resisting them. We should therefore observe multiple small transfers involving different groups of suppliers.

The main cost element facing groups that are either seeking or resisting wealth transfers are start-up costs, but once they are borne they no longer affect marginal costs. Established interest groups, then, enjoy an advantage in both seeking and resisting wealth transfers. This advantage amounts to a strong incentive for an established clientele of transfer recipients. A transfer may be large and durable, yet only affect each supplier to a small extent. Still, the larger the group of suppliers and the larger or more durable the transfer (or both), the higher the benefits will be from resisting. Votes and wealth can be assumed to be convertible. Since brokers compete for wealth or votes, political entrepreneurs may seek out groups of suppliers and, in return for their votes, oppose transfer programmes on their behalf. The larger the group of suppliers involved, or the larger or more durable the transfer sought, the higher the probability that a competing broker will organize resistance to a proposed wealth transfer.

It follows that 'deal law' should be of relatively shorter durability than 'background law'. Likewise, 'deal law' should strongly benefit established groups and only mildly harm small, scattered groups; that is, 'deal law' should not impose considerable welfare losses on the general public. There are clearly tendencies in society that contain the social loss from rent seeking.[19]

Assuming convertibility between wealth and votes, legislative brokers can either seek to serve established interest groups or appeal to large groups of general interest voters. They will probably do both; they have an incentive to produce legislation that benefits many, while harming few. Generous transfers are largely precluded since a transfer that is perceptibly to benefit many must impose a heavy burden on a few. Such a transfer will not be supplied because the benefits from resisting it will generally exceed the opportunity costs of forgoing the resistance. It follows that legislative brokers have an incentive to produce legislation that is capable of producing wealth for the general public; the more durable this wealth-producing legislation is, the larger the benefit is from it and, presumably, the larger the expected return in votes. Legislators face incentives to produce durable wealth-enhancing legislation side by side with incentives to broker transfers of relatively limited duration. This holds true under the assumption that legislators have sufficient information. While obviously legislators are not omniscient, they can rely on their clients to possess and process the relevant information. Wealth reducing legislation will be brought to the attention of the legislators by those whose wealth is being affected as well as the press.

We conclude that brokers in the legislature face incentives to produce both efficient 'background law' as well as (mildly) inefficient 'deal law'. 'Mildly' inefficient is a deliberately loose term, since the argument is cast in terms of tendencies, not precisely quantifiable magnitudes. I mean to suggest that the (negative) welfare costs of deal law in this scenario will be relatively minor as composed to the (positive) welfare effects of background law.

8.7.2.2 The open jurisdiction

The second model differs from the first in two respects. It assumes that the jurisdiction is open in the sense that citizens and corporations can either resist or evade unwanted legislation. They may evade into other jurisdictions or into an extralegal domain within the jurisdiction, such as an underground or shadow economy. The first alternative is relatively straightforward, the equivalent to the small open economy in international trade theory. The smaller the jurisdiction and the more flexible the agents it comprises, the more elastic we can expect the evasive response to be. Even if the jurisdiction is 'big' and closed, however, the room for evasion may be substantial. Regulations can be avoided by taking up other lines of business. Conflicts can routinely be settled out of court or conflict prone transactions can be avoided altogether. Alternative forms of dispute resolution can be resorted to or initiated. Finally, producers can withdraw from market transactions and shift exchanges of goods and services into an organization designed to reduce transactions costs.[20]

None of these developments are included in what has been labelled the shadow economy, which itself is reputed to be a sizable extralegal sector in the advanced Western economies.[21] The shadow economy, then, can be assumed to provide scope for evasion in addition to the evasion strategies already listed above.[22]

This modification of our model has two implications: the larger the potential there is to evade, the smaller the citizens' incentive will be to resist 'deal' law that aims at extracting transfers, and the smaller the extracted transfer, particularly in the long run. While this leaves the demand for transfers unaffected, increasing the scope for evasion dries up the supply and raises the legislators' cost of providing transfers, or 'deal laws'.

Secondly, the larger the scope for evasion, the stronger the competitive pressure will be on legislators to produce efficient legal arrangements. And the stronger those competitive pressures are, the more likely it is that the economy will experience an expansion of its production possibility frontier.

The efficiency effect of 'deal law' when supply dries up is essentially secondary, that is, that efficiency loss occurs in terms of productive activities forgone in an economy. These are the opportunity costs of 'deal law'. Obviously, they depend on the extent to which opportunities for wealth production are foreclosed by 'deal law'. This effect implies that the general welfare loss of 'deal law' increases with the scope for evasion.

Where resistance to 'deal law' weakens and transfers decline, a large number of 'deal laws' will be enacted. This observation reinforces the aforementioned tendency for 'deal laws' to be numerous, but of relatively limited direct impact on attained wealth. By the same reasoning, however, 'deal laws' contract the production possibility frontier of the economy at large and hence affect citizens' attainable wealth positions.

We can conclude that in an 'open' jurisdiction, legislators face even stronger incentives to produce efficient 'background law', whereas incentives to produce 'deal law' become weaker relative to the first model.

8.7.2.3 Introducing Leviathan

The third model expands on the second in featuring an open jurisdiction, a Leviathan legislature[23] that seeks to maximize revenues from taxation, and a judiciary that adjudicates litigation by professional standards of jurisprudence and remains unaffected by the revenue maximization behaviour of the legislature. Hence, an independent judiciary is assumed. This model is designed for the long-run implications of legislators' activities on the efficiency of the whole body of law.

In Leviathan models legislators are again assumed to maximize political profits from taxation, on the one hand, or regulation (i.e. 'deal law') on the other. Taxation and regulation are not only interchangeable as political means. Inasmuch as policies based on either invariably burden the citizenry, the size and fertility of the tax base is affected by the extent of regulation;[24] whereas conversely the regulatory domain shrinks as the burden of taxation increases, and vice versa: reducing the burden of taxation opens up the regulatory domain. From this simple argument it follows that the production of 'deal law' impairs the fertility of the tax base. Hence, 'deal laws' generate negative externalities for the legislature at large by reducing the tax pie.

In the Leviathan literature[25] it is customary to assume that Leviathan acts myopically. The long-run tax rate is assumed to exceed that rate which would yield the maximum stream of tax revenues; likewise the long-run regulatory intensity exceeds that regulatory intensity which would maximize the production of 'deal law' in the long run. Frey and Ramser (1986) have shown, however, that the short-run optimization of tax rates as well as regulatory intensities (considered simultaneously) can yield overregulation in tandem with undertaxation. It then appears that Leviathan's myopia is at odds with the beast's appetite. Short-run optimization does not yield a maximum political profit.

By way of clarification suppose there is a unicameral legislature[26] and delegates are allowed to be re-elected. Then we can classify the delegates into cohorts according to the length of their tenure in the legislature. Whereas seniority can safely be assumed to carry additional power, there will always be a cohort that contains more members than a given one chosen at random. The larger cohort will be composed of younger delegates than the smaller one. This rule applies to all but the youngest cohort, which will be the largest. Hence, votes tend to be concentrated with younger delegates. The longer the tenure of a delegate, the shorter his expected future tenure, and thus the shorter his time horizon can be in taking political decisions. Empirically we also observe that elected officials' re-election probabilities are a positive function of the length of their past tenure.

The relatively lower re-election chance of younger representatives affects the length of their time horizon only insofar as political gains and losses of 'deal law' can be more heavily discounted in the immediate future where re-election is uncertain. Long-run effects, however, will be important for younger elected officials who can expect to be held responsible for 'deal' legislation they supported. Hence, elder delegates should be observed to be more prone to 'deal law' than younger delegates. Conversely, the 'newcomers' are more likely to take a long-run view, since they stand a greater chance not only of being confronted with the adverse consequences of sizing down the tax base of regulatory domain but of profiting individually from a large future tax base and unimpaired regulatory domains. Their opportunity cost of exposing deals is lower than that of longer serving legislators; it may even be nil. Since powerful interest groups will turn primarily to senior legislators who can deliver better deals, exposing those deals may be the best strategy in trying to depose long serving incumbents. Thus, gains from exposing 'deal law' and introducing 'background law' are likely to be highest for junior candidates, even if their expected tenure in office may remain relatively low due to lower (re-)election chances. In turn, delegates who take a long term view outnumber their elder colleagues; more particularly, they have an incentive to produce 'background law' that broadens the tax base and increases its fertility by expanding the production possibility frontier of the economy. All this suggests that 'deal laws' will often be opposed by younger politicians who try to build political coalitions of transfer victims, thus seeking votes in the present while preserving their political power base for the future. This tendency should be observable in particular where politicians can claim revenue sources or regulatory domains, i.e., when political property rights are allowed to develop.

With this sequence of three models we have established conditions under which background law is more likely to appear than deal law. The legislature which initiated codetermination legislation can clearly be described as meeting these criteria. The legislature was under intense pressure to generate law that would facilitate the reconstruction of Germany under difficult conditions, attract investment and motivate workers. Potential for rent seeking was next to absent, and legislators of widely different political persuasions were forced to agree on the project. These observations support the presupposition that at least in 1950, codetermination created efficient background law.

Will democratic legislatures largely engage in producing 'deal law' at the expense of providing the economy with 'background law'? Under the strict assumptions that legislatures consist of political brokers who act in a Leviathan environment, the conclusion is a resounding no. Brokers in the legislatures face incentives to produce efficient 'background law' as well as (mildly) inefficient 'deal law'.

Although these incentives hold in a closed jurisdiction, in an open jurisdiction legislators face even stronger incentives to produce efficient 'background law', whereas incentives to produce 'deal law' become weaker relative to the first model. Finally, taking a long-run view, one notes that 'deal laws' will often be opposed by younger politicians who try to build political coalitions of transfer victims, thus seeking votes in the present and preserving their political power base for the future. This tendency should be observable in particular where politicians can claim revenue sources or regulatory domains, i.e., when political property rights are allowed to develop.

8.8 APPLICATION TO THE LEGISLATION OF CODETERMINATION STRUCTURES

In the previous section, we have shown that under standard public choice assumptions, it is quite likely that efficient law is being legislated. Hence, even holding on to strict public choice assumptions does not lead to the suggestion that inefficient or redistributive legislation is likely. If, as in the case of the Federal Republic of Germany when deciding on codetermination structures, the jurisdiction had to be assumed as open and companies could easily avoid the application of the legislation, it is extremely likely that members of parliament faced strong incentives to produce efficient law. Not only the legislative history but also standard public choice analysis points in the direction of this conclusion.

8.9 THE PARADOX OF MONITORING

The theory of the classical firm assigns one factor of production, typically capital, the role to assign the monitor of, on the one hand, its own performance and secondly the performance of the other factor, i.e. labour. Monitoring is in itself a productive task, since it prevents shirking, that is a suboptimal use of the means of production, typically in the interest of one of those involved in the process of production but not coincident with the purpose of the operation. Williamson calls this the problem of sub-goal pursuit. The marginal productivity of either factor of production, both labour and capital, depends on managerial services, and in particular the marginal productivity of labour depends on managerial inputs, as the marginal productivity of management depends on the willingness of workers to be efficiently managed. The marginal productivity of either one of these factors determines, ultimately, its remuneration. Both wages and managers' earnings depend, ultimately, on their marginal productivity, measuring errors notwithstanding.

Hence, when in both line work and management there is an element of discretion, a system of monitoring needs to be found that does not depend on any one of these factors.

If we look at the situation as it existed in West Germany in 1949 when the newly elected government with its hair thin majority announced its intent on passing the legislation that would introduce codetermination, setting up an efficient governance structure amounted to a substantial organizational and legislative challenge. Six elements of that situation stand out to be mentioned:

1. To begin with, German companies in 1949 had virtually no access to international capital markets. Since there were no local capital markets either, investments had to be made out of profits not yet realized. These profits, in turn, obviously depended on the size of investment. The larger the investment could be, the larger could be the marginal and total productivity of labour, and hence the wage. However, no capital markets being available and investments having to be paid out of gains not yet being made, the larger the net profits of the firm the larger the wage, but the larger the wages fund the smaller the net profits of the firm and hence the smaller the investments to be made, and hence the smaller the marginal productivity of labour. This strange paradox called for a resolution.
2. Due to both the war destruction and the ensuing demountation campaigns, many firms found themselves with insufficient or no equipment. The firms' book assets having been reduced by war and ensuing inflation, currency reform and depreciations to next to nothing, the real assets consisted in the firm's history, a site which often resembled a pile of rubble, and a willing workforce. The history also included the memory of how to produce, how to organize, how to link up with former suppliers and customers, and how to work with the local government.
3. Some of these former customers, however, were not currently available. German companies had to re-establish their previous international customer relationships, itself a time consuming process, and a difficult one as, due to the war, technological advances had not been realized in civilian production.
4. The reputation of those former owners and managers was often tainted. Immediately after the war, some of the owners had been detained in camps, and what had been a business relationship with the government was now seen as criminal complicity. Hence, firms also often lacked the credit that they had hitherto enjoyed through the reputation of their owners. Partly, the new managers who to a

large extent had also been recruited from the labour movement formed a part of the reputation on which credit could be extended.

5. On the other hand, firms in 1949 invariably met strong market demand, as citizens were trying to rebuild their lives, as either refugees or survivors of the bombing raids. Many people had lost their household possessions and were eager to rebuild a normal life. The strong materialism characteristic of the fifties and sixties in Germany bears ample witness to these initial shortages.
6. Finally, political life was reconstituting itself from the bottom up. Only in 1949 had a limited federal government been formed. In 1945, first local, then regional and later state governments had been formed. Only the year of 1948 saw the currency reform with the emergence of markets. In 1949, the war and post-war period was still to a great extent dominating people's minds, the experience with the newly created market, in many ways the first free market after 1914, was still very fresh and equally short.

What then is the appropriate governance structure of corporations to rise out of these precarious conditions? It is obvious that the classical firm, under these conditions, is not the appropriate answer. The monitors themselves needed to be monitored.

8.10 THE SOLUTION OF BONDING

Under these circumstances, both owners and workers with their representatives had an interest in rebuilding the companies and creating an investment fund through wage restraint. Thereby, of course, the workers had to become co-owners, but the solution suggested by the Free Democrats of gradually giving them ownership certificates such as stock in exchange for wage concessions was not a feasible alternative, since co-monitoring of the investment had to start right away. How could the workers have accepted stock in worthless companies that could only gain in value through their commitment to create credit? The solution suggested by the (legally trained – all four had a doctorate) managers in 1947 indeed was a stroke of genius. By building on the concept of the two-tier board, labour could be invited to assume an equal position on the supervisory board and management could proceed, as professionally as possible, under the joint supervision of labour and capital. In fact, the investment of the workers had been bonded. Only through the bonding process was it indeed forthcoming. In this sense, codetermination can be assigned an important rank in explaining the 'economic miracle' West Germany lived through in the fifties and sixties.[27]

The stark consensus that marked the position of all parties in the parliamentary debate thereby finds its logical explanation. The situation required a new solution which was indeed hit upon, and there was no relevant alternative. This, however, may be said not to have been true afterwards. To that question we now finally turn.

8.11 PATH DEPENDENCE

Ultimately, the question needs to be addressed as to why the institution of codetermination was not only continued but also extended to cover the entire German corporate landscape (of companies having more than 1000 employees).

The answer has to be given in different parts. To start with, two common misconceptions have to be avoided. The first misconception concerns the firm's capital access at the time when codetermination was introduced. Henry Hansmann (1966) writes:

> I can, however, hazard a theory of my own: that the firms involved would probably have to raise new capital at some point, and that they might want to sell large amounts of stock for the purpose – stock that would dilute the worker's earnings and control. Codetermination assured them 50% control, and through that control they could assure themselves wages yielding an appropriate fraction of the companies' earnings. (p. 2)

This alternative theory is factually wrong on two points. First, companies for some time to come had no access to capital markets and therefore had to rely on self-financing. International capital markets were not accessible to German corporations (at the time of the deliberations still suffering under demountations), and domestic capital markets were extremely thin during the first part of the fifties.

Secondly, codetermination did allow workers control over the investments in terms of siting and (through co-decision-making in the works councils) the technologies used, and therefore could indeed have been used in order to shape any specific capital increases through issuing new stocks or bonds. Codetermination, however, does not allow any access to decisions over wages.

Hence, in order to explain the further extension of codetermination, we have to stick to the specific German case which is not generalizable as it depends on a historical starting point not to be found anywhere else in the industrialized world.

The first part concerns the act of 1965, which was part of the corporate reform act needed because the national socialist government had written the leader principle into corporate law. This complicated reform package also included all those element of codetermination that the speaker of the Free Democratic Party in the parliamentary debate had outlined in 1951, including the one third representation of labour in the supervisory boards. That act covers every joint stock company with more than 1000 employees.

Different is the act of 1976, which was the result of the big coalition between the original two large parties that had in 1949 supported codetermination, although only one of them had been part of government. The price for taking part in government that the Social Democrats exerted was the extension of codetermination over all industries beyond coal and steel. Here, the echelon was finally decided to be a minimum of 2000 employees. However, Biedenkopf in 1965 had already found that codetermination in the industries covered worked, in that it did not lead to frictions and conceivably had benefits. Since 1965, companies were aware of the pending legislation. Easy escape routes were built early on. The act requires specifically corporate forms which can be changed, it is bound to a specific size which can be undercut by reproportioning or regrouping enterprises, it requires a location of the seat of the company within the German jurisdiction which can be easily avoided (for instance by locating headquarters in German language Switzerland), even a simple change in the bylaws of the supervisory board can render codetermination under the act of 1976 meaningless. All of these activities took place to a certain extent, but not to a very large extent. When the act was passed in 1976 with more than 90 per cent of the vote in parliament, and without even a hint of union action, it was widely perceived as a logical evolutionary development in German corporate law. No perceptible effect on the stock exchange has ever been documented. There was litigation surrounding the implementation and there was litigation in front of the constitutional court in order to test the future of such legislation. However, the general perception is that there is not going to be a future in this legislation. Codetermination as a part of German corporate law is firmly in place, and the only point of further argument is to defend it against future developments in corporate law initiated by the European Commission or the European Parliament. Since under the Maastricht Treaty, that treaty has to be read through the German Basic Law, and since codetermination has been tested against the German Basic Law, through the constitutional court case against the codetermination act of 1976 and the ensuing verdict, codetermination has been chiselled in stone for the time being and under the restrictions mentioned above.

The further development of codetermination after 1951 can only partly be seen as path dependent. The other and more important part is the experience the German industry has gained with the institution of codetermination, and that experience has not varied much from the original conditions. Since in Germany the different stakeholders are expected to invest heavily in the company, the stakeholders including the workers, the local community, capital owners, of course, title needs to be given to all these investment commitments. Since such title is difficult to imagine, codetermination may have proven to be the most adequate vehicle to protect investments that can be jeopardized when industrial strife, antagonism, intolerance or managerial hubris endanger specific assets, these being either specific human capital investments or specific capital investments.

8.12 CONCLUSION

In this chapter I have tried to render an account of the history of German codetermination from the point of view of why it actually came about. The chapter tries to suggest that the solution, although innovative, was virtually the only one that German decision-makers in both industry, trade and politics could hit upon. As it turns out, the solution was suggested, independently or not, by four academically trained industry leaders in the industrial heartland of West Germany. Although the implementation through various legislatures of the solution required a circuitous route, the final outcome seems logical enough. However, it is an outcome that has a very specific origin. It is not clear under which circumstances German codetermination could be an interesting or even an attractive model for corporate America.

The legislation on codetermination created a type of player in the labour market which was substantially different from employers operating under different rules. Codetermination emphasizes the specific location of the works, it has an impact on the product mix, it is not irrelevant with respect to technology choice, it requires heavy investment in research and development as well as a long-term view to human capital formation, where the expectation is that the human capital will remain with the firm, as long as the firm exists. Such a player will be more steady in the labour market than a player not similarly constrained and motivated. It may create, in the short run, fewer jobs, but can be expected, in the longer run, to sustain more of them than the comparable corporation.

NOTES

1. For further references and documentation of this example, see Jürgen Backhaus, 'Die Überuhrung von Produktionsmitteln in Gemeineigentum', *Zeitschrift für öffentliche und gemeinnützige Unternehmen*, 18.4, 1995, 465–76.
2. Printed matter nr. 2, German Parliament [Deutscher Bundestag] 1, 1949. The term 'demountation' refers to the dismantling or disassembling of industrial plants. According to Allied agreement, Germany was to be demilitarized, and this could be interpreted by removing its productive capacity. Lists of militarily relevant productions sites had been drawn up, and demountation teams systematically implemented the policy by following these lists.
3. German Parliament 1 (1949), 15th session on 4 November 1959, p. 352.
4. Printed matter nr. 117, Deutscher Bundestag 1, 1949.
5. German Parliament 1 (1949), 15th session, 4 November 1949, p. 353.
6. German Parliament 1 (1949), 117th session, 14th February 1951, pp. 4431–60.
7. German Parliament, 117th session on February 4, 1951, p. 4436.
8. As printed matter number 2168 still of the first period of the German parliament 1949, submitted on April 18, 1951.
9. German Parliament, 140th session, 9 May 1951, p. 5587.
10. BundesVerfassungsGerichtsEntscheidung (BVerfGE) 50, 1979, 290.
11. Cooter & Kornhauser 1980, Goodman 1978, Hirshleifer 1982, Landes & Posner 1979, Posner 1977, Priest 1977, and with reservations, Rubin 1977, 1982, Terrebonne 1981. There are others who disagree, for example Richard Posner is 'distinctly skeptical about the claim' (personal communication). The notion has nevertheless become so deeply rooted in the folklore of the law and economics subdiscipline that it has rendered meaningful discussions about efficient legislation by code or statute very, very difficult. The purpose of this section is to help overcome these mental obstacles.
12. See notably Posner 1981, the Hofstra Law Review Symposium 1, 11, 1980 and, critically, Samuels 1981.
13. 1780, Works 1838- Hart 1843, Collected Works 1968.
14. This begs a related question: Where will those parties turn that have been frustrated by inefficient court rulings? Answers to this question of substitute re-litigation will, of course, hinge on the availability of alternative sources of adjudication.
15. Michelman calls it 'background law'.
16. McCormick & Tollison 1981.
17. See Posner (1987) at note 12.
18. This assumption is standard in the American context. One should wonder whether it contains a reasonable description of political processes in Europe. In Europe, political parties tend to play a much greater influence than in the United States. Still, important interest groups are expediently and reliably being served by their parties or caucuses, and particular politicians specialize in particular interest groups.
19. Tullock (1980).
20. Williamson (1981).
21. Simon & Witte 1982, Tanzi 1982.
22. Frey & Ramser 1986, Frey & Weck 1983.
23. Buchanan & Brennan (1980).
24. Posner (1986). The trade-off has long been noted in the economics literature. See Backhaus & Wagner (1987).
25. Buchanan & Brennan 1980, Buchanan & Lee 1982.
26. According to McCormick & Tollison 1981, a unicameral legislature is more conducive to interest groups, i.e. 'deal law' legislation than a bicameral legislature, especially if the two houses are of uneven size.
27. An American commentator has cast the matter differently; the workers, afraid of future stock emissions and thereby a dilution of their shares, preferred the statutory board seats to shares. This may be a good start for didactical purposes. Yet German

companies tend not to rely on stock issuance, for their expansions, not even today, and certainly not then (in 1951) when there were yet no viable capital markets.

ACKNOWLEDGEMENTS

Thanks to Henry Hansmann and Stephen Bainbridge for helpful comments and to Reginald Hansen, who provided many useful suggestions and pointed to new evidence. Three anonymous referees also deserve thanks.

REFERENCES

Backhaus, Jürgen G. and Richard E. Wagner (1987), 'The cameralists: a public choice perspective', *Public Choice*, **53**, 3–20.

Bentham, Jeremy (1978), *An Introduction to the Principles of Morals and Legislation* (printed 1780).

Bentham, Jeremy (1970), *Of Laws and General* (written before 1789).

Bentham, Jeremy (1838–1843) *The Works of Jeremy Bentham (11 Volumes)*, Bowering, (Dir.), Edinburgh 1838–1843.

Bentham, Jeremy (1968), *The Collected Works of Jeremy Bentham*, London.

Buchanan, James M. and Geoffrey Brennan (1980), *The Power to Tax. Analytical Foundations of a Fiscal Constitution*, Cambridge: Cambridge University Press.

Cooter, Robert and Lewis Kornhauser (1980), 'Can litigation improve the law without the help of judges?', *Journal of Legal Studies*, **9**, 139–63.

Frey, Bruno S. and Hans Jürgen Ramser (1986), 'Where are the limits of regulation?', *Journal of Institutional and Theoretical Economics*, **142**, 571–80 (Zeitschrift für die gesamte Staatswissenschaft).

Frey, Bruno S. and Hannelore Weck (1983), 'What produces a hidden economy? An international cross section analysis', *Southern Economic Journal*, **49**, 822–32.

Goodman, John C. (1978), 'An economic theory of the evolution of the common law', *Journal of Legal Studies*, **7**, 393–406.

Hansmann, Henry (1996), 'Comments', Conference on Employees and Corporate Governance, Columbia Law School, November 22.

Hirshleifer, Jack (1982), 'Evolutionary models in economics and the law: cooperation versus conflict strategies', *Research in Law and Economics*, **4**, 1–60.

Landes, William M. and Richard A. Posner (1979), 'Adjudication as a private good', *Journal of Legal Studies*, **8**, 235–84.

McCormick, Robert E. and Robert D. Tollison (1981), *Politicians, Legislation, and the Economy. An Inquiry into the Interest Group Theory of Government*, Boston/The Hague: Martinus Nijhoff.

Michelman, Frank I. (1980), 'Constitutions, statutes, and the theory of efficient adjudication', *Journal of Legal Studies*, **9**, 431–61.

Posner, Richard A. (1977, 2nd edn; 1986, 3rd edn), *The Economic Analysis of Law*, Boston: Little Brown.

Posner, Richard A. (1981), *The Economics of Justice*, Cambridge: Harvard University Press.

Posner, Richard A. (1987), 'The Constitution as an Economic Document', *George Washington Law Review*, **56** (1), November.

Priest, George L. (1977), 'The common law process and the selection of efficient rules', *Journal of Legal Studies*, **6**, 65.

Priest, George L. and Benjamin Klein (1984), 'The selection of disputes for litigation', *Journal of Legal Studies*, **13**, 1–55.

Rubin, Paul H. (1977), 'Why is the common law efficient?', *Journal of Legal Studies*, **6**, 51–63.

Rubin, Paul H. (1982), 'Common law and statute law', *Journal of Legal Studies*, **11**, 205–25.

Samuels, Warren (1981), 'Maximization of wealth as justice', *Texas Law Review*, **60**, 147–72.

Simon, Carl P. and Anne D. Witte (1982), *Beating the Systems: The Underground Economy*, Boston: Auburn House.

Tanzi, Vito (ed.) (1982), *The Underground Economy in the United States and Abroad*, Lexington: Heath.

Terrebonne, R. Peter (1981), 'A strictly evolutionary model of common law', Journal of Legal Studies, **10**, 397–407.

Williamson, Oliver E. (1981), 'The modern corporation: origins, evolution, attributes', *Journal of Economic Literature*, **19**, 1537–70.

Index